WOMEN IN ACADEMIC LEADERSHIP

Also available in the Women in Academe series:

The Balancing Act:
Gendered Perspectives in Faculty Roles and Work Lives

Most Students Are Women:
Implications for Teaching, Learning, and Policy

WOMEN IN ACADEMIC LEADERSHIP

Professional Strategies, Personal Choices

Edited by

Diane R. Dean, Susan J. Bracken,
and Jeanie K. Allen

Foreword by Claire Van Ummersen

STERLING, VIRGINIA

Published by Stylus Publishing, LLC
22883 Quicksilver Drive
Sterling, Virginia 20166-2102

Library of Congress Cataloging-in Publication-Data
Women in academic leadership : professional strategies,
personal choices / edited by Diane R. Dean, Susan J.
Bracken, and by Jeanie K. Allen ; foreward by Claire Van
Ummersen.—1st ed.
    p. cm.—(Women in academe series)
    Includes index.
    ISBN 978-1-57922-188-1 (hardcover : alk. paper)
    ISBN 978-1-57922-189-8 (pbk. : alk. paper)
    1. Sex discrimination in higher education—United
States.   2. Women college administrators—United States.
3. Educational leadership—United States.   I. Dean, Diane
R., 1967–   II. Bracken, Susan J.   III. Allen, Jeanie K.,
1951–
LC212.862.W66   2009
378.1'11082—dc22   2008055007

13-digit ISBN: 978-1-57922-188-1 (cloth)
13-digit ISBN: 978-1-57922-189-8 (paper)

Printed in the United States of America

All first editions printed on acid free paper
that meets the American National Standards Institute
Z39-48 Standard.

Bulk Purchases

Quantity discounts are available for use in workshops
and for staff development.
Call 1-800-232-0223

First Edition, 2009

10 9 8 7 6 5 4 3 2 1

CONTENTS

ACKNOWLEDGMENTS

This project would not have been possible without the hard work and support of many people who believe in and work toward equity issues for women in higher education. We sincerely appreciate everything you do! We especially want to thank John von Knorring, Judy Coughlin, Karen Haley, Mary Dee Wenniger, and, of course, all the contributing authors.

Diane R. Dean
Susan J. Bracken
Jeanie K. Allen

FOREWORD

Claire Van Ummersen

Women in Academic Leadership: Professional Strategies, Personal Choices focuses attention on the progress women have made in advancing in higher education careers and at the same time reminding us of the road yet to travel. Its central message is clear: Women remain underrepresented in academic leadership and must exercise personal agency for fostering their own advancement and challenging inequities. This volume takes the view that gender inequity is embedded in organizational culture, and therefore the academy must focus on proactive strategies to advance gender equity in academic leadership, such as providing professional development, creating opportunities for experiential learning, and encouraging mentors to support and coach more women as they work to advance within administrative roles.

Several of the authors use a feminist post-structuralist perspective to highlight the barriers women face in institutions with rules created by and for the comfort of men. Academic careers are structured around an outdated assumption that academics are either single or have at-home partners. It is critical for all to understand that society has changed. No longer are stay-at-home wives the norm. Even though 70% of child caregiving is still carried out by women, the parents of most families today are both employed and are seeking more balance. Yet institutional cultures continue to block talented women and men from flourishing, and therefore we lose their potential contributions to the knowledge base. The challenge of navigating the male norms that define the academy can be daunting. Several chapters in this book delineate the differences among sectors in American higher education and the different approaches women have taken to excel in these contexts. In faith-based colleges and universities, for example, gender inequalities are especially difficult to address because of the biblical construct of women's roles.

Recurring themes in *Women in Academic Leadership* speak to the clear need for women to build leadership skills and acquire the confidence necessary to use their skills to achieve strategic goals. But much more is needed.

Women need structured opportunities to practice their acquired competencies and they need to be recognized for their talents. Women as well as men attempt to negotiate critical junctures in academic administrative career paths despite the widespread lack of opportunities to enhance or hone their skills to be effective leaders at that next level. For example, the transition from dean to chief academic officer is rather like leaping across a crevasse hoping an updraft will sustain you until you land squarely on the far side and learn how to navigate the terrain, including the interpersonal as well as the competency challenges required to be successful. Chapters in this volume explore various professional strategies for building skills and building confidence. The need for academic leadership development cannot be overstated. Several of the book's contributors, for example, delineate the importance of program availability and experiential learning for skill building and the need for additional resources to achieve equity. Other contributors write about the importance of mentors, role models, and informal support networks in providing developmental opportunities and recognition, as well as supporting and coaching more women as they work to advance within administrative roles.

Advancing to, surviving, and thriving in academic leadership depends on personal choices almost as much as on professional strategies. Women set high standards for themselves; they lead from a value-based core; they seek continuous learning, formally and informally, throughout their careers; and they are concerned with balance in their lives. *Women in Academic Leadership* addresses the particular barriers and choices women face, especially women of color, in their search for balance between their professional and personal lives. This book speaks to leadership at all levels. It is as relevant to the leadership of program coordinators and department chairs as it is to senior positions.

As a whole, the volume addresses all women in academic leadership, yet it carefully attends to concerns facing women of color who remain vastly underrepresented in academe. The lack of women of color in the professional faculty ranks chokes the pipeline, leaving few to advance to academic leadership positions. In chief academic officer roles, for example, women of color remain anomalies. Most women who rise to this critical position and the formal leadership ranks below it (e.g., dean, department chair) are the first within their institutions to hold that role. For women of color, barriers to these roles and the pressures within them are more intense as they face the overwhelming responsibility of breaking gender and color barriers.

As we look at the road before us, we see that chilly climates must be warmed not by using rising CO_2 levels but by deliberate, honest discussions to effect changes in the rules of institutions and attitudes of their members, especially faculty. Topics related to equality, diversity, and social justice in higher education must be given a more prominent place in the curricula of leadership programs.

Several contributors in this volume comment on the women presidents who have been willing to use their authority to model and create change in the academic culture to make it more welcoming and supportive of people of both sexes. These courageous presidents will be instrumental in changing the culture throughout higher education. It is important to note that an increasing number of our male colleagues support and welcome these changes as well.

We must be particularly attentive to the constrained fiscal landscape, which is limiting the number of full-time tenure-track faculty colleges and universities can employ. While we have unparalleled opportunity to diversify the faculty as a large portion of our senior faculty retires, we have seen a drop in new tenure-track entrants. According to the U.S. Department of Education (as cited in American Association of University Professors, n.d.), the percentage on tenure track has dropped from 57% in 1975 to 31% in 2007. Perhaps the time has come to discuss seriously nontraditional pathways to senior academic leadership roles.

The good news is that increasing numbers of women and people of color are graduating with PhDs and moving into the academy. Women presidents and senior administrators along with male colleagues are leading the efforts within colleges and universities to hire more women faculty and people of color and to assist them in achieving tenure. Institutions are beginning to address balance issues broadly for all faculty and at all stages of faculty careers. Creating flexibility within faculty careers by offering part-time opportunities, caregiving leaves of absence that stop the tenure or promotional clock, and opportunities for reentry are critical to recruiting and retaining women. We have an unparalleled opportunity to change the composition of our faculty and we must take advantage of this.

Eliminating gender and other stereotypic barriers that limit access to opportunities for previously excluded groups is critical to serving our students—now 58% female and increasingly of color—so that we can attract, retain, and advance faculty role models who can then teach, mentor, support, and model the new culture of the academy. This will assist in socializing and mentoring new underrepresented students.

Preparing women for leadership is essential. The American Council on Education (as cited in *The Chronicle of Higher Education*, 2008) reports that only about 23% of college and university presidents are women, and of that number less than 14% are members of underrepresented groups. Women presidents must demonstrate attitudes for success and competencies in leading, managing budgets, and fund-raising. Presidents must create a sense of community and a shared vision of the future of the institution. Constant communication with the multiple, diverse constituencies assists presidents with gaining and maintaining legitimacy. Relationship building is as important to presidential success as are adaptability and balance.

Yet leadership resides not only in a president's position but also throughout the institution. Preparing women for leadership means providing professional development to improve leadership skills at all levels as well as prepare for advancement. Competency counts, as does demonstrated ability, so women must seek out experiential opportunities, enlist outstanding mentors, and join support networks. Most important, they must develop attitudes for success. Regardless of one's position, all leaders must be motivated by core values, have passion for their work, and have a vision of where they are headed and why.

Women, you are the keepers of your own careers. Be prepared, be the best at what you are doing, make your choices confidently, and be fulfilled.

References

American Association of University Professors. (n.d.). *Trends in faculty status, 1975–2007: All degree granting institutions, national totals.* Retrieved March 10, 2009, from http://www.aaup.org/AAUP/newsroom/Highlights/IPEDSo7.htm

The Chronicle of Higher Education. (2008, September). A profile of college presidents, 2006. [Electronic version]. *Almanac Edition: 2008–09, 55*(1), 27.

INTRODUCTION

THE BALANCING ACT REVISITED

Professional Strategy and Personal Choice on the Path to Academic Leadership

Diane R. Dean, Susan J. Bracken, and Jeanie K. Allen

The Women in Academe series presents gendered research and writing on issues that influence women's experiences in higher education as faculty, students, and academic leaders. An advocacy work, the series aims to stimulate interest, dialogue, and collective action in creating positive and equitable working and learning environments for women and men in the academy.

The first volume in this series, *The Balancing Act* (Bracken, Allen, & Dean, 2006), focused on faculty work lives, presenting multiple views on how faculty struggle to balance their professional roles with their family and personal lives. We know from the collection of writing in *The Balancing Act* that women are not entering academic careers at rates proportional to their degree attainment, and when they do enter academia, they are less likely to gain tenure-track positions and achieve tenure and promotion. We further know that it is difficult for men and women to establish families and meaningful personal lives while pursuing tenure, and it is particularly more difficult for women to do so.

Women in Academic Leadership complements *The Balancing Act*, turning attention to the low numbers of women in academic administration. The volume features a collection of research studies, scholarly essays, and personal narratives that converge on a coherent and central problem: the challenges women face in attaining, surviving, and thriving in academic leadership roles.

The authors are faculty and administrators in junior, midcareer, and senior positions. They are or have been college presidents, deans, department chairs, and program coordinators. They speak from experience, research, and observation. They hail from public and private institutions at the 2-year, 4-year, and graduate levels. They include women who have walked the long road of academic leadership, and women who are just beginning their careers. Their scholarship and reflections featured in this volume share a feminist post-structural perspective for understanding the pervasive barriers that limit women's opportunities in higher education. Individual chapters focus on the professional strategies that women pursue on the path to academic leadership, and the personal choices women make along the way.

Professional Strategies on the Path to Academic Leadership

Women remain significantly underrepresented in top academic leadership positions and in key positions along the academic career ladder (American Council on Education, 2007; Corrigan, 2002; Dean, 2003). They continue to experience bias in the hiring process; inequitable workloads, salaries, and resources; and limited opportunities for professional development and advancement. *Women in Academic Leadership* addresses the various formal and informal professional strategies women employ to increase their leadership capacity, position themselves for opportunities, and reach their career goals. Chapters 3 and 7, for example, look at research findings on the effectiveness of formal development programs. In chapter 3 Sloma-Williams, McDade, Richman, and Morahan demonstrate how formal programs not only impart specific skills for developing women faculty as leaders, they also are an important origin of self-efficacy beliefs. Formal programs can increase women's self-perceived capabilities to seek, attain, and effectively engage in academic leadership positions. Turner and Kappes, however, remind us in chapter 7 that such programs are not one size fits all. Women of color have specific developmental needs in addition to those shared by their White, or Caucasian, counterparts. Their chapter includes a valuable appendix detailing the foci and logistics of several renowned national academic leadership development programs.

Chapters 5 and 6 look at informal development strategies. In chapter 6 Dean presents national research on the mentoring experiences of women academic vice presidents, revealing the relationships among their mentoring, professional development, and career aspirations. Gonzalez Sullivan investigates women presidents' strategies for and experiences with informal on-the-job learning. In a career ladder that lacks clear preparation for and progression between positions, and an environmental context of rapid change, informal learning becomes critical for women and men. Gonzalez Sullivan offers us a myriad of strategies and helps dispel the myth that leaders should be expected to step into their roles already knowing everything they need to perform well and succeed.

Even women who have advanced to the highest academic office can still face difficulties in leadership. In chapter 9, Bornstein, drawing from her research on academic presidents, illuminates how internal and external environmental contexts can affect women presidents in attaining and sustaining presidential legitimacy. She discusses strategies women must use to gain and maintain legitimacy in positions staunchly located within taken-for-granted gendered structures.

Personal Choices

We know from *The Balancing Act* that women face and make a variety of difficult choices as they negotiate between their personal and professional lives. *Women in Academic Leadership* continues to explore the balance between the personal and professional, exploring five major tensions: values-based versus political leadership, hierarchical versus collaborative visioning and direction setting, self-marginalization versus mainstreaming, self-isolation versus community building, and the influence of women's complex and multiple identities.

In chapter 1, Eddy researches the gendered nature of leadership itself. She examines the extent to which academic leadership is male normed, revealing important differences in how men and women presidents perceive their own leadership and how they are perceived by their campus constituents. The male imagery the presidency is steeped in is an advantage for men and a disadvantage for their women counterparts who never quite fit and are always "other." Ultimately Eddy proposes a multidimensional model of leadership, one that can help us transform how we think about and practice leadership.

In chapter 2, Tarule, Applegate, Earley, and Blackwell analyze the personal-narrative discourse of four women academic deans, illustrating the kinds of dilemmas women leaders face in their quest to lead from personally authentic and feminist leadership styles. They examine these stories from theoretical and reflective positions that enable readers to think carefully and critically about some of their own leadership quandaries and to examine the significance of the intersection of what we collectively think of as effective leadership and the gendered nature of leadership itself.

Chapters 4 and 8 explore the influence that women's complex and multiple identities and affiliations have upon their opportunities and effectiveness as agents of change. In chapter 4, Wood presents a scholarly piece on the unique barriers to women's advancement in faith-based colleges and universities as well as systemic and institutional equity change efforts under way. In chapter 8, Moses distills career advice from 25 years of scholarship and lived experience to address issues and opportunities for African American women in academe. Confirming the writings of Turner and Kappes, she illustrates how a one-size-fits-all strategy toward advancing women in academe cannot work.

Personal Agency

Ultimately *Women in Academic Leadership* calls forth and champions the power of personal agency. *Agency,* by definition, refers to an action or means through which something is accomplished (*Encarta,* n.d.). An agency can refer to a business that conducts a specific kind of work, a government organization charged with specific administrative duties, or a legal relationship between two individuals when one is charged with the responsibility and authority to act on behalf of the other (*Encarta*). We the editors define human, or personal, agency as individuals accepting the responsibility and claiming the authority to be the means through which they accomplish their desired goals. Personal agency involves the individual capacity to act independently and make free choices and the responsibility to do so. This necessitates ability, intentionality, authority, and accountability.

The concept of agency as applied to academic careers was introduced by Neumann, Terosky, and Schell (2006) in *The Balancing Act.* In their chapter they explored and called for a greater sense of agency among tenured professors in developing their own posttenure careers. The authors in *Women in Academic Leadership* collectively carry that concept forward, applying it to academic administration. The feminist post-structuralist viewpoint in this volume illuminates gender inequities as originating from a male-normed organizational culture, embedded in organizational structures that limit or influence women's opportunities. However, women need not succumb to these structures. Although individuals "vary in their access to context-embedded resources and privileges and in their abilities to draw on such resources" (Neumann et al., p. 94), and these variances influence an individual's effectiveness in activating personal agency (Marshall, 2000), this does not prevent people from charting and directing their own life path (Clausen, 1991; Elder, 1994; Lerner & Busch-Rossnagel, 1981; Marshall, 2000; Neumann et al.). Women academic leaders can and do exercise their individual capacity and responsibility to set and reach desired career goals, employing requisite professional strategies and making inevitable personal choices.

It is our hope that this collection of research and writing may help women realize their capacity for self-determination. May they become more knowledgeable about professional strategies they might employ and not be constrained by myths and assumptions that perpetuate ineffective strategies. Further, may they expand their awareness of the range of personal choices available to them and have the boldness to pursue those choices.

Yet we also strive for something more. Students, faculty, and administrators are socialized into academe, and their scholarly and work lives are informed and shaped by the organizational culture around them. Although organizational structures and cultures constrain choices and actions, organizational contexts are not unalterable. The effects of human agency can be far reaching, as people individually or collectively affect the world around them. It is our larger hope that the *Women in Academe* series will stimulate the awareness, advocacy, and action necessary to change the social and organizational systems we inhabit, thereby creating positive and equitable working and learning environments for all in the academy.

Suggestions for Building Awareness, Advocacy, and Action

Continuing what we established in *The Balancing Act,* we would like to offer concrete suggestions for women and men who would like to take tangible steps within their own work environment to effect change for the better. This list reiterates several of the steps suggested in volume 1, extending them and adding additional steps emanating from *Women in Academic Leadership.*

Awareness

1. **Maintain vigilant awareness of campus work life and environment and question what we define and accept as normal.** We can ask ourselves how this collection of research and writing confirms or differs from the experiences that we live or observe on our own campuses, why we participate in shaping imbalanced or inequitable workplace practices, and what we can actively do to make changes.

2. **Reflect on what we and our campuses identify as the traits and behaviors of effective leadership and question what leadership traits**

we accept and reward. Leadership is culturally defined. We can ask ourselves whether the leadership traits we accept and reward are truly effective and whether they are consistent with those required to create and sustain equitable environments. Further, we can challenge inconsistencies revealed through such analysis.

3. **Maintain awareness of multiple dimensions of identity and their intersections.** As we continue to understand and challenge the barriers that limit opportunities for women in academe, we must remain aware of other dimensions of identity that constrain or enable individual choices and actions. Strategies and choices appropriate for one group of women may be inadequate for another. Racial, religious, socioeconomic, and other differences necessitate different strategies and compel different choices.

Advocacy

4. **Embrace the "personal is political" in your work and look for it in the work of others.** In terms of equitable, healthy work environments, what is viewed and framed as good for women is also good for all members of the campus community *and* essential for the longevity of the academy. We can and should be critically reflective of our own and others' participation, leadership, and agency in creating positive and equitable work environments.

5. **Balance the process of problem identification with inquiry into noteworthy, positive structures and practices.** In *The Balancing Act*, we cautioned against focusing exclusively on identifying and labeling problems within the academy and on viewing solutions as lying outside of ourselves and residing in actions others should take instead. We can become solution seekers, asking ourselves what are the best practices for developing and practicing academic leadership, and what more may be achieved on our own campuses.

Action

6. **Reenvision ourselves as adult learners in addition to experts in our respective fields.** Leadership begins with the self. In *The Balancing Act* we appealed to academics to perceive themselves as lifelong adult learners in need of ongoing personal and professional opportunities to grow and learn. Here we suggest leadership development for individuals at all levels of academic administration. In the context of flattened administrative hierarchies and shared governance, successful

norm, making it difficult for women to lead from a more authentic perspective (Curry, 2000). This chapter asks, How do women and men community college leaders construct their perspectives of presidential leadership? Furthermore, do these presidents lead in traditionally gendered ways?

Theoretical Framework

Nidiffer (2001) posited an integrated model of leadership that blends historically gender-related leadership competencies. Her model argues for a fuller array of leadership competencies drawing from the best elements of models that have favored men in the past, that is, traits of power, decisiveness, hero, and so on; and those that favored women's attributes, that is, traits of generative leadership, collaboration, participation, and so forth. She argues that when using an integrated approach "the typically female traits are more advantageous than typically male traits. Thus, choosing a man for a leadership role has no automatic advantage" (p. 112). The integrated model of leadership Nidiffer proposed builds on two perspectives of leadership competencies: socialized competencies and acquired competencies. Her integrated model of leadership values the feminine and masculine proficiencies. In contrast, the feminine deficit model discriminates against the socialized or more traditional female competencies, devaluing the very essence of female strengths and approaches to leadership relative to the preferred male socialized norms. Likewise, the masculine deficit model discriminates against male attributes, which come up short when using female strengths as the measure of success.

The study underlying this chapter tests the applicability of an integrated model of leadership theory in practice by analyzing the leadership of sitting presidents. It applies Nidiffer's (2001) conceptual model of integrated leadership using a feminist standpoint. "Feminist standpoint theories focus on gender differences, on differences between women's and men's situations, which give a scientific advantage to those who can make use of the difference" (Harding, 1991, p. 120). Standpoint theory places value on women's experiences, acknowledges the different experiences of women relative to men, and does not equate difference with inferiority. Hartsock (1987) points out that standpoint theory allows the invisible to become visible. Rather than a simple dualism, standpoint theory "posits a duality of levels of reality of which the deeper level or essence both includes and explains the 'surface' or appearance, and indicates the logic by means of which the appearance inverts and distorts the deeper reality" (p. 160). Thus by looking at leadership from the perspective of women, we may discover an alternative interpretation of the construction of leadership, one that moves beyond the traditionally male attributes often associated with leadership theory and toward the integrated model espoused by Nidiffer.

Literature Review

In framing this research, I drew upon three areas of literature. I began with the history of leadership in community colleges, then expanded those historical foundations using current findings of pathways to the community college presidency, giving particular attention to female forms of leadership as it relates to male-normed traditions, including the role of work-life demands. Finally, I considered and incorporated the influence of gendered language.

Historical Foundations

Twombly (1995) reviewed four eras of community college leaders. From 1900 to the 1930s trait theory dominated, epitomized by the "great man" theory. The leaders of the 1940s to the 1950s sought to become independent from secondary schools and forge an identity of their own. The 1960s–1970s detailed the present-day version of the community college in which colleges served the function of educating transfer students, meeting local economic needs, and educating a vocational workforce. Typical leaders exemplified strong, dominant leadership representing male norms of leadership deemed necessary during those pioneering days. Finally, the 1980s–2000 focused attention on resource issues, employing models from business that emphasized efficiency and strategic planning. These eras of community college leadership drew heavily upon male imagery, traits of strength, power, and dominance. Recent writing on community college leadership, however, argues for the need for a more cognitive approach to leadership, one that places greater emphasis on acquiring skills in learning to lead than on the acquisition of a particular set of traits (Amey, 2005).

Further study by Amey and Twombly (1992) deconstructed language to study leadership at community colleges over time. Their review illustrated that a group of White male scholars and practitioners reinforced their own ideals of the typical leader. Having a White male as the norm leaves women and people of color struggling to conceive of ways to authenticate their own leadership, as it does not fit the images portrayed in the community college literature.

Current Pathways

Recent research (Amey et al., 2002) noted that while the pathways to the presidency in community colleges have become more varied, historical patterns prevail. The majority of college leaders obtain their positions after a trek through the administrative hierarchy from faculty to department chair to dean to vice president of instruction, finally arriving at a presidency. Further study by VanDerLinden (2003) argued that women face barriers in promotion, given their inability to move and the lack of advancement possibilities within their current institution, hence limiting their promotion options and, ultimately, the number of female presidents. Women with family responsibilities and those who are part of a dual-career couple with spouses whose careers are coequal or elevated from their own face burdens not experienced by their male counterparts because women are less able to move. Men with families, on the other hand, more often will have a wife who either does not work or whose career is subservient to their own, thus allowing for more flexibility to take advantage of promotions offered through a move to another institution.

Regarding family issues, women face even further differentiated experiences than men do. Recent research (Mason & Goulden, 2004) has problematized these differences, highlighting that having a family may slow the career progress of women faculty—most often the stepping-stone to administrative ranks. Notably, women presidents (all institutional types) altered their job for children 25% of the time compared to men (2% of the time; Corrigan, 2002). Moreover, women in heterosexual relationships still handle the majority of household chores and are the major child care providers, establishing a differentiated and added work experience that their male peers do not share. The inevitable tensions and choices between the primacy of family versus career, or of having a family at all, inserts another barrier for women who would seek advancement.

Female Versus Male Forms of Leadership

Previous research on women and leadership (Helgesen, 1995; Rosener, 1990) argued that men and women lead differently. Literature on women's leadership assumes more sharing of power and a participatory orientation to leading (Chliwniak, 1997; Townsend & Twombly, 1998). For example, successful women leaders operate within a web of inclusion, rejecting traditional hierarchies and relying instead on a web of relationships (Helgesen). Likewise, traditional male leaders rely on transactions of rewards and punishments, whereas women focus on transforming individual self-interest into meeting institutional objectives via increased participation and power sharing (Rosener).

Yet other research suggests that leadership may not be so rigidly gendered. For example, juxtaposed with this perspective is the research of Gillett-Karam (1994), which studied men and women presidents at community colleges. Although her findings mirror current demographics outlined above (age differentials between male and female presidents, experience differences, etc.), she concluded that leadership actions were strongly tied to situations, not gendered differences. Eddy (2003) found that while campus members spoke about their presidents in gendered terms, perceiving that men exhibited authoritative leadership and women generative leadership, the actual leadership behaviors of the presidents were not stereotypically gendered. Jablonski (1996), despite research that has shown that women have more generative leadership orientations (Sagaria & Johnsrud, 1988), discovered that although women presidents believed they led in more participatory and collegial ways, faculty members at their colleges disagreed.

Furthermore, although conceptualizations of college presidents' approach to leadership have changed from the "take-charge," "great-man" approach to an emphasis on participatory and shared decision making, an approach more often associated with women leaders (Chliwniak, 1997), the faculty members in Jablonski's (1996) study were conflicted about what they desired and expected in a leader. On the one hand, faculty members wished for more participatory leadership, but on the other they also wanted strong, aggressive leaders—the latter attribute most often linked with male leadership. Thus, women often are caught in the double bind of trying to meet male norms while also meeting the expectation of their gender.

Maintaining such limited definitions and images of leaders leaves women with a narrow band of acceptable leadership behavior (Amey & Twombly, 1992). A dilemma for women involves the choice they must make between adhering to traditional norms and expectations based on male ways of leading or enacting a more personally genuine and therefore perhaps a more female construction of leadership (Amey, 1999). Glazer-Raymo (1999) referred to women who opted to adapt as they move through the male-normed system as "playing by the rules" (p. 157). A dangerous option, playing by the rules reifies the strict male-female conceptions of leadership. When faced with this double bind, women cannot win. This deficit model of leadership positions women as constantly judged against the male norm, facing the choice of attempting to meet these expectations by rejecting a sense of self. Tedrow and Rhoads (1999) added two more options for women—reconciliation and resistance. Reconciliation involves striking a trade-off for women, in which they recognize the limitations of the male norms but work within the system for change. Resisters, on the other hand, reject this Faustian bargain and strike out against the boundaries that male norms establish with active opposition.

The Influence of Gendered Language

Language construction also plays a central role in the enactment of leadership on campus. As with research on leadership, communication scholarship asserts that women communicate in gendered ways, with men serving as the norm (Tannen, 1994). Male norms of communicating allow for men to be directive, assertive, and in charge, whereas female norms expect women to be agreeable and nonconfrontational to allow for broader participation. For instance, women speak in a manner that offers suggestions rather than absolutes, often doing so in the form of questions (Spender, 1981).

West and Zimmerman (1987) posited that men and women are "doing gender" in following traditional gendered schemas along sex lines. In this scenario, individuals are penalized for acting in a manner inconsistent with their gender. Thus, an assertive or dominant woman is viewed as acting outside her proscribed gender role and is penalized versus a man acting in the same manner who would be rewarded. As a result, individuals lock themselves into activities supporting the socially acceptable behavior for their gender. Doing gender builds on creating differences between men and women that are then "used to reinforce the 'essentialness' of gender" (West & Zimmerman, p. 140). Valian (1998) describes this concept as *gender schema*. "Gender schema assumes men and women are different based on a combination of nature and nurture and as a result, each gender manifests different behaviors in various aspects of life" (Nidiffer, 2001, p. 109). Language then acts to reinforce what it means to be a male or female leader based on essential features, with the male and female speakers themselves reinforcing certain kinds of gender identity (Cameron, 1998).

The influence of male language usage affects organizational culture (Morgan, 1997). Of particular concern for leaders is how organizational culture creates social reality. The use of language feeds into the creation of reality in determining what is valued (Berger & Luckmann, 1966). Thus, an organization with male language norms consequently creates a male-normed reality, ultimately setting the bar or definition of success as imbued with male attributes. Gilligan (1982) and Helgesen (1995) suggest that male domination of normative behavior also occurs in organizations. "Women moving into [institutions] are generally seen as interlopers, and are at greater pains to prove that they belong" (Eckert, 1998, p. 67). Language use serves to reinforce the cultural ideal of male hegemony within organizations where a patriarchal frame of values interprets reality. Despite research on the role of male symbols of privilege within organizations (Spender, 1981), gendered issues still remain (Ropers-Huilman, 2003). Thus, while we in academe are aware of having organizational reward structures that value men and profess a concern for the advancement of women to leadership positions, our institutions of higher education still harbor gender discrimination practices and barriers to advancement. The recent coverage of the treatment of women in the academic sciences (Fogg, 2005; Wilson, 2004) exemplifies and reinforces that gender issues remain for women on college campuses.

Research on the perceptions of male and female leaders highlighted that "leaders were viewed more positively when they used a leadership style that was typical of and consistent with their gender" (Griffin, 1992, p. 14). Thus, leaders were rewarded for doing gender (West & Zimmerman, 1987), which reinforced historic assumptions of male and female leadership characteristics.

Summary

The history of community college leadership builds upon and establishes male norms as the measure of what constitutes successful presidencies. The impact of more women entering the presidency shifts the historical definition of the type of leaders needed. In addition, present circumstances and the anticipated press to find new presidents to replace retiring chief executives at 2-year colleges demands that we rethink what it means to be a good leader. On the one hand, a historical dominance of male norms of leading creates a gauge for what it means to lead a community college. On the other hand, the contemporary push for more participatory leadership and collaboration values more female norms. The literature serves to provide a means to investigate and discern more clearly the distinctions between male and female attributes of leading, and how a theoretically gender-integrated style of leading might manifest in practice.

Methodology

For this study, I interviewed a total of nine community college presidents. Site visits were conducted at all locations, with face-to-face interviews occurring with all participants, as well as with campus members from the leadership team, faculty, and support areas. In total, I conducted 73 interviews. A broad range of geographic and institutional diversity was represented by the sites; full-time student enrollment ranged from 2,000 to 10,000, with rural and urban campuses represented. Five of the colleges were part of a community college district, but each campus had its own president. The gender composition of the campus presidents was five men and four women, which is an overrepresentation of women relative to the percentages of women leading 2-year college campuses (44% for the study, compared to 27% nationally;

Corrigan, 2002). To discover more about the gendered nature of community college leadership, I employed a phenomenological research method. Phenomenology research searches for the central underlying meaning of an experience, in this case the construction of leadership by community college presidents, and uses data reduction to analyze specific statements and themes for possible meanings (Creswell, 1998). This research methodology focuses upon how individuals consciously develop meaning via social interactions (Creswell,1998). I also employed a heuristic lens to allow for deeper interpretation of the experiences described (van Manen, 1990).

For this study, I reviewed verbatim transcripts of the interviews for elements that reflected the integrated model of leadership posited by Nidiffer (2001), reading and rereading to obtain a sense of overall themes. I then coded all transcripts for language referring to the presidents' leadership, reviewing their statements to discover how the participants constructed their ideals of leadership based on the gendered schema of the model. Categories for male and female language included sentences and phrases based on male descriptors or inferences, such as authoritative, directive, hero oriented, or male norms. Coding for female language included sentences and phrases using language invoking ideals of generative, participatory, consensus building, relationships, or based on a female norm. Because my own bias in terms of what constituted male or female language presented a potential limitation, discussion of findings with a peer reviewer addressed this issue and aided in category validation. Thematic groupings put assorted statements in separate categories that indicated various perspectives on how the participants framed leadership. I identified patterns and categories using what Marshall and Rossman (1999) referred to as "reduction" and "interpretation" (p. 152). The process of reduction allowed for sorting data into manageable portions with similar themes. I brought interpretation of meaning to these categories and insight, given previous research and the voices of the participants.

Findings

Several findings emerged after analysis of the data. First, gendered stereotypes were evident on some level for all participants, with individuals playing out the expected roles of their gender. Second, whereas some of the women presidents noted differentiation of experience based on their gender, none of the men did. For men, their gender was invisible, thus supporting the idea that male imagery remains the hegemonic norm. Finally, the integration of leadership appeared to involve one-way movement, with men still operating from an authoritative perspective but using relationship skills mainly to obtain results—not relations. However, when the women spoke of their leadership being participatory, in reality their descriptions involved more use of hierarchy and directives despite the value they placed on relationships. Thus, while the data supported Nidiffer's (2001) notion of an integrated model of leadership that values male and female competencies, the beneficiaries of the integrated model favored men, not women. Men were rewarded for using female competencies involving relationship skills, whereas the leadership women exemplified relied more on traditional male norms of authority at a cost of a less-authentic female leadership style that integrated competencies.

Playing Gender Roles

Previous research (Getskow, 1996; West & Zimmerman, 1987) emphasized how roles tightly link to the expectations others have of individuals based on their gender. This study reinforced such gender schema. For example, two of the women spoke specifically of seeking their presidencies when their husbands retired and their children were on their own, reifying the female expectation of caring and nurturing one's family. One woman, when speaking of how she delayed entry into administration, noted:

> It was just clear to me at that point when my son was just 3 or 4 years old that I could not take an administrative position and protect what was important to me, which was the stability of my marriage, my son's growing up in a stable environment. So, the only thing I did, I left the associate dean's position, took a sabbatical, got back into teaching.

Each woman in the study also reported a circuitous route to the presidency, often with stop-outs for family obligations or lack of support for advancement.

Another gendered difference in routes to the presidency involved mentoring. Often, men receive more mentoring than their female counterparts (Hall & Sandler, 1983), establishing another facet of what constitutes male norms for leadership. One participant noted the lack of mentoring she received versus what she assumed her male counterparts were obtaining. Indeed, all of the men in the study commented on the help they received during their careers from mentors. Two men spoke specifically of mentoring they received from women. The approach both of these men in turn took in their presidencies highlighted more work on relationships and communication within the organization, presumably learned from their women mentors, than the approaches of the presidents who had only male mentors.

In an act of reinforcing gendered stereotypes, one of the female presidents stated:

> I spoke in my first convocation piece that I was particularly well suited to this challenge [a cut in campus budget] because we had raised a family on a single faculty member's salary, since I didn't work when our children were young, but I was always pinching pennies and managing, so I was very well equipped for this job, but it's tough.

This woman president specifically called attention to her female gender during this event of public discourse. Moreover, in describing this female president, one campus member said, "The president is willing to use her authority, but she uses it fairly gracefully." The feminine descriptor of "gracefully" reifies the gender of this president, distinct from ways campus members described their male presidents. The men in the study did not refer to their gender with respect to their family roles; the exception being one male participant who commented that his wife was a librarian and when seeking his presidency, he was conscious of the need to find a location that could accommodate her career.

The double bind women face when they act outside their prescribed feminine roles was evident for the participants. One participant recalled an event that shaped her desire to ultimately become a president:

> I can remember a night that I met with the president and I was interim dean of academic affairs at this point. I was going to apply for the permanent position and I met with him. I did apply for the position. But I met with him and I don't even remember what got us started but there was something that he wanted to do that I had a strong disagreement about and I told him that in my firm way [laugh] which was probably too blunt and bitchy. And he called me a bitch! I remember walking out of there, I mean I held my own, but I walked out of his office and said, "I can't work for this man. And what's more, I probably can't work for anyone. I've got to be my own boss." And what does that mean? If you're not in academia, I supposed you go into business for yourself. If you are in academia, you look for a presidency. And that's when I knew I was going to have a rocky time.

In this instance, when a woman tried to assert herself, she was punished for acting out of her prescribed feminine gender role. In a similar situation a man may have been called strong willed or tough, which would have reified the prescribed male attributes. Most likely, he would not have been demeaned or categorized in the same manner.

The men in the study often spoke of their leadership from the perspective of being the hero for the institution who arrived to save the day. The image of the hero-leader originates in male imagery and reinforces the gender schema of male leaders. The ideals of men's being authoritative and ultimate arbitrators of campus direction were clearly manifested in the interviews. One male president commented:

> The campus faculty were ripe for change. Ripe is my choice of words. They were ready. They were simply looking for someone to say, "What should we do?" So, there was receptiveness to any idea and a willingness to try things. . . . I think that to a great extent they were so appreciative that we wanted to go somewhere that even if they didn't agree with where we were going that overcame their disagreement. And I'm still riding that sleigh.

Evident in all of the presidents' comments were images of being the person in charge on campus. Regardless of the amount of participation by campus members, there was a sentiment that the "buck stops here" at the desk of the president. As the highest positional leader on campus, each participant took his or her role as the final arbitrator of decisions as given. The role of ultimate decision maker is rooted in male norms and characteristics.

A Women's Perspective

Putting women's perspectives at the center, how did these women talk about what it means to be a leader? As noted, only the women in the study commented on their gender with respect to their leadership. Other themes in their views on leadership included relationships, campus fit, community, family and timing, and a lack of career planning.

All the women participants held relationships in high value. For example, one of the female presidents commented, "One of my division chairs says that I'm Jimmy Carter, [since] I don't like to think the worst of people." These women worked closely with campus members as a critical and core component of the way they led. Several described how they spent the first months on the job hosting various small-group gatherings to meet with different campus members. While some of the male presidents also commented on doing the same form of beginning introductions, it appeared that such acts of relationship building held different intents for men. For the women, it created a sense of their individual ownership of the process of change on campus. They often used the words "my plan" when reviewing change initiatives, indicating a more personal connection with the process in which they were tightly invested in the outcomes. The men, on the other hand, seemed to look to relationships not so much on an individual level, but rather as a collective lever to use in enacting the broader goals of change. The men exhibited less personal investment in the process, instead interacting with more detachment. Men did not tie outcomes as closely with a sense of personal responsibility. Rather, they attributed any missteps to process or context.

The women in the study often referenced a sense of "fit" with their campus. As one president noted about her experiences as a candidate in the search for her current position:

> Each time I left [one of the interview meetings, I was] feeling pretty comfortable about it and pretty relaxed, and saying to myself, "If this is the kind of fit that I think that it is or that it feels like, then it will go forward and be successful. And if it's not, then one of us is not meeting the other's needs and this is probably not a place where I could be successful." You know, it just felt good.

Another woman in the study defined fit a bit differently, not merely noting the fit with college but rather the region. She commented:

> I fell in love with the state. I never really spent any time in the West. I was born and grew up in New York and New England, and that was it. I was struck by how much I liked the arid West. I like the sunshine, I like the absence of a lot of insect life, I like that dry, sterile, sort of environment. And there is wildlife, there may not be a lot of insects, but there's a lot of other kind of wildlife. We walk every night. Two nights ago, we were followed by a couple of coyotes. So that happens. So my reaction was not so much to the school but this is where I want to live, this part of my life.

Statistics indicate that women hold fewer presidencies and obtain them later in life. Only one of the four women in this study came from a previous presidency, and it was within the same district. Given the lack of opportunities for multiple presidencies, these women gave added consideration to the positions they took. The fit of the position and the locale became justifiably critical in their choices.

In contrast, three of the five men in the study had held previous presidential positions. With greater odds for subsequent presidencies, men did not reference the qualities of fit and locale as critical considerations. Only one man noted the location of his institution: in his home state near his elderly mother. But, he also commented, "I would have gone other places but don't tell my mother that. She's convinced I came back here to see her."

The women participants all spoke of the role of community on the campus. Attentive to building relationships, they sought to foster a sense of cohesiveness and oneness. One woman president commented: "I think the lack of community is a concern for me here and I'm trying to see what we can do in terms of traditions." Another president described her intentions for community on campus:

> I'm really trying to maintain regular face-to-face contact with staff. . . . you know bonding and making sure we involve people so that they meet, everybody knows each other and really can share informally—really that's one thing which I think is important that they understand, [that] they know who we are.

Women valued their roles in creating a sense of connection on campus. In contrast, although men spoke of relationships on campus, they focused on maintaining open communication and awareness of strategic goals, not on fostering an interpersonal connection or a sense of oneness.

The role of family and timing of career moves influenced career progression for the women participants. The issue of dual-career families also had a bearing on the timing of their moves into the presidency. For the women such a move was easier to make at the end of their husbands' careers. The men participants, in contrast, did not note that their career choices were based on the obligations of their partners. Family and working spouses presented barriers en route to the presidency only for women. They clearly were rooted in gender. The existence of barriers and ways that women overcome such roadblocks ultimately influenced how these women lead and what they view as important issues, both for themselves and for others in the college.

A lack of career planning and intentionality about becoming a president were evident for all the women participants. As one of the women presidents noted,

> It wasn't something that I felt strongly about [getting a presidential position]. I mean, I was considering it and I guess I kept thinking what harm would it do to apply for this position here and what harm would it do to pursue the next step. It was kind of like, well, I'd take one step and see if that felt okay and then take the next step.

Since women did not always intentionally think about ascending to a presidency, they did not necessarily expose themselves to opportunities that would help them prepare for leading a college.

Men, on the other hand, sought their presidencies through encouragement of mentors, through promotions throughout the years, and often with an intentionality that was lacking in the female participants. Two of the men participated in the League for Innovation in the Community College presidential sessions, while another obtained his doctorate in the University of Texas at Austin program that holds a strong track record for training presidents. Those men who had strong mentoring also exposed themselves to opportunities that allowed them to obtain skills—the acquired competencies noted in Nidiffer's (2001) model—relative to their female counterparts. The gender schema evident for the women leaders was primarily invisible to them. Men did not comment in specifics about their gender or on the influence of gender on being campus leaders; they operated instead with an assumed right to the position and an unquestioned link between their gender and position.

One-Way Integration

In moving toward an integrated model of leadership, an underlying tenet is the acquisition of attributes of the opposite gender. For men, this means acting more collaboratively and allowing for more participation on the part of campus members. For women, integration means exhibiting traditional male characteristics of power, authority, and directives.

The findings from this study indicate that the male participants have begun at a minimum to use the language of collaboration and teamwork. Of course, not all the men in the study exhibited more generative forms of leadership in the same manner. At a minimum, however, each of the male participants spoke of the value of relationships with campus members and the role that listening to input from others had on their own decision making. For instance, one president, who exhibited many "herolike" characteristics, also noted,

> Just because I had the vision [didn't mean I could] implement it. I needed to do something before that. I needed to develop a consensus. Consensus is the wrong term. I needed to develop strong support for that from a group of faculty and staff.

Yet although men valued relationships and gave attention to individual voices, ultimately they did not seek true collaboration. Rather, they used collaborative behavior to garner support for achieving their intended and outlined presidential goals.

However, two different male leaders did show a more authentic style of collaboration. One described his leadership as follows:

> I see my leadership style in ways similar to a team. A team like baseball in that I play multiple roles. At the same time I'm the team manager. I play that role. I'm also the coach. So I'll take people aside and be a mentor. At times I'm a player. Not in today's vocabulary—I play in a band but I play the game with them, meaning we are all there, we are doing that. I'm also a cheerleader. When things are going well I don't need to wave a flag oh, I'm the president no, no but I'm cheering. Keep doing that and everything and I'm also a scout. I go out and I check out what is happening there. You notice [in] all of this I didn't mention the team owner. I'm not a team owner. It's ours. We are all in this together. And we have various roles.

Interestingly, when a campus member reflected on this president's leadership he noted, "My sense is, and I'm not speaking for myself, but my sense is, my reading of this is what [campus members] say, they feel there is a leadership vacuum at this campus. They don't feel that the president is taking charge and getting us the direction that we need." The language of this description highlights the penalty for male leaders who act outside their prescribed gendered roles: Campus members perceived the more collaborative orientation of this male president's leadership as less effective.

The other male president with a more cooperative orientation understood the way in which his position as president created distance between him and campus members. To combat this, he held individual meetings with each campus member when he first arrived at the college. As a result, he commented, "No one's afraid of me."

Importantly, the integrated model of leadership promoted by Nidiffer (2001) assumed that women operate from a more feminine perspective of leadership: one oriented toward the female values of democracy and participation. The data from this research do not support this notion. Instead, the women participants appeared to obtain their positions of power by enacting the very male features that have been traditionally held in esteem. Namely, the women worked within the hierarchy and assumed power by position. They relied on traditionally female characteristics of relationships and participation in ways similar to their male counterparts.

Each woman spoke of ways in which she used the hierarchy of the organization to gain control and also spoke of instances in which she used directives. As one female president noted,

Well the organizational structure was terrible. There were any number of serious problems. The most serious was that I had deans that I did not trust. . . . The first thing I did was to group areas under two vice-presidents. The appointment of the two vice-presidents was right away, like the fall of my first year, when I realized I needed to get some space. I needed basically to get some control.

Other women participants noted how they used shifts in the hierarchy to better align the organization to oversee changes. These women used the bureaucracy to set up a structure they could exhibit influence over. Key in the reorganization efforts was the placement of trusted individuals in positions of power.

One of the women set up a system of program review in which various degrees were labeled "In Jeopardy," implying a risk of elimination if they did not improve their cost-effectiveness for the college. Other women in the study exhibited similar directives.

Only the president who led a newly forming campus exemplified a truly cooperative leadership style. Here, with no preestablished organizational norms to follow, she could use the features of a learning organization to begin to build the structure of the new college. The core team used a consensus-building model to make decisions on how to structure the new college and its systems. The president commented that collective learning was a goal: "Almost all the decisions so far were done in a collaborative way so we really reach consensus on those as we developed it." She feared, however, whether she could keep this format of decision making operating once the college was fully staffed and operational. As she said,

One of the things that I fear a little bit. . . . One thing is to get them to accept our vision, and have them understand it and to believe it and embrace it. A bigger challenge might be for us to be open to the new ideas that they will bring. And not to just say well no, you can't do that because that's not the way we planned it.

The fact that only this one woman participant truly exemplified leadership from a more authentic female perspective might be attributed to context. She was charged with creating a new college versus assuming a leadership position in a college already established. While other women had the daunting task of infusing collaboration and participation into the traditional, hierarchical structures they inherited, she could root these attributes in her organizational culture as the new college formed.

Discussion

Nidiffer's (2001) integrated model provides a strong foundation to consider how to get the best of both male and female leadership competencies. The visible clues of a leader's sex may obscure our ability to see true integration, because they serve as the first clue we react to in establishing our expectations of them. These visual cues alert us to what to expect from a female leader versus a male leader based on past experience and socialized expectations of leadership based on gender. Consider the traditional desire for a "hero" leader, who is always male and who lives on in these times of tight fiscal constraints. Our challenge, assuming this continues as a valued form of leadership, is how to get ourselves and others to see a variety of acceptable forms of what a hero may look like.

Women face the difficult double bind of being expected to act according to their gender while being measured against male norms of leadership. Men do not face this same problem. Expected to behave according to the very norms they are measured against, most men are not even cognizant of the benefits their gender provides to them relative to women. For men, their gender is invisible, and they neither address nor comment upon it when they think of their own leadership.

Men realize the value of relationship building, traditionally a female characteristic, but have the advantage of still being seen as the hero at the same time. The men in the study often used relationships to foster and build on their hero image. The women, instead, used the relationships to foster more of a fit within the institution, with an eye toward the development of community. Paradoxically, although women leaders valued relationship building for community, they predominately operated within a directive hierarchy. The integrated model proposed by Nidiffer (2001) appeared to work more to the men's advantage than to the women's. A contributing factor to this assessment includes the forms of evaluating leadership. Research by Bensimon (1989) challenged how leadership perspectives might be biased given a male orientation to the conceptual models. When the models themselves are questioned, gender evaluations begin to look different. Thus, evaluating the participant's leadership based solely on the competencies outlined may have favored male attributes over female even when acknowledging that both types of competencies are valued. Historically, leadership theory originates in the study of men. This creates a dilemma when measuring women against male-originated norms. This shortcoming was evident in how the male and female presidents viewed, defined, and articulated intended outcomes for relationships. Men used relationships but often with different intents than women did. Women saw relationships as integral to the internal fabric of the college, whereas men viewed relationships as a mechanism to affect their own change agendas.

An alternative representation of the model might better address the multidimensional aspects of leadership (Figure 1.1). This model allows for the presentation of the underlying gendered schema proposed by Valian (1998). Valian based definitions of gender schema on assumed gender differences and behaviors reinforced as appropriate to and associated with masculine and feminine attributes. Depending on past experiences and underlying identity construction, individuals may see themselves along a continuum ranging from male to female. Given that gender is a socially constructed ideal, an individual may be located at different points along the continuum depending upon individual identity construction. Seeing gender as more multifaceted allows for a more nuanced discussion regarding leadership. Similarly, the continuum of attributes that have traditionally been more male or female in classification allows for a range of leadership behaviors. The attributes themselves do not rely on gender but rather on how an individual approaches his or her leadership. Thus, the male leader noted above who believed in a team structure for his organization would be located farther on the female side of characteristics on the continuum. Likewise, the female president who was using the structure of

FIGURE 1.1
Multidimensional Leadership

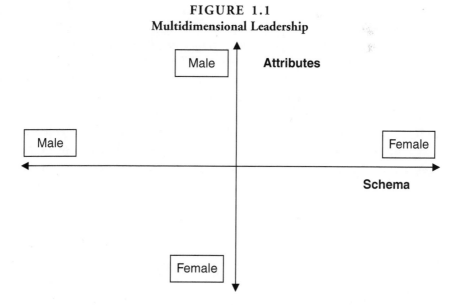

the hierarchy to gain control would be positioned more on the male side of the range of attributes.

The availability of more dimensions in discussing leadership allows for a more authentic evaluation of leaders. Rather than a simple duality of male or female leadership perspectives, a multidimensional model allows for expanded conceptions of what it means to be a good leader. An individual with a higher male-oriented schema and more male characteristics of leadership would be located in the M-M quadrant of the model. Likewise, an individual with a female schema and corresponding female characteristics would be found in the F-F quadrant. Using the argument of Nidiffer's (2001) integrated leadership model, individuals within an integrated model would be located in either M-F or F-M. The advantage of the multidimensions within this model is that even within this integrated formation, individuals may be located in a large range of locations. A multidimensional perspective allows for the deconstruction of the dualism often present in conversations regarding men and women and how they lead. Rather than being limited to an either/or situation, or even a blended concept as Nidiffer suggests, a continuum model allows for both genders to lead more authentically. A key to the successful implementation of a more holistic conception of leadership involves rewarding a variety of styles, not just those favoring men.

Conclusion

As the findings from this research indicate, women still do not fully lead from an authentic perspective. We still judge "good" leadership against the male norms of success. Change is evident, however, as highlighted by the woman president in charge of opening a new campus and who uses a more cooperative model of leading. Likewise, the two men presidents who valued teamwork and relationships within their colleges highlighted how male leadership has become infused with the traditionally female attributes of collaboration and participation. Pointedly, each of these men had women mentors. This implies a need to think more critically about the role of intentional mentoring for men and women.

Given the lack of parity in the numbers of women community college presidents relative to men, several questions arise: Are women opting out of pursuit of the highest leadership position since they feel they can be more authentic at lower levels? Are women being shut out of the highest positions because they are not perceived as herolike with the ability to save the day? Do women have to first lead like men to be recognized for advancement?

Once in positions of power, are they able to lead from a more gender-authentic perspective?

The viewpoint of a multidimensional perspective of leadership allows for more choices of what constitutes an integrated form of leadership. In this case, a variety of male and female attributes are recognized as appropriate for and suitable to leading a campus—ultimately allowing men and women to lead more authentically. If we envision the model of leadership more complexly, containing multiple planes of attributes and characteristics, individual leaders may be located in a variety of points within the model and still be effective and genuine. Currently, we might view one of the quadrants as historically more valued, that is, the M-M quadrant, and one as undesirable, that is, the F-F quadrant. The goal is to value more variability of location within the quadrants.

Hiring committees must think more complexly about gender in choosing new leaders. As this research shows, while campus members perceived presidents in gendered terms, the presidents did not necessarily lead in strictly gendered ways. The women employed traditional male leadership in using the hierarchy, whereas some of the men used expanded concepts of teamwork in making decisions. If committees base hiring decisions simply on gender, then community colleges will miss out on potentially good leaders. Given the leadership crisis facing these institutions, we must think more expansively about what it means to lead.

Women are becoming more accepted as college leaders and more numerous in positions of responsibility on college campuses. Deeply engrained perspectives of what it means to be a leader remain rooted in male norms, however. As more women become presidents, it may become easier for others to see women and their leadership perspectives as more typical—if women presidents lead from a degree of gender authenticity. The good news: We are looking at a markedly different profile of presidents now than we did even a decade ago. As the number of women presidents increases, it will help us to envision other ways of leading. In times of crisis, we may still desire a hero to save the day. More and more women, however, are becoming the heroes of their campuses and leading the way for expanded understanding of what it means to lead.

References

Amey, M. J. (1999). Navigating the raging river: Reconciling issues of identity, inclusion, and administrative practice. In K. Shaw, R. A. Rhoads, & J. Valadez

(Eds.), *Community colleges as cultural texts: Qualitative explorations of organizational and student cultures* (pp. 59–82). Albany, NY: SUNY Press.

Amey, M. J. (2005). Conceptualizing leading as learning. *Community College Journal of Research and Practice, 29*(9–10), 689–704.

Amey, M. J., & Twombly, S. B. (1992). Revisioning leadership in community colleges. *The Review of Higher Education, 15*(2), 125–150.

Amey, M. J., VanDerLinden, K., & Brown, D. F. (2002). Career mobility and administrative issues: A twenty year comparison of the changing face of community colleges. *Community College Journal of Research and Practice, 27*(7–8), 573–589.

Bensimon, E. M. (1989). A feminist reinterpretation of presidents' definitions of leadership. *Peabody Journal of Education, 66*(3), 143–156.

Berger, P. L., & Luckmann, T. (1966). *The social constructivism of reality: A treatise in the sociology of knowledge.* Garden City, NY: Doubleday & Company.

Cameron, D. (1998). Performing gender identity: Young men's talk and the construction of heterosexual masculinity. In J. Coates (Ed.), *Language and gender: A reader* (pp. 270–284). Oxford, UK: Blackwell.

Chliwniak, L. (1997). Higher education leadership: Analyzing the gender gap. *ASHE-ERIC Higher Education Reports, 25*(4), 1–97.

Corrigan, M. (2002). *The American college president: 2002 edition.* Washington, DC: American Council on Education Center for Policy Analysis.

Creswell, J. W. (1998). *Qualitative inquiry and research design: Choosing among five traditions.* Thousand Oaks, CA: Sage.

Curry, B. (2000). *Women in power: Pathways to leadership in education.* New York: Teachers College Press.

Eckert, P. (1998). Gender and sociolinguistic variation. In J. Coates (Ed.), *Language and gender: A reader* (pp. 64–75). Oxford, UK: Blackwell.

Eddy, P. L. (2003). Views of gender in the community college presidency. *Community College Enterprise, 9*(2), 49–64.

Evelyn, J. (2001, April). Community colleges face a crisis of leadership. *The Chronicle of Higher Education, 47*(29), A36.

Fogg, P. (2005). Harvard's president wonders aloud about women in science and math. *The Chronicle of Higher Education, 51*(21), A12.

Getskow, V. (1996). *Women in community college leadership roles.* Los Angeles: ERIC Clearinghouse for Community Colleges. (ERIC Document Reproduction Service No. ED400025)

Gillett-Karam, R. (1994). Women and leadership. In G. A. Baker III (Ed.), *A handbook on the community college in America: Its history, mission, and management* (pp. 94–108). Westport, CT: Greenwood Press.

Gilligan, C. (1982). *In a different voice: Psychological theory and women's development.* Cambridge, MA: Harvard University Press.

Glazer-Raymo, J. (1999). *Shattering the myths: Women in academe.* Baltimore: Johns Hopkins University Press.

Griffin, B. Q. (1992, March). *Perceptions of managers: Effects of leadership style and gender.* Paper presented at the annual meeting of the Southeastern Psychological Association, Knoxville, TN.

Hall, R., & Sandler, B. (1983). *Academic mentoring for women students and faculty: A new look at an old way to get ahead.* Washington, DC: Association of American Colleges.

Harding, S. (1991). What is feminist epistemology? In S. Harding (Ed.), *Whose science? Whose knowledge?* (pp. 105–132). Ithaca, NY: Cornell University Press.

Hartsock, N. C. M. (1987). The feminist standpoint: Developing the ground for a specifically feminist historical materialism. In S. Harding (Ed.), *Feminism & methodology* (pp. 157–180). Bloomington: Indiana University Press.

Helgesen, S. (1995). *The web of inclusion: A new architecture for building great organizations.* New York: Currency/Doubleday.

Jablonski, M. (1996). The leadership challenge for women college presidents. *Initiatives, 57*(4), 1–10.

Marshall, C., & Rossman, G. B. (1999). *Designing qualitative research* (3rd ed.). Thousand Oaks, CA: Sage.

Mason, M. A., & Goulden, M. (2004). Do babies matter (Part II)? Closing the baby gap. *Academe, 88*(6), 21–27.

Morgan, G. (1997). *Images of organization.* Thousand Oaks, CA: Sage.

National Center for Education Statistics. (2003). *Digest of education statistics, 2002.* (Department of Education, NCES 2003-060). Washington, DC: U.S. Government Printing Office.

Nidiffer, J. (2001). New leadership for a new century: Women's contribution to leadership in higher education. In J. Nidiffer & C. T. Bashaw (Eds.), *Women administrators in higher education: Historical and contemporary perspectives* (pp. 101–134). Albany, NY: SUNY Press.

Ropers-Huilman, B. (2003). *Gendered futures in higher education.* Albany, NY: SUNY Press.

Rosener, J. B. (1990). Ways women lead. *Harvard Business Review, 68,* 119–125.

Sagaria, M. A., & Johnsrud, L. K. (1988). Generative leadership. In M. A. Danowitz Sagaria (Ed.), *Empowering women: Leadership development on campus* (pp. 13–26). San Francisco: Jossey-Bass.

Shults, C. (2001). *The critical impact of impending retirements on community college leadership.* Leadership Series Research Brief, No. 1. Washington, DC: American Association of Community Colleges.

Spender, D. (1981). *Man made language.* London: Pandora Press.

Tannen, D. (1994). *Talking from nine to five: How women's and men's conversational styles affect who gets heard, who gets credit, and what gets done at work.* New York: William Morrow.

Tedrow, B., & Rhoads, R. A. (1999). A qualitative study of women's experiences in community college leadership positions. *Community College Review, 27*(3), 1–18.

Townsend, B. K., & Twombly, S. B. (1998). A feminist critique of organizational change in community colleges. *New Directions for Community Colleges, 26*(2), 77–85.

Twombly, S. B. (1995). Gendered images of community college leadership: What messages they send. *New Directions for Community Colleges, 23*(1), 67–77.

Valian, V. (1998). *Why so slow: The advancement of women.* Cambridge, MA: MIT Press.

VanDerLinden, K. (2003, April). *Career advancement and leadership development of community college administrators.* Paper presented at a meeting of the American Educational Research Association, Chicago, IL.

van Manen, M. (1990). *Researching lived experience: Human science for an action sensitive pedagogy.* Albany, NY: SUNY Press.

Weisman, I. M., & Vaughan, G. B. (2002). *The community college presidency, 2001.* AACC research brief (ED466261). Washington, DC: American Association of Community Colleges.

West, C., & Zimmerman, D. H. (1987). Doing gender. *Gender & Society, 1*(2), 125–151.

Wilson, R. (2004). Louts in the lab. *The Chronicle of Higher Education, 50*(20), A7.

2

NARRATING GENDERED
LEADERSHIP

Jill Mattuck Tarule, Jane Henry Applegate,
Penelope M. Earley, and Peggy J. Blackwell

Story: A few months after assuming my first university leadership position, I attended what I was told was an important professional meeting—a place where critical networking occurs. The conference began with a reception, and as I entered the room I noticed that most attendees were men who seemed to know one another already and formed conversation groups in closed circles. I saw a woman standing near the buffet; she was alone and occupying herself by selecting and slowly nibbling vegetables while she scanned the dynamics in the room. I recognized her from presentations she had given at other meetings, and as I walked in her direction, she offered a welcoming smile. Having attended these meetings before, she pointed out various people who were current or emerging powerbrokers in the group. As we chatted, another woman entered the room. "That's Marleen," the woman said, explaining that Marleen was dean at a major university and served on a number of important boards and committees. We watched as Marleen punctured and joined the closed circles.

The next morning I saw Marleen at a coffee break and introduced myself. She expressed pleasure at meeting another woman dean, and we made tentative plans for dinner that night. Later I found my colleague from the vegetable buffet. She introduced me to another new dean who had arrived that morning. I mentioned that I had plans for dinner with Marleen that evening and invited her to join us. The new arrival was pleased and said she'd find a nice restaurant and make a reservation, then went on to tell us that a woman who had been her mentor would be flying in. She said she would include her as well. Later, I spoke to Marleen to confirm our plans

31

and told her that I had found three additional women colleagues to join us. She stared at me for a second and then said, "Of course, that's fine. I'm participating in the dean's golf tournament this afternoon but if I'm late, please go ahead without me."

The four of us (absent Marleen) met in the hotel lobby and after waiting a while decided to go ahead to the restaurant. When we arrived I saw Marleen at a table across the restaurant having drinks with four male colleagues. Uncertain what to do, I walked to her table to let her know that our group was there. I saw her evaluate the situation. "Hello, Kathy," she said, "how are you, dear? Sorry we missed connections. Let's touch base tomorrow." As I walked away, I could feel the eyes of her male colleagues on my back. Incidentally, my name isn't Kathy.

I recounted this conversation to my new friends and dinner companions. The senior dean in our group—who I learned had mentored several women—explained that Marleen had chosen to adopt a traditional leadership style—hierarchical, closed—saying, "She keeps trying on male skin but it never fits quite right; she just doesn't know it."

T hat was a beginning. We did not know at the time that this dinner meeting would lead to the creation of an ongoing group of women leaders. Over time it has expanded as new women leaders were appointed and contracted as others retired. A core group of four has remained. We live and have lived all over the country and overseas, and we have learned that a nonproximate support group such as ours is an unusual resource for building support and considering theory. We have written this chapter to tell our story about what we have learned in that process, to share the importance of such networks, and to encourage other women to develop similar groups of their own. Marleen is a fictional character based on people each of us has encountered in our professional life. We respect and honor the Marleens of the world; we just don't want to be like them.[1]

Introduction

For more than a decade, we, the four women authors of this chapter, have met every year at a fall and at a spring professional meeting. Our casual dinners grew into an ongoing discourse about effective leadership and how that intersected with what we saw as the gendered nature of leadership. Over time, the discourse moved from simple sharing to a more analytic form. The mode of inquiry that emerged included examining each story, issue, or problem we experienced, such as the one preceding, for meaning in three ways:

(a) how what we shared was linked to and "illuminated" (Hoshmond, 1989) theory about leadership; (b) how it informed theory about women and leadership; and (c) frequently, how an exploration of whether considering the gender of the leader—what we came to call the gender lens—provided any further clarification or understanding about the issue or problem we were addressing.

This chapter examines four major themes that emerged from our discourse by using the same approach or method that became our way of making meaning in our conversations about our experiences as leaders. Each theme is introduced with a story. The story is then considered reflectively, drawing on leadership theory, gender theory, and each other's articulated ideas about leadership practice.

This process of meaning making is firmly grounded in our individual narratives and the continuing stories about our separate experiences of leading and of leadership. Over time, this process of narrating our experiences twice a year not only became an important outlet for each of us, it also began to take on a life of its own. It became as much a theory-building seminar as a support network. Supporting this transition, the group was able to find other venues for what was becoming our work together, from getting a conference funded to consider how gender issues had been largely ignored in education reform reports to organizing to ensure that certain perspectives were reflected in the work of professional associations through our membership on committees, boards, and the like.

There were, of course, differences among us as individuals and in the institutional contexts in which we led. And over the years there would be changes in the jobs we held for all but one of us, changes that led one of us to be a dean in another institution, another to go "forward" to the faculty after being an administrator, one to become a department chair, and another to fall in love and retire to follow a new partner. The group was at one time as large as eight, but the four who are writing now ended up being constant over time, despite the changes in our lives. Unquestionably, it was through those regular face-to-face meetings that the form of the narrative process was developed. One or more of us would come to the group with a new dilemma, concern, or thought. Often, these were issues that for political or personal reasons we felt could not be raised on our campuses. The value of having a safe place to bring these issues to is immeasurable. Furthermore, over time a shared vocabulary began to develop as well as, to a certain extent, a shared worldview about leadership and about us as women engaged in being leaders.

Theoretical Framework

We contend that the fact we are all women is a critical factor in what has emerged from our group and its work. However, we recognize that gender in and of itself is a problematic analytical frame or lens. On the one hand, it can be argued that there are fundamental differences in how women and men view the world, themselves, their relationships, and power (Aiken & Tarule, 1998; Astin & Leland, 1991; Helgesen, 1990; Rosener, 1995).

On the other hand, it can also be argued that as a woman or a man becomes a leader, more is alike than different between them, and the situation itself shapes similar responses. That is, there is a cultural definition of what a leader is and does, and all who move into leadership roles enact, at some level and to some degree, their acculturated view of leader (Coleman, 2003). It has also been argued that since men have unquestionably dominated the population of leaders, any definitions of the role logically grew from and reflect the practices of that dominant group (Chliwniak, 1997; Coleman, 2003). Those definitions in turn shape the new leader's way of thinking about and enacting the role as well as what is identified as the traits and behaviors of an effective leader.

While the jury is clearly still out on the gender question, we take the stance, rooted in our own experiences, that there do appear to be some differences, but that those differences are gender related, not gender specific (Belenky, Clinchy, Goldberger, & Tarule, 1986; Gilligan, 1982). Thus, using gender as an analytic frame to examine leadership behavior is useful because it encompasses a constellation of attitudes, skills, and dispositions that are most commonly identified with males or with females but not exclusively so.

In addition, using a gender lens for analysis of fundamental assumptions that shape institutional leadership practice or to search for differences in style, traits, or beliefs may be important for another reason. Coleman (2003) argued that the identification of a woman's way of leading may actually create significant opportunities for more variety in leadership models and more use of what she refers to as the transformational model:

> One interpretation of the espousal of a more transformational model on the part of men is that they are recognizing the benefits and popularity of the more feminine style and annexing it in order to maintain their preeminence as leaders. Another may be that education as an environment is one which predisposes its leaders, both male and female, towards a more democratic and participative style. (pp. 45–46)

It is probably not a coincidence that this theoretical perspective about leadership generally, and about the role of gender in leadership specifically, gained strength in our thinking as we participated over the years in our non-proximate network that was notably marked by the style Coleman (2003) describes. If we could not get it on our campuses, the network and our stories and analyses helped us to keep this leadership model alive in our work and in our thinking.

The Narratives of Leadership: Stories and Analyses

The Power of Merging the Private-Public Self

Story: In the middle of my third year as dean, my husband of 25 years decided to leave me. I was deeply hurt, emotionally fragile, and devastated. But I had a responsibility to my institution, and fortunately that is just what I needed to keep me going—responsibility. During the long days that come with academic administration, I had much to occupy my thinking. There were always those institutional and collegiate demands on my time that took me out of myself. My weekends gave me time for grieving.

For reasons unknown to me at the time, I did not want to share my personal pain within my university. Now I know that I was afraid my personal issues would reflect badly upon me in the public realm, that there would be untoward gossip and speculation about me, and those kinds of hallway conversations might lead to considerations about me as dean that would make me appear weak or worse. Who knew how losing a husband would be interpreted?

That summer I needed a break, a real getaway to relax and regroup. I had read about a new spa that sounded like just what I needed. I'd never been to a spa, but my image was of rest and relaxation. Off I went. One day for lunch I sat with a group of women who had just returned from "the horse experience." They were completely and obviously taken with it, though vague about the details. "Just sign up and go," they insisted. So I did, even though my childhood history was filled with bad experiences with horses. I thought that by doing the horse experience I might just be able to shed those fears from childhood and learn to enjoy riding.

The session was not at all about learning to ride. It involved a series of exercises that each participant performed with a horse: selecting, grooming, and walking with the animal. I did just fine selecting my horse, a large chestnut mare named Lucy. Our instructions involved brushing, combing, and cleaning the horse's hooves. I began with the easy tasks, brushing the horse and talking to the horse to gain my confidence, before undertaking what I thought was the difficult job of cleaning the hooves. When the time came for that job, I simply could not get Lucy to lift her leg. The more I tried, the more frustrated I became. Other participants were moving along, and there I stood feeling alone and helpless in the face of what I thought was an insurmountable task. Failure was in my face. I couldn't do the job. Finally, the leader came over to me to see how I was doing. I started to cry, and Lucy, of her own free will, lifted her hoof and stepped on my foot. The leader asked me what the tears were about and a rush of emotion came. Why had I not asked for help? Why had I not asked another member in our group to assist me? Why did I think I had to do all the work privately and alone?

At the fall meeting, when our group convened, I finally had the courage to tell these stories. First came the horse experience, then the story of my impending divorce. It was time to trust my friends with my private pain. It was time to let my colleagues see my vulnerabilities. Through them I could gauge with whom and in what ways I needed to share my personal life with my campus.

Analysis: We all related instantly to the general fear of being perceived as weak or ineffective when circumstances of our personal life are imposing and all-consuming. But the horse event had helped our colleague, and soon all of us, to differentiate a more specific issue from the general fear—how could she present her divorce to her college and campus colleagues? While we worked to answer that question, the group began a dialogue about how the public and private domains of one's life intersect with one's role as a leader, which has relevance for this theme and the last one discussed in this chapter.

Women's work was originally entirely in the private domain—the domestic life of the family. Men's work was of the public domain. Albeit that in the preindustrial era the differentiation between the genders was far less sharp, the postindustrial norm is that leadership is a public domain role—whether industrial, governmental, academic, or elsewhere—and that a leader should not bring issues of the private domain to the workplace. The assumption that the private domain remains outside the workplace is still the predominate one. Although some progress has been revealed in the notions of the family-friendly workplace, for example, the fact remains that there is a rather uneasy resolution about what the balance really ought to be between private and public domains for leaders. Leaders with young children often feel this intensely. Given that women carry the predominance of the work of the private domain even when they also have public roles in the workplace, they frequently are faced with choices that keep the differences between these two domains in their daily consciousness. For example, women leaders sometimes need to pick a child up after school even though important meetings may be scheduled from three to five.

The horse story focused our inquiry on these concerns and on how much one can or should integrate one's personal and professional lives. Stories abound about leaders whose personal life has had a disastrous influence on their role: We all knew leaders who have lost jobs because they were in an affair that went public.

We began to understand that the horse experience had helped our colleague to want to adjust the public-private domain balance. Moreover, as she did, it became apparent that integrating the personal back into the public role of leading could produce a renewed sense of efficacy. Energy that is no longer being devoted to masking pain or to being cautious and careful to keep the personal information out of one's work and thoughts is released and refocused on one's work and on leading (Bolman & Deal, 1995). Arguably, the task of integrating private and public roles and lives is a complex dance (Heifetz, 1994) that requires vigilance. According to Block (as cited in Perreault & Reyes, 1994), the goal is to be authentic enough to oneself and to others without allowing the personal to become overbearing or all-consuming. One somewhat surprising outcome from achieving a balance may be an increased sense that others perceive one's leadership as somehow more trustworthy—probably because if one can speak the truth about hard personal issues it is likely that she or he will do so about the hard issues the organization faces. Yet there are dangers here as well. The balance is key; too much personal is no better than too little.

The horse story also serves as a metaphor about how a leader who is stuck and cannot ask for or find ways to get help is likely to get stepped on, may become immobilized, isolated, and, perhaps worst of all for women leaders, end up crying. This type of dilemma itself is a relational issue—relational changes in a personal life have an impact and reverberate on workplace relationships, the public sphere. For the leader so endangered, the downward spiral described in the horse story needs to be interrupted through the relationships themselves by finding ways to share appropriately what is having an impact in the leader's life that may be influencing how one is leading.

In this case, until a few people know about the divorce, there can only be speculation about why their leader seems so pained ("It must be us," is the frequent assumption made in the absence of information) or about why she needs to be away from campus (in reality to deal with lawyers and the like, but speculation is more likely to be something along the lines of, "She must be looking for a new job"). In short, all the relationships in the workplace are affected when a leader has significant personal issues that are demanding and absorbing energy or time or both.

The power that relationships wield in leading has been understood more in recent leadership literature and frequently is seen as specifically related to women as leaders. Much of gender theory asserts that women tend to emphasize connection, care, and responsibility in their thinking and ethical decision making as well as in their interpersonal relations (Belenky et al., 1986; Gilligan, 1982), and thus this emphasis is taken into their leadership roles. We are struck with how many of our conversations began with dilemmas that cast the moral and ethical problems faced in relational terms, like the horse story. While we would not argue that this is how all women lead, we believe that it creates a particular set of opportunities and challenges. And in agreement with the Coleman (2003) quote (p. 34), it is a critical factor in creating a particular, new, and badly needed kind of leader and leadership.

Value-Based Practice: Dilemma, Discourse, and Disappointment

Story: Each summer the president of our university holds a retreat for campus leadership. For two days we focus on timely issues related to the many functions of a large campus, always with an eye toward the state and national political agenda that has an impact on higher education funding. Generally these are very full days with intentional and serious dialogue related to present and future challenges. Last year the university's media relations consultant ran a session focused on getting us to consider ways to enhance the public image of the university. We were reminded about the importance of letting the public know the outstanding work of our faculty and students. I made notes to consider all the exciting projects under way in the departments, which I thought deserved recognition.

About 2 weeks after the retreat a faculty member sent me an e-mail with a news article attached describing the funding of a new piece of federal legislation promoting alternative certification for teachers. This new legislation encouraged people who want to teach to bypass all courses in education. Instead, the article said, now all that is needed to become a certified teacher is a degree and a passing grade on a test. The faculty member's anger reflected what many of us believe is a misguided plan to increase the teaching workforce that reveals at best a misunderstanding of what it takes to learn to teach and at worst a general disregard for how children learn and a discounting of colleges of education.

In the e-mail, the faculty member wanted to know what I was going to do to make known our position about the value of having well-educated teachers in classrooms. He felt it was imperative that our college and university take a stand on the matter and let the public know the value that a well-qualified teacher adds to a child's learning environment. I was reminded of the media consultant's message to get the word out about the excellence of the university. This was the perfect opportunity to do just that while also being able to tell how well regarded our college was for the quality of our graduates and for their work in the schools.

I thought for a while about the approach I might take and decided to write an editorial for the local paper. I consulted with national leaders in my professional network to get the facts straight about the legislation. I discussed this approach briefly with my leadership team, who fed me several important points about the values we hold for well-educated teachers. Then I wrote. When I finished the piece I called the editor of the paper to let him know what I was doing. He encouraged me to submit the piece right away. I felt energized by this and I knew I was doing the right thing for my college and the profession of teaching. The editorial was printed in the Sunday paper.

On Monday morning when I arrived in my office there was a call from the provost. He needed to speak with me ASAP. When I phoned his office, his secretary asked that I come over to his office right away; he was conferring with the president of the university but would be back shortly and wanted to see me. When I queried her about the substance of the call, she said it was about my editorial. Hmm. My curiosity was aroused. Maybe he wanted to thank me personally for doing such a fine job in representing the university? With text in hand, off I went across campus to see him.

When I entered his office he did not move. Instead, he demanded to know where I got the idea that I could write an editorial for the local paper and use the university's good name to degrade a piece of national legislation. Did I not know that the governor's good friend wrote that bill? How did I think my article reflected on the president of the university? I was stunned. I thought I was speaking out on an issue of vital importance to my college and was making the university look strong in the public eye. Now I was being chastised for stepping into a political minefield that I hadn't even known existed! Later, I asked myself if the values of my college were out of sync with the provost and president, and if so, what this would mean for my leadership.

Fortunately, the next week there was a conference where my colleague deans and I would meet. I needed their help in thinking this through. Here I thought I was doing the right thing by my college and my profession, but the power and politics of the university had trumped speaking out on an issue of critical importance to my college. Were other deans having these sorts of dilemmas on their campuses? When did higher education change from being mission driven to being a political arm of the state?

Analysis: From this story came a long discussion about the intrusion of political ploys on campus and how, especially in colleges of education, there is always the dilemma of getting caught between holding to a values-based stance and playing the political game. But the editorial story was illustrative of a particular form of that dilemma that faces women and men leaders: the clash between values and management. Management in this case does not only mean those, such as the provost, who are responsible for making sure things run smoothly. Rather, management is the process by which organizations or governments set policy applicable to particular issues (Spolsky, 2004).[2] Setting policy within an organization requires attention to meaning and values. Looking first at meaning, unless there are common understandings, such as what "getting the word out" means, or what common good getting the word out is to serve, there cannot be unambiguous policy agreements. Clearly the presentations on public relations at the president's retreat jumped straight to this leader's desired end—visibility for the institution—without engaging the deans and other campus leaders in conversations about the meaning behind the message.

So our colleague left the university retreat with the understanding that her responsibility was to promote the ways in which her college contributed to advancing the university's goals and mission and thereby, in her mind, advancing the common good for both. But in this case, for the president, the "common good" actually meant protecting the university by not irritating any influential outsiders. In considering this problem, we also speculated that perhaps the president was being pushed by the board of regents to increase the level of institutional recognition in the state. If the regents made this request (a management decision) without consideration of what they intended by "recognition," then another level of complexity and potential conflict emerges.

In the realm of values we see the transformational lens of gendered leadership as an illuminating perspective. The central value revealed in this situation is the notion of general welfare. Our colleague and her faculty hold the core value of serving the broad goal of advancing the lives of children by preparing thoughtful, professional teachers. This is what Labaree (1997) refers to as advancing a *public good.* In teacher education, a public good in education is preparing educators who can help children learn and prepare to be productive citizens committed to social justice. As illustrated by the provost's actions, the university also values what Labaree labels as a *private good:*

positioning the institution to be more competitive, more powerful, or ahead of other universities. Thus, the role of the leader in this situation is to foster and develop what Shapiro and Stefkovich (2001) describe as *communal understandings*. The emphasis on the value of the community, on its discourse, and even, some would argue, on children's development as a social responsibility (Ruddick, 1980) can be identified as gender-related capacities of women leaders. Our colleague's dilemma also illustrates problems that arise when there are different understandings of meaning and values within the university's governance structure: faculty, dean, provost, president, and board of regents.

The dilemma represented by this story and the clash between values and management is particularly challenging for leaders. All of us are responsible to a more senior administrator, a board, or possibly an elected official. It may not be feasible or appropriate to launch a frontal assault on the values of those to whom we are accountable. Yet deans hold the powerful responsibility of serving as translators between their constituents (faculty, schools, teachers, school administrators, and parents) and their provosts, and in that capacity we can influence understanding and perhaps values in the larger culture. The conversation in our group took a more practical turn: what strategies our colleague could use to (a) advise the central administration not just of the college's mission statement but the values that are embodied in the statement and how they are reflected in the work of the unit; (b) engage the faculty in conversations about the nexus of meaning and values in their own work; and (c) share this information with the college's K–12 partner schools, and in that manner enlist them as allies on behalf of the unit. None, we understood, was without risk.

Nurturing Power

Story: I have always been a bit perplexed by the notion of "the vision thing." When I became dean, people whom I had known for years began immediately to ask me what my vision was for the college. Since the college was under assault by the regents, my vision was simple: survive. That was surely not what others thought a vision should be. In attempting to meet the more grandiose expectations, we—faculty and administration—worked on a vision for the college for a couple of years, wordsmithing down to syllables, before finally agreeing. My experience was that the process of attempting to reach consensus was a long and painful one. The next dean's experience (from my vantage point back on the faculty) was smooth and relatively rapid. For my successor, a task force worked on the vision for a few months and then brought it to the faculty. It was passed. The question I've asked myself is, "What was different?" Is it possible that in trying to be collaborative, I gave the impression of a lack of leadership and indecision, thereby causing the faculty to engage in endless debate? Did the listeners perceive my willingness to share power as a sign of weakness because of a belief that real leaders don't share their power?

Or did faculty impose the stereotype of a "weak" female leader simply because I was the first female dean? Perhaps my experience could be explained as a power issue in which the faculty attempted to demonstrate that they held *real* power over the new female dean. I admit that I found it difficult in the first few years as dean to accept the status and the fact of power.

Yet, there are those—men and women—who believe that if power is not wielded like a magic wand, then it does not exist. That certainly was true for many of the senior men whom I had worked with for years and who made it plain that the status quo—curriculum, department structure, college structure, positions—was their vision and legacy. They not only resisted change but actively undermined any efforts that might result in diminishing their influence on the college. Several of these men had held the actual power in the college for years, using various strategies to control actions of successive deans. Power was *their* property. They employed what I now understand to be well-established strategies of control, using fear and conflict to divide faculty into groups. In contrast, many of the senior women, while often not enthusiastic about change, supported it for the good of the collective organization, downplaying their own preferences. Their strategies included building community through lunches, task forces, meetings, and discussion groups. The consequence was two extremes: individuals who worked to sustain themselves and keep their legacy and property—power—versus those who worked to sustain and transform the organization by building community.

I'd thought for years that faculty members tend to be highly individualistic. Thinking about the vision of the university as an organization from the perspective of an individual, as opposed to the perspective of the organization, leads to different views. Indeed, gender differences certainly exist in leadership, and how we think about effective leadership may well transcend these gender differences just as thinking about the larger organization may well transcend individual differences. These were issues I brought to our network, and connecting with others became a link to understanding. Yet the vision thing still perplexed me.

Analysis: Issues of vision and authority have been at the heart of many of our conversations, and arguably they are underlying themes in each of the scenarios we present. In a fundamental sense, of all people who identify themselves as collaborative leaders, women are especially prone to this self-identification (Beatty, 2000; Rosener, 1995; Wheatley, 1999) and are confounded by hierarchical organizations that embody traditional concepts of privilege. These organizations embrace competition as a core value and assume that if there is to be a winner, then others must be losers. Advancement of an individual or a unit comes at the expense of the advancement of others. As we struggled with issues of power, we came to discover that even as we talked about sharing power, we were accepting a traditional way of thinking about power as a finite commodity. If I have more power, someone else must have less.

A gendered leadership style, we contend, must be grounded in an understanding that power is infinite. As we considered this concept we began to see our roles and relationships with others very differently. Rather than thinking about how we can parse out bits of our authority to faculty or others, we need to consider how to nurture and develop power in others, particularly, we felt, among women. By doing this, how we think about or define power becomes connected to the notion of liberty. That is, we can engage in actions to literally grow power as long as our actions are not harmful to individuals or our larger organizational community (Stone, 1997). As we explored the idea of power as infinite, we realized that the endless faculty debate over a vision statement, as described by our colleague, was possibly because the faculty felt constrained or bound by invisible parameters on the vision statement and the amount of input they thought they could have, or because they could not transcend their individual perspectives for fear of losing what little power they had. We speculated that were a university to operate on the premise that power is infinite, then discussions such as those over vision might well be very different.

All of us have struggled with power and what it means. However, we concur with our colleague's suggestion that while gender differences certainly exist for leadership, how we act on our leadership challenges may well transcend these differences. Yet, life for any leader who deliberately and systematically acts to increase power may be risky. The organizational culture may be too ingrained with traditional behaviors to offer the fertile environment that developing power as capacity rather than commodity requires. The leader may be perceived by others in the organization as attempting to make them weaker (the clash between power as infinite and power as finite). Or the leader herself may be seen as weak by those who employ a linear management style. We believe this concept of power as infinite is one of the most important outcomes of our group discussions, but each of us would acknowl-edge that we have been neither highly nor consistently successful in imple-menting it in our organizations.

The Power of Being Marginalized

Story: I am sitting with the deans of my institution being interviewed by the Provost Search Committee chair and the headhunter from a search firm regarding the qualities we want in a provost. We are all a bit jaundiced, hav-ing had a string of provosts in the past 5 years come and go. Anticipation and hope are obvious in the conversation, along with a bit of caution. The group works hard to articulate what a leader would need to be a successful provost with us, with the president, and with the regents.

The conversation is thoughtful, all are contributing, and a picture begins to emerge of what at least the deans of the university, diverse as we are, can agree really matters for a person who will fill this role. I am thinking we have done a pretty good job when the headhunter says, "Well, this seems pretty thorough and helpful. Thank you. But just before we end, I want to ask one more question. If the provost candidate is a woman, are there other qualities or expectations that should be included?"

I am beginning to ponder the question when my colleague dean (she, I, and one other woman were the only women in the group of fifteen) leans forward. "Huh," I think (and confess with some chagrin as I write), "she looks mad." She speaks: "The qualities for a woman provost would be *exactly* the same as the ones for *any* provost!" She slaps her paper down on the table and leans back, clearly disgusted by the question. "Of course," I mutter, trying too little and too late to support my colleague.

Driving home, I can barely stand the fact that I totally missed her very accurate and acute observation and comment. Worse, I *was*, just before she spoke, actually thinking about what different qualities might be relevant. I realize during the drive that (a) the institution has never had a female pro-vost, and (b) I may have begun to lose something in this 15th year of being a dean. I muse on the notion of sympathetic resonance in leading. Sympa-thetic resonance is the phenomenon of involuntarily moving with or aligning with an action. It happens, for example, when a perfect note is played or sung near a piano, and the piano strings of that precise note also vibrate—involuntarily resonating to the note. It has been argued that a similar reso-nance occurs between people, such that a certain kind of energy emitted by one person calls forth the same in another (Guzetta, 2000).

Fact or metaphor, this notion of sympathetic resonance captures what is becoming for me a really serious worry. Am I beginning to unwittingly or unconsciously think more and more like the majority of leaders, primarily male, with whom I have been working during my many years of being a dean? I know that one of my strengths is being able to listen and discern what someone is and is not saying. Deeply committed to keeping relationships in the forefront in my leadership, I do resonate with how others are viewing and seeing the world. Moreover, in my early years in leadership, there were few alternatives to the cultural majority's view about what leadership is. So I can be pulled back to that earlier dominant view and resonate with it whenever I am working with or listening to someone who holds that perspective.

Yet, deep down and somewhat subtly, when that happens it feels like I am losing something really important that has helped me to be successful as a leader and has certainly been one of the things I have admired in my colleague: the fresh and sharply critical perspective that being a feminist, and thus a bit marginal, brings to one's work. It was in that moment when my colleague spoke that I had caught myself out of touch with the margin as I busily and compliantly tried to respond to the question.

By the time I get home, I am deeply disturbed by the whole event. But it feels very risky to talk about it on campus. I am relieved that next week is a conference where the group has set up a dinner.

Analysis: We began this chapter with a description of Marleen, a fictional woman leader whom all of us know. The reason we feel discomfort about the Marleens of the world is that at a certain level we fear we may become one of them and in doing so lose our connection to the margin that is deep in our soul. For marginalized—or slightly marginalized—groups, the danger is always there of adopting the cultural majority's perspective and losing one's own. Yet maintaining the marginal view is also challenging. "When being known means being known for one's authentic self, and one's authentic (female) self is inherently marginal to the dominant organizational culture, the resulting potential for cognitive and emotional dissonance is worthy of consideration" (Beatty, 2000, p. 340). Like the issue of balancing the private and public domains or the personal and the professional lives, the issue of one's feminism or one's female status as a leader requires thought and negotiation. There is no way to erase the fact that one is a female and in a leadership role. It leaves, thus, the issue of how much one assimilates and resonates with dominant practices and how much one does not.

In addition, our colleague's anxiety over whether she was losing something profound raises the core reason for why our nonproximate group has been so important to us. One of us was asked recently to write a short essay describing how national organizations address gender equity issues. It is true that many, although not all, professional education organizations devote some attention to issues of gender. This generally is done by establishing a committee, hosting a workshop or special event for women, or publishing books or articles on gender issues. These activities are important for organizations to demonstrate their commitment to gender equity or helping women advance. But to some extent, these efforts are often created as an addition to and in the margins of the dominant work and practices of the organizations and, thus, have little influence within or upon the organization itself in any way. Nonetheless, we assert that when an organization creates these opportunities, they frequently act as a catalyst for women to establish strong proximate or nonproximate support networks, which is, we would argue, a very important factor in promoting the development and success of those members who join such groups.

Finally, it seems clear that such groups are in fact not all that novel. We all have male leader friends who have a similar group of professional peers. But we were struck, as we began to discuss it, with the apparent difference between the groups. Theirs, our male friends' group, seems more focused on public work together, on finding ways to collaborate or consult together usually in their discipline, whereas our group, this chapter notwithstanding, remains focused on our own processes of becoming leaders and on women as leaders. We are creating new thinking for ourselves. One marker of this difference, which never fails to amuse, is that whenever our group gathers in a hotel lobby or is seen at a restaurant, it invariably evokes a comment from a passerby such as, "Uh-oh. There's the power group plotting," or words to that effect. We assert that such reactions signal that women as leaders really are still marginal. As such, women—when convened in a group—elicit the unintentional but predictable public response to a marginal group that their purposes are suspect, a bit opaque, threatening, or all these.

Concluding Reflections

Our stories were told to illustrate the kinds of dilemmas women leaders face and to examine these stories from theoretical and reflective positions that would enable the reader to think carefully and critically about some of her or his own leadership quandaries. We recognize that these narratives are socially constructed and dependent upon the social, situational, and contextual nature of our particular higher education environments. Yet, there are common threads that ring true for us in these narratives regardless of our place, role, or institution. As we conversed and wrote these expressions of our lives as leaders, we became more and more convinced of the value and power that is represented in our collaborative and supportive kinship. As Astin and Leland (1991) noted in their study of women leaders, "Our study makes clear that leadership cannot prosper fully as a solitary phenomenon. On the contrary, most experienced leaders . . . needed opportunities for colleagueship that promote the sharing of wisdom and insight, away from the heated battles of the activism they generated. . . . We need the insights [that] continued discourse among leaders might offer" (p. 161).

In reading through these stories, there are questions we hope the reader will ask to prompt her or his own reflection. We thought this conclusion could provide a beginning to such inquiry. In "the power of merging the private-public selves" we can see the value of being human. To what extent are you willing to open your private life to the scrutiny of your colleagues? How vulnerable are you willing to be, personally and professionally? Why do we view opening our personal lives as "risky business"? Under what circumstances is it best to keep personal issues or concerns hidden? How does a leader develop that sensibility of knowing to whom and at what time private information is best brought to light?

In "value-based practice" we can see the leader being blindsided by institutional politics. To what extent is it your responsibility to raise questions of meaning when a university officer issues broad calls to action? How do you privately or publicly check your assumptions and seek a common language? When your professional values are counterproductive to the organizational values, how do you maintain your integrity while supporting the goals of the institution?

In "the vision thing" we see a leader who is committed to a collaborative process in setting direction and building commitment, yet she wonders if the process makes her appear weak. The construct of power as infinite is introduced. How do you make organizational exercises like writing vision and mission statements meaningful? How do you honor the strengths of the faculty in building unity for the collective whole? To what extent does a leader need to be explicit about the rationale for the processes she chooses, or is the cultural power of the hierarchical tradition so strong that collaborative planning simply is not viable in one's setting? How do you augment power with others?

In "the power of being marginalized" we see a leader in the study of herself and the development of her own perspectives about being a woman and being a leader. How important is it for a leader to be self-reflective in these ways? What has surprised you about your own leadership behaviors? Under what conditions have you seen yourself grow as a leader and a woman? To whom do you turn for advice and validation?

Finally, our work would not be complete without a note of encourage-ment to seek out other women leaders for their experiences and their strength. The Marleens of the world will not give such aid easily, but there are many successful women leaders who enjoy and gain strength by actively encouraging others. You who wish to join or start a peer support network may find similarly interested women leaders through professional associa-tions or in community action groups. The value of such networks is in the dialogue, reflection, and colleagueship. You do not have to live in the same community. We encourage you: Find it—or create it. Engage. Enjoy, and grow as thoughtful, supported leaders.

Notes

1. The "Marleen story," as with all the stories in this chapter, is a composite drawn from our group's conversations and work but altered to ensure anonymity.

2. Bernard Spolsky (2009) developed the framework of meaning, practice, and management to apply to the development and evolution of language policy. We find his model useful to help analyze our experiences.

References

Aiken, J., & Tarule, J. (1998). The centerpiece in women's leadership: Perspectives from the field. In C. Funk, A. Pankake, & M. Reese (Eds.), *Women as school executives: Realizing the vision.* College Station: Texas A&M University-Commerce Press.

Astin, H., & Leland, C. (1991). *Women of influence, women of vision: A cross-cultural study of leaders and social change.* San Francisco: Jossey-Bass.

Beatty, B. R. (2000). The emotions of educational leadership: Breaking the silence. *International Journal of Leadership in Education, 3*(4), 331–357.

Belenky, M., Clinchy, B., Goldberger, N., & Tarule, J. (1986). *Women's way of knowing: The development of self, voice and mind.* New York: Basic Books.

Bolman, L. G., & Deal, T. W. (1995). *Leading with soul: An uncommon journey of spirit.* San Francisco: Jossey-Bass.

Chliwniak, L. (1997). Higher education leadership: Analyzing the gender gap. *ASHE-ERIC Higher Education Reports, 25*(4), 1–97.

Coleman, M. (2003). Gender in educational leadership. In M. Brundrett, N. Bur-ton, & R. Smith (Eds.), *Leadership in education* (pp. 36–53). London: Sage.

Gilligan, C. (1982). *In a different voice.* Cambridge, MA: Harvard University Press.

Guzetta, C. E. (2000). Music therapy: Nursing the music of the soul. In D. Camp-bell (Eds), *Music physician for the times to come* (pp. 146–166). Wheaton, IL: Quest Books.

Heifetz, R. A. (1994). *Leadership without easy answers.* Cambridge, MA: Harvard University Press.

Helgesen, S. (1990). *The female advantage: Women's ways of leadership.* New York: Doubleday.

Hoshmond, L. L. S. (1989). Alternative research paradigms: A review and teaching proposal. *Counseling Psychology, 17,* 3–79.

Labaree, D. (1997). Public goods, private goods: The American struggle over educational goal. *American Educational Research Journal, 34*(1), 39–81.

Rosener, J. (1995). Ways women lead. In J. T. Wren (Ed.), *The leader's companion: Insights into leadership through the ages.* New York: The Free Press.

Ruddick, S. (1980). Maternal thinking. *Feminist Studies, 6,* 70–96.

Shapiro, J. P., & Stefkovich, J. A. (2001). *Ethical leadership and decision making in education: Applying theoretical perspectives to complex dilemmas.* Mahwah, NJ: Erlbaum.

Spolsky, B. (2004, September). *Does the US need a language policy, or is English enough?* Paper presented at the Bowen Lecture Series, Center for Education Policy, George Mason University, Fairfax, VA.

Stone, D. (1997). *Policy paradox: The art of political decision making.* New York: Norton.

Wheatley, M. (1999). Goodbye, command and control. In F. Hesselbein & P. M. Cohen (Eds.), *Leader to leader: Enduring insights on leadership from the Drucker Foundations' award-winning journal.* San Francisco: Jossey-Bass.

3

THE ROLE OF SELF-EFFICACY IN DEVELOPING WOMEN LEADERS

A Case of Women in Academic Medicine and Dentistry

Lorraine Sloma-Williams, Sharon A. McDade, Rosalyn C. Richman, and Page S. Morahan

On a macrolevel, this chapter explores the role of self-efficacy in the development of women leaders in academic medicine and dentistry. On a microlevel, it considers how the Hedwig van Ameringen Executive Leadership in Academic Medicine (ELAM) Program for Women contributes to increasing self-efficacy beliefs among participating Fellows, using Bandura's (1997) four principal sources of self-efficacy as a guide. After setting a context, the chapter lays out its conceptual framework, presents ELAM as a case study, and then categorizes and analyzes Fellows' comments to highlight their growth of self-efficacy beliefs during and after participation in the ELAM program. Derived from our analysis, the chapter concludes with three main implications for developing women academic leaders, particularly in medicine.

Context

In the field of academic medicine, women face many barriers in achieving positions of leadership. Although women have made progress toward gaining equal representation in the field (Association of American Medical Colleges [AAMC], 1996, 2002, 2004; Benz, Clayton, & Costa, 1998; Bickel, 2001; De Angelis, 2000; Fried et al., 1996; Morahan et al., 2001; Nonnemaker, 2000;

Richman, Morahan, Cohen, & McDade, 2001; Tom, 1997; Valian, 1998; Yedidia & Bickel, 2001), they work and conduct research in a male-dominated environment that influences their career and leadership development. While women enter medical schools at the same rate as men (50% vs. 50%) and graduate medical schools in almost the same number (46% vs. 54%; AAMC, 2004), the proportion of women in leadership positions in academic medicine has not increased during the past 20 years (Carr, Friedman, Moskowitz, & Kazis, 1993; Morahan et al., 2001). Despite beginning at a comparable proportion with men as medical students, women move toward leadership positions, for example, as tenured faculty, department chairs, and deans, at far lower and slower rates than men do (AAMC, 2002). Few women achieve leadership roles in academic medicine.

Many factors limit women's potential to assume leadership positions. A hypothesis often raised is that women may not aspire to reach high levels of leadership. Despite the popularity of this assertion, we found only one study in academic medicine that showed that women medical school faculty do not aspire to national visibility in the same manner as men do (Buckley, Sanders, Shih, Kallar, & Hampton, 2000). While presenting intriguing data and conclusions, their study needs replication and expansion before definitive conclusions may be reached.

A plethora of additional possibilities relate to the lack of women's advancement in academic medicine. Hewlett and Luce (2005), writing about barriers to women's advancement in corporate America, conceptualized and detailed the many "off-ramps" and few "on-ramps" available to women as they navigate the career advancement highway. In academic medicine, these off-ramps include women's lacking necessary knowledge about tenure and promotion criteria in their institutions (Buckley et al., 2000). Data reveal a higher turnover rate among women academics than men (8% vs. 6.6%), resulting in women's leaving the medical professoriate at higher rates (Colletti, Mulholland, & Sonnad, 2000); the reasons are not yet completely understood. Another barrier may be a result of exclusion from informal networking because of gender (Colletti et al.), or because men and women are drawn naturally to groups of their own gender (Etzkowitz, Kernegor, & Neuschatt, 1994; Sandler & Hall, 1986). As women maneuver through the world of academic medicine, they face a multitude of obstacles. These easily available (or difficult to avoid) off-ramps, combined with a lack of on-ramps, limit their ability to become leaders in the field. Abundant literature acknowledges the off-ramps. This chapter examines one possible on-ramp: self-efficacy growth as it relates to leadership development.

Conceptual Framework: Bandura's Theory of Self-Efficacy

Self-efficacy theory has emerged as a way to understand and influence behavior change across many settings (Bandura, 1986, 1992, 1993, 1994, 1997). People direct their lives according to their perceived self-efficacy, or their beliefs in their capability to plan and follow through on courses of action required to attain their desired goals (Bandura, 1997). Those who feel positive about their abilities to complete certain tasks are more likely to succeed in those endeavors (Pajares, 2002). It is the basis for personal successes and achievements (Bandura, 1997). Fostering and empowering women with a greater sense of self-efficacy, therefore, may greatly influence their leadership development in the field of academic medicine.

Self-Efficacy and Women's Leadership Development

There are ways to bolster the advancement of women into leadership positions (Ely & Meyerson, 2000; Ruderman & Ohlott, 2002). Among these, research has clearly established the development of a positive self-concept as an important building block (Birnbaum, 1988, 1992; Heifetz, 1994; Ruderman & Ohlott). Self-efficacy beliefs can positively affect leadership aspirations, as well as predict a leader's self-perception of his or her own effectiveness (Woods, 2004).

Leyens, Desert, Croizet, and Darcis (2000) suggested that inadequate self-efficacy may restrict women and minorities from moving forward to the same leadership status as Caucasian men in particular fields. Therefore, development of self-efficacy may provide a viable on-ramp for women as they aspire to academic leadership positions. Although other institutional and structural barriers (off-ramps) remain, providing opportunities for women to develop self-efficacy may foster their aspirations for higher leadership positions and enable them to better maneuver through the world of academic medicine and dentistry.

Supporting this hypothesis, research has linked self-efficacy to career development. Bandura (1997) described self-efficacy as the belief in one's own capabilities to organize and execute the sources of action required to manage prospective situations. Self-efficacy serves as a primary influence on career choice and development (Murray, 2003). Underlying many of the behaviors helpful for leadership positions, it functions as a major predictor of goal-setting behavior, the degree of effort devoted to a specific task, and actual task performance (Choi, Price, & Vinokur, 2003).

Further research specifically links self-efficacy to leadership development. McCormick, Tanguma, and Lopez-Forment (2002) found self-efficacy and confidence as critical components of leadership development and leadership behavior. Singer (1991) examined gender differences in self-efficacy among middle managers across varied organizations and found that women based their leadership aspirations on self-efficacy beliefs coupled with what they anticipated as the benefits and payoffs of becoming a leader. The higher her sense of self-efficacy, the more likely a woman would aspire to a leadership position. Enhancing self-efficacy, therefore, can help women develop as leaders.

While reasons for women's underrepresentation in academic medicine vary, social cognitive researchers have suggested that women's self-beliefs about their capabilities may provide valuable lessons for future leadership development (Bandura, 1997; Hackett & Betz, 1989; Pajares, 1996).

Confidence or Self-Efficacy?

When discussing capacity in the workplace, authors often interchange or confuse the terms *confidence* and *self-efficacy*, warranting a brief definition as part of our study's conceptual framework.

Confidence refers to a positive belief about oneself in general, a self-assurance that arises from appreciating one's own abilities.[1] Self-efficacy, on the other hand, refers to believing in one's sense of agency. It goes beyond believing in ability, isolating and identifying the critical belief that one's ability can actually produce specific and desired results in particular contexts (Bandura, 1997). Self-efficacy refers to affirmation of capacity and strength of belief in that capacity (Bandura). Although confidence and self-efficacy are closely related, these subtle differences are important to note.

Because our analysis is built upon Bandura's (1997) framework, we present his articulation of these differences in his own words. "Confidence," wrote Bandura,

> is a catchword rather than a construct embedded in a theoretical system. Advances in a field are best achieved by constructs that fully reflect the phenomena of interest and are rooted in a theory that specifies their determinants, mediating processes and multiple effects. Theory-based constructs pay dividends in understanding and operational guidance. The terms used to characterize personal agency, therefore, represent more than merely lexical preferences. (p. 382)

Self-efficacy is not a commonly understood term. In our study, interviewed Fellows referred to indicators such as *confidence, self-assurance, ability*, and *skill development*, as well as evidence of taking on new responsibility or acting differently in professional situations because of what they had learned as a result of their ELAM experiences. For this research we operationalized Bandura's (1997) definition of self-efficacy to reflect the comments of the ELAM Fellows. When a comment contained references to self-confidence, coupled with a specific action, task, or skill set, we coded the comment as an indication of self-efficacy. Then, we examined these examples using Bandura's framework to explore whether they may be indications of one of his four sources of self-efficacy.

Developing Self-Efficacy

Conceptual and empirical work has described how best to measure self-efficacy for different behaviors in different populations (Bandura, 1997; Garman, Wingard, & Reznik, 2001; Lenz & Shortridge-Baggett, 2002). What can be defined and measured can also be developed.

Self-efficacy can be cultivated in a number of ways. Bandura (1997) identified four principal sources for its development: (a) mastery experiences, (b) vicarious experiences/social models, (c) verbal persuasion, and (d) physiological and affective states. Formal professional development that attends to providing specific experiences in these four areas can cultivate and increase self-efficacy beliefs. Indeed, Garman et al. (2001) found that a formal mentoring process in an academic medical center improved self-efficacy among junior faculty concerning critical professional skills. In this chapter we explore how one professional development program—ELAM—helps women develop self-efficacy among the skills required to succeed and advance as leaders.

Methodology: Case Study of the ELAM Program

Our chapter presents an exploratory case study of the ELAM Program for Women. Through an exploratory single-case design with a single unit of analysis (ELAM Fellows; Yin, 1994), we examined Fellows' interviews from three ELAM classes after completion of the ELAM program. To shed light on the Fellows' comments, we used Bandura's (1997) self-efficacy framework to interpret what appeared to be self-efficacy learning and to identify sources of self-efficacy development. This allowed us to pinpoint the sources even further and, through the example of ELAM, to present this as a potential model for other programs.

The ELAM Program—The Single-Case Design

ELAM addresses the gap in women's leadership in the field in academic medicine and dentistry (Drexel University College of Medicine, n.d.). Established in 1995, it serves senior women faculty in medical and dental schools at the associate professor level or higher. The nation's only in-depth program focused on preparing women academic leaders in medical sciences, ELAM helps women develop skills useful to entering new leadership ranks or enhancing their current positions.

ELAM's curriculum aims to optimize leadership learning for its Fellows. Developed under the guidance of an advisory committee of national leaders, the year-long, part-time course of study attends to many professional and personal skills required to lead and manage successfully in today's complex health care environment. Program content is divided into three main curricular themes: financial, organizational, and systems management; emerging issues in academic health; and personal and professional development with special attention to the unique challenges facing women in leadership positions. ELAM reaches out to all learning styles through individual and small-group learning, including the use of in-depth case analyses, simulations, teamwork, reflective work, mentoring, coaching, and traditional interactive lectures. Fellows graduate from the program with increased skills and knowledge to continue in or aspire to leadership positions.

Data Collection and Analysis—The Single Unit of Analysis (ELAM Fellows)

Since its inception, ELAM has maintained a robust program evaluation strategy and long-term follow-up with participants. Members of the ELAM classes of 1996, 1997, and 1999 participated in follow-up telephone interviews of 45–60 minutes between 0 and 13 months after program completion (average interview was 6–8 months after program completion). Forty-one interviews were examined for this research (19 interviewed of 23 who gave consent from the 1996 class of 24 Fellows = 82.6% of the consented members who provided interviews, 7 interviewed of 18 who gave consent from the 1997 class of 30 Fellows = 38.8% of the consented members who provided interviews, and 15 interviewed of 28 who provided consent from the 1999 class of 37 Fellows = 53.5% of the consented members who provided interviews). The interview protocol had two foci: to uncover specific skills acquired through ELAM and to investigate Fellows' subsequent leadership development in their home institutions. Sharon A. McDade conducted all the interviews. Each interview was audiotaped, fully transcribed, and then analyzed for commentary in both focus areas. Themes emerged from inductive analysis of responses using standard qualitative techniques managed through ATLAS.ti software. The research protocol was approved through the Institutional Review Board process of all the institutions involved in the study

(Columbia University Teacher's College, Drexel University College of Medicine, and George Washington University).

For the purposes of this chapter, we isolated statements related to Bandura's (1997) four sources of self-efficacy and analyzed and interpreted what appeared to be self-efficacy learning, including identifying sources of self-efficacy development (Tab. 3.1). Using a constant comparative technique (Strauss, 1987), we reviewed each file for confirmation of or challenge to Bandura's sources. Grouping across years allowed for measurement of stated objectives across three different classes to ensure robustness of the themes. References to all four of Bandura's sources of self-efficacy development were found in the interviews.

Limitations

We note two limitations to this study. First, the theme of self-efficacy emerged from an analysis of the interviews. Fellows were not explicitly asked about their self-efficacy, nor were follow-up contacts made with Fellows to clarify their comments to uncover whether they were indeed and specifically referring to self-efficacy. However, using Bandura's (1997) framework as a guide, this lexical and contextual analysis and our operationalization of the framework is grounded in Bandura's theory. For example, ELAM Fellows throughout the interviews referred to increases in confidence. Keeping in mind the differentiation between confidence and self-efficacy, in some

TABLE 3.1
Summary Table of ELAM Impact on Self-Efficacy

Source of Self-Efficacy	Mastery Experiences	Vicarious Experiences/Social Models	Verbal Persuasion	Physiological and Affective States
ELAM curricular component	• Finance sessions • Emphasis on communication	• Role models in ELAM faculty facilitators and peers • Network experiences in ELAM	• Linkages to home institutions • Mentors • Relationships with dean fostered	• Built-in time for self-reflection • Personal reexamination
Percentage indicating improvement in this area (out of 41 total interviewed)	82.9	71	48.7	65.8

instances their comments clearly indicated a reference to self-efficacy, particularly when they coupled it with words such as "self-assurance," "ability," and "skill development," as well as evidence of taking on a new responsibility or acting differently in professional situations because of ELAM. Every effort was made to ensure that analysis was in keeping with the intent of the Fellow and the context of her comment about her leadership development.

Second, we used participants' self-assessments of their ELAM experiences and subsequent leadership development. No research data were collected about the leadership development of the Fellows from the supervisors or colleagues. Relying on self-reports and self-assessments presents limitations on several dimensions. We have only the Fellows' commentary concerning their leadership development and the relationship of that development to ELAM. More importantly for the purposes of this analysis, respondents may have enhanced or neglected aspects of their experiences and subsequent performance. This affects not only what we can report, but more significantly, selective self-monitoring actually affects beliefs of personal efficacy (Bandura, 1997). If one especially notes and remembers successes or selectively ignores poor performances, self-efficacy beliefs increase. Conversely, dwelling on poor performance and selectively ignoring successes can diminish self-efficacy, especially if the individual began with a low perception of self-efficacy. The degree of attention given to external validation or recognition (remembering or selectively ignoring it) also influences self-efficacy (Bandura). This limitation means that a professional development program such as ELAM can go only so far in fostering self-efficacy among its participants. Individual proclivity toward remembering the positive or the negative mediates outcomes.

ELAM and Self-Efficacy

In our examination of these interview data, 95% of 41 interviewed ELAM Fellows from classes 1996, 1997, and 1999 indicated the program provided benefits in building self-efficacy. We present our findings on how the Fellows specifically indicated self-efficacy development according to Bandura's (1997) four sources, providing excerpts from the Fellows' statements as illustration.

Mastery Experience

Bandura (1997) concluded that successful experiences produce stronger and more generalized efficacy beliefs than do the other three sources. Mastery experience, according to Bandura, refers to the way individuals gauge and interpret the effects of their actions. The perception of a successful performance raises efficacy beliefs, whereas the perception of failure lowers them. Mastery experiences are built upon instruction in cognitive strategies and practice in applying learned skills. Individuals need sufficient experiences to learn and prove their abilities before development will accrue. Mastery experiences are the most influential of the four sources of efficacy, producing stronger and more generalized efficacy beliefs than do the other three sources. They "provide the most authentic evidence of whether one can muster what it takes to succeed" (Bandura, p. 80).

ELAM Fellows participated in active learning experiences designed to increase their performance in specific skill areas and received verbal affirmations and guidance in a nonjudgmental environment. From our analysis, the ELAM program increased the Fellows' sense of competence by providing opportunities for them to feel successful, resulting in an improvement in self-efficacy in very specific content-related areas. The following statements exemplify ways that ELAM created mastery experiences for Fellows through skill development, testing the waters, speaking out, and broadening their horizons. Note the specific references to ELAM educational sessions that helped Fellows increase their self-efficacy levels with relation to the tasks at hand. Bandura (1997) reported that such early gains are important for increasing self-efficacy, creating positive memories to draw upon later.

Mastery experience through skill development. Nearly 83% of the interviewees (34 Fellows) reported an increased sense of capacity on the job as a result of their practical skill development at ELAM. Although referencing other areas, Fellows most often referred to increases in financial management and communication skills, and a general sense of overall skill development. Their comments indicated an increased sense of capacity to tackle tasks on the job, which led us to classify this as indication of self-efficacy development.

Fourteen interviewed Fellows (34%) reported improving financial management skills, enabling them to take on tasks at their own institutions with increased competence and to maneuver through their institutions with increased ease and capacity. For example, as one Fellow described:

> Well, for me the learning highlight was all of the finance exercises and the mini-MBA, especially the hands-on ones where we were given numbers and we were asked to crunch them or come up with a solution to a problem involving budget. . . . That was a brand new skill set for me. That was something I came into ELAM knowing zero about. . . . the day [the ELAM facilitator] introduced herself to us . . . she gave that speech that said, "If

you want to know how your institution runs you must know how the money flows." And I looked at her and I thought, "My God, she is right. Of course, she is right. That's why I'm so frustrated about at my own institution, because I can't get a handle on why the money is disposed in the way it is. If I could just understand the mystery of it and I could get myself in a position where I could express my opinion, or use some of my creativity in that way, maybe something good would happen for my institution." So I did these finance exercises at ELAM. I loved it. Everybody at my home institution knew that I loved it, too, because I had to deal with all the finance people. At the end of ELAM I came to my dean and said I want to follow up on everything I learned on finance.

The financial training provided at ELAM contributed to the Fellow's increased sense of self-efficacy. Other Fellows reported that after ELAM they were able to tackle financial aspects at their home institutions without feeling as intimidated as they did prior to ELAM training.

ELAM's concentration on development of communication skills also fostered mastery experience in that area. Five interviewed Fellows (12%) commented that their communication skills improved because of ELAM training and were most apparent in the areas of conflict resolution, team building, and negotiating. About 22% of Fellows (9) referred to their acquiring a range of overall management and leadership skills.

Some Fellows reported gaining confidence as a result of skill development, such as the woman who said,

> On a personal level it gave me a lot of self-confidence; and networking, which I found very invaluable on a professional level. I've been able to open my horizon regarding new skills which I need to develop. You know, providing me with the base line for some of those skills and also showing me how I need to grow and develop in a professional sense. . . . at several levels that has changed my mind as to how I view things. You know, I mentioned self-confidence and that's a big piece of it, and I can give you some specific examples. I've given . . . five talks this week, my sixth being Saturday, and I have gotten outstanding kudos for those talks. Why am I better than I was two weeks ago? It's a self-confidence issue. It's that I can say something well, I can communicate it well, and I got that feedback through . . . ELAM.

Others defined the program's benefits using the language of self-efficacy. One Fellow said that ELAM helped her build,

> well, confidence. Just reinforcing the assumption that there's no reason that you couldn't do as well or better than anybody else. I think the other

skills in terms of organizational structure, managing performance analysis, managing conflict, all of that was there before. But I think what mattered most was just that sense of "well, of course you could do it."

Another Fellow said,

But what I realize, more as a result of ELAM, is that I really am a very good team-builder, and in that sense I think my ability to be a leader and to see myself in leadership positions was very much enhanced as a result of ELAM. The development of a general skill-set helped increase confidence among the Fellows.

Significantly, these Fellows' statements illustrate not only an appreciation of their abilities, which were there before but they had not recognized (confidence), but also a newfound sense of agency to use those abilities toward specific ends (self-efficacy), in this case leadership.

As Bandura (1997) claimed, mastery experiences, such as improving one's tangible skill set in a given area, produce generalized self-efficacy relating to leadership skills and capacities.

Mastery experience through testing the waters. Mastery learning also requires individuals to have an opportunity to try new, previously untested skills (Bandura, 1997). We found that Fellows not only believed in their skills and ability to succeed—indicators of self-efficacy development—but through their budding sense of self-efficacy, they started reaching out and testing the waters relating to leadership capacities using their skills in transferable applications in their home institutions and elsewhere. One ELAM Fellow captured this experience particularly well, saying that ELAM gave her

a willingness on my part to take on more responsibility and to embark on projects where I really haven't any fundamental experience, just the experience of organizing people and process. For example, the dean asked me to be the chair of a committee, a task force on making a set of recommendations on computer assisted instruction in the medical school curriculum. Five months ago I didn't have a clue what that was about, I knew that there were a few rudimentary attempts at this commercially but I really hadn't delved into it, so I just tried it. I figured I didn't have a whole lot to lose, in three months I could only make so much of a fool of myself. [So, the committee formed a set of recommendations and the result was] we did a good job . . . . he has allowed us to form a standing committee for at least the intermediate term to complete the project.

Nearly 24% of interviewees (10 Fellows) indicated that as a result of ELAM they had either taken on new tasks that they would not have otherwise attempted prior to the program, or felt ready and able to do so.

Mastery experience through speaking out. Speaking out—or having the confidence to voice an opinion with the belief that one's words will have an impact—is an experience distinct from general communication skills. Thirty interviewed ELAM Fellows (73%) indicated that they now felt confident enough to speak out where otherwise they would have remained silent. This figure includes those who reported that their voices were now being heard and acknowledged at their institutions, as well as those who demonstrated an increased sense of self-efficacy because of a more fluent vocabulary.

One Fellow described her experience this way:

> I'm different because of ELAM, I'm different in so many ways. . . . One is I was working with a colleague who did something in his laboratory that I thought was absolutely amoral. . . . So I decided I was going to talk to him about it and I did, and I didn't have a lot of time to mentally rehearse it because he called me and wanted to come and talk to me about this research project and I decided . . . it was the first time I was face to face with him since I discovered this thing happened and I was going to say something so I could try to get it off my chest. He did something. . . . I don't know if I learned this at ELAM exactly, but I used body language to not let him leave the room until I had a chance to bring it up. . . . Like he tried to escape, and I actually moved myself into a position where he couldn't get out the door. And I think I was brave enough to do that for two reasons: one, because at ELAM we learned that people will try to intimidate you and try to weasel out. I was reading his behavior, he wanted to weasel out of that conversation and if I were him I would try to weasel out of it too. . . . That was very different. Confronting someone is something that I would almost rather die than do, I would eat a bottle of Maalox before I would confront someone. But when I had those nightmares I knew that it was time.

Another Fellow spoke of learning to speak authoritatively, of learning "how to form [a] sentence and how not to weaken [her] knees before [she] even open[ed her] mouth." She noted that although she may be quaking at the knees, she could work through it and still convey authoritative speech. A third Fellow spoke of this from a different perspective, saying,

> I think the other piece is just a tougher skin. The networking and the validation gives you a tougher skin. . . . like in study section last week a man

started talking over me in the group and I just don't put up with it any-more. I looked straight over at him and said, "Can I finish my comment please?" It's like I don't really care to devalue women anymore. We are out there and unless we start to change some of the subtle garbage it's going to be there forever. So, it's a tough skin kind of thing.

In general, these and the other Fellows who gave examples of speaking out linked this development of self-efficacy to an increase in their visibility within their institutions.

Mastery experience through broadening horizons. One of the biggest chal-lenges is creating an outward and forward-thinking focus for individuals to recognize where their newly developing leadership abilities can take them. The acknowledgment of new horizons requires individuals to alter self-appraisal, an important step in self-efficacy development. According to Bandura (1997), while redundant information reveals nothing new about an individual's efficacy, new experiences require an alteration of preexisting self-schemata. Further, the degree of importance given to new experiences and the resulting memory of the events depends on the degree to which an indi-vidual's self-beliefs are positive and negative (Bandura, 1992).

Thirty-five interviewed Fellows (85%) indicated a broadening of hori-zons as a result of the ELAM program. Fellows indicated that ELAM opened their eyes to new professional possibilities in academic medicine. Fellows now regarded areas as accessible to them that were either not reachable or perceived so before participation in ELAM. This new self-awareness of what they may be able to accomplish may have required varying degrees of adjust-ment to their existing conceptual frameworks relating to themselves as lead-ers and self-efficacy beliefs, a process that takes time. However, over the year-long program Fellows had the time needed to make such alterations and, importantly, were able to do so in a safe, supportive, and nonjudgmental environment. The following interview comments indicate how ELAM helped Fellows broaden their horizons. One said,

> It's opened my eyes to some opportunities that are out there. . . . And it's really got me thinking of how am I going to strategize for this next job. That's real important.

Another articulated it this way:

> I think that ELAM has helped me focus on what my abilities are, it's increased my self-confidence, it's made me aware and realize the strengths within myself and all the possible things that are out there waiting for

me. . . . Yeah, and I didn't really realize this coming to ELAM, one of the things ELAM's done for me was make me realize what I want to do next because I wasn't really sure.

Such statements illustrate how Fellows broadened their horizons, learning about opportunities in the field, and believing those opportunities to be within their reach based on their belief in their own capacity and personal agency.

The mastery learning fostered through ELAM—skill development, testing the waters, speaking out, and broadening one's horizons—is only the beginning of a developmental process. Most leadership competencies develop over a long period of time. For complex competencies, "different sub-skills must be acquired, integrated and hierarchically organized under continually changing conditions that can enhance or mar particular performances" (Bandura, 1997, p. 86). A long-range process, persistence in leadership development becomes important. Efficacy beliefs affect the amount of effort expended on an activity, the length of time persevering in the face of adversity, and how resilient individuals will be even when severely disappointed by their efforts (Pajares, 2002). This becomes critical on the long road of career development. "It is one thing to select a career field of study but quite another to stick with it and master it when the road to success is strewn with countless difficulties" (Bandura, p. 425).

Vicarious Experiences/Social Models

According to Bandura (1997), people do not rely on active experience as the only source of information about new and existing capabilities. "Efficacy appraisals are partly influenced by vicarious experiences mediated through modeled attainments" (Bandura, p. 86). The social models, however, must be similar enough to learners for them to be able to envision themselves in similar leadership positions. "The greater the assumed similarity, the more persuasive are the models' successes or failures" (Bandura, 1994, p. 86).

Twenty-nine interviewed Fellows (71%) indicated that vicarious experience from the ELAM program had an impact on their self-efficacy development relating to leadership. ELAM provided formal venues for social modeling, such as the Meet the Leaders series, opportunities for Fellows to meet and work with leaders in academic medicine, and also through informal venues, such as observing and interacting with other Fellows and ELAM facilitators. In addition to ELAM itself, seven interviewed Fellows (17%) spoke about vicarious experiences they had through ELAM mentors whom they met either before or subsequent to the program.

By seeing successful women similar to themselves, Fellows recognized that they too possess similar capabilities necessary for leadership success. One Fellow said that the models ELAM formally provided through its programming benefited her, "in many, many ways—it would take a really long time, I think, to describe all of them—but exposing me to women who were confident, competent, and who had achieved a variety of different things in a variety of different ways. So, to sum that up in one word, I would say possibly [that they were] role models and/or mentors." She also spoke of the benefits of peer interaction, saying,

> The peers . . . the same thing for the peers, looking at each peer and seeing how each woman had achieved . . . and one of the things that struck me was if you looked at what each person had achieved . . . I think getting to know each other was wonderful because you could see how their achievement matched their personality and their style of interaction. And it gave a very realistic and insightful view of what I can achieve given what I know about myself and where my limitations are and where my opportunities are.

As this Fellow indicated, social models not only helped women envision themselves as future leaders, they also served as benchmarks women could use to assess themselves and discern areas requiring improvement. ELAM provided many structured and informal opportunities for women to do such self-appraisals. As one Fellow noted,

> I found [Faculty A] particularly generous in some of her insights and she had talked to me at one point about kind of the caring versus the caretaking which I think was, personally, very beneficial to me in kind of thinking critically about my own behaviors and hopefully improving on them. I think that it forced me to think critically about where I perceived my abilities compared to a group of people that an outside body had defined as emerging or potential leaders in academic medicine.

These Fellows, and others like them, perceived the leadership skills of other women and used those insights to assess and judge their own performance and skills, processes identified by Bandura (1997) as important components of positive role modeling that can lead to self-efficacy and subsequent positive action.

Verbal Persuasion

Verbal persuasion—through affirmations and recognition—is another important source of efficacy information (Bandura, 1997). People, Bandura noted, expend and sustain greater effort when persuaded verbally that they possess the capabilities to master given tasks. Having a wealth of remembered affirmations and positive recognition to draw upon sustains people through difficulties. Although not as strong as mastery experiences, it can be a particularly powerful source for those who are unsure of their own abilities. Without a store of such verbal persuasions, one may "harbor self-doubts and dwell on personal deficiencies when difficulties arise" (Bandura, p. 101).

Nearly half of all interviewed Fellows (49%, or 20 Fellows) reported receiving external validation of their current leadership abilities or on the new leadership skills they brought back from ELAM. For example, one participant reported receiving "a lot of very positive reinforcement. It's almost like providing a mirror, you know, or a shiny surface and you do look at yourself and it's a mirror that makes you look good or better."

Another spoke of the external validation she received in the following way:

> The other benefit is, I think for me at my institution, is the external validation of my potential. Because I think certain people in my institution thought [before I went to ELAM] that I might have leadership potential, but for me to be selected [for ELAM] was a signal event that's been repeated in print and in verbiage over and over and over. And I think, to some extent, that stuff becomes a self-fulfilling prophecy. So, it's made me larger than life in my own institution in a way that nothing I could do at home would do for me. . . . Well, my dean says it publicly all the time, and every time he introduces me to someone in a one-on-one or a small group situation he introduces me as being a rising star and a future leader of our college and that kind of thing. . . . Now that did not happen before I was accepted to ELAM, and I think if he survives as dean long enough he will see me in some sort of leadership position.

Fellows indicated that the verbal persuasions and reinforcements helped them to recognize the leadership talents they possessed. As Bandura (1997) noted, "For many activities, people cannot rely solely on themselves in evaluating their level of ability because such judgments require inference from indicants of talent about which they may have only limited knowledge" (p. 104).

In some cases, interviewed Fellows reported that other faculty members, coworkers, or staff recognized and commended them on jobs they were already doing well but had previously gone unrecognized or without validation. When ELAM Fellows returned to their institutions after the successful completion of the course, they were looked upon with increased respect because of the reputation of the program. From their comments, Fellows indicated that the ELAM experience changed their institutional image to that of an emerging leader. This external recognition coupled with the validation of their new skills to match the reputation enhanced the Fellows' sense of self-efficacy.

Physiological and Affective States

Physical well-being, mood states, and mental strengths have an impact on one's performance level and on one's perception of self-efficacy. They play an especially influential role in the functioning of the individual during high levels of stress that often accompany leadership positions. Many individuals interpreted their stress reactions and tension as signs of success or failure, and a reinforced ability to perform well under stress contributes to improved self-efficacy and self-concepts as leaders. Although ELAM Fellows processed their experiences differently (internally vs. externally), the majority reported an improved ability to perform during occasions of stress.

Affective states also include one's emotional reaction when engaging in self-reflection. Indeed, Bandura (1997) considered self-reflection as the most uniquely human capability and indicative of self-efficacy development. In this study, 27 interviewed Fellows (65.8%) expressed an increased sense of self-awareness and a better perception of themselves after participating in the ELAM program. As this Fellow commented: "It's also sort of helped bring me out of a shell I think, because I've been used to being extroverted in the doctor-patient or the teacher-learner situations when I'm in my comfort zone. . . . this has sort of extended my comfort zone." Many others reported that they could now embrace their positive and negative attributes without feeling threatened, as previous statements in this chapter have indicated. Their increased confidence enabled them to work on their weaknesses and seek help when necessary instead of regarding weakness as a sign of failure.

Implications of the Study

Bandura's (1997) four sources for the development of self-efficacy provide a useful framework for understanding how ELAM Fellows developed important foundations of self-efficacy for leadership. Interviewed Fellows reported growth aligned with the themes of mastery experiences, vicarious experiences/social models, verbal persuasion, and physiological and affective states. Now we examine the practicality of these findings for the development of leadership among women in academic medicine today. From the analysis of the interviews three main observations emerged: (a) self-efficacy growth as it relates to leadership development is a gradual process, (b) self-efficacy growth relating to leadership development is a collaborative (involving the support and nurturing of other people) and independent process (self-testing, self-reflection), and (c) informal and formal support networks help women who are developing as leaders to thrive.

The Gradual Process of Developing Self-Efficacy

From our data we propose that organizers of leadership development for women must recognize that with self-efficacy at the core of leadership development the process is gradual and requires patience for authentic and lasting growth. We have found that it takes about 3 years after completion of the ELAM program for most of the Fellows to demonstrate moves into leadership roles. As Bandura has noted, the development of the important foundation for leadership—the development of self-efficacy—is usually a gradual process. Although there may be rapid growth in self-efficacy initially, early development plateaus and the gradual nature of the learning process soon emerge. "Rate of improvement varies with stage of skill acquisition. Improvements come easily at the outset, but rapid gains are harder to come by in late phases of skill development" (Bandura, 1997, p. 86). The process usually consists of a gradual increase in self-efficacy development over time.

Thirty-nine (95%) of the interviewed Fellows confirmed the gradual nature of self-efficacy development. For many Fellows, ELAM was the catalyst that started the process, as reflected in the following comment from a Fellow:

> You've given us tools to begin that process. . . . I don't think it's given us everything but I think it's given us the beginnings and the sense of resources and the beginnings of a network [and the recognition that] there's something that you can do . . . to improve and enhance your own ability to survive in an ever increasingly complex world.

For others, self-efficacy grew incrementally after an initial boost. One Fellow spoke of the process this way:

> I [came to] peace in my professional development. [ELAM] provided the opportunity for me to look at myself along a continuum and it also provided me with an opportunity to develop parts of my skill set that had to be deepened. You know some [leadership skills] were just starting to emerge and it helped me deepen those skills in some areas and in some things it gave me a whole fresh dimension.

Skill refinement requires time for study, for trial and error, and for repetition and mastery, especially when attempting particular techniques and strategies. When new self-efficacy information is gathered, the individual also requires time and energy to process and translate this information. She must fit her new knowledge into preexisting self-knowledge structures or create new structures where none existed before (Bandura, 1997). This takes time. Fellows reported that continued support and post-ELAM feedback positively influenced their leadership development at their home institutions. As this development occurs, there is a relationship among the tasks an individual accomplishes, the impact they make on the individual's sense of efficacy, and ultimately an impact on their leadership development that then influences career advancement.

For women in academic medicine, the gradual nature of self-efficacy development has important implications. From our analysis of this group of interviews, the Fellows' comments indicate that self-efficacy develops over time, and expansion requires persistent cultivation. Continued support and feedback even after the completion of the course of study were factors identified by the Fellows as having an impact on their leadership ability within their home institutions.

The Collaborative and Individual Process of Developing Self-Efficacy

Forty interviewed Fellows (95%) referred to the collaborative and individual nature of their self-efficacy development. Bandura (1997) recognized that collaborative learning through the modeling of peers and superiors was important so that one could measure oneself against others; developing self-efficacy is not done in isolation. "People must appraise their capabilities in relation to the attainments of others" (Bandura, p. 86). With this in mind, self-efficacy development can be an individual and a collaborative process. From the Fellows' comments, they reflected both types of development. We suggest that optimal self-efficacy development initiatives for women in academic medicine will encompass opportunities that allow for collaboration with mentors and peers, while also ensuring time alone to process information.

Collaborative development. Competency modeling—a collaborative process—is crucial for development of self-efficacy. In the field of academic medicine, which has so few women in leadership positions, constructed environments such as that of ELAM provide crucial opportunities for women leaders to collaborate and share with those on lower rungs of the career ladder. As one Fellow articulated,

> You have all these ideas [about leadership], but in our place [very few] women are full-professors, so very few women are there to share those thoughts and ideas with. . . . You don't realize until you go to ELAM, and

get some validation, that those truly are good models of leadership and that women do have a lot to offer.

Having women role models helps women develop a vision of themselves as future leaders and measure their own growth and development. In a sense, ELAM provided constructed mentoring experiences (or vicarious experiences in Bandura's [1997] framework) for participants to use as examples in forging their own subsequent mentoring and role-model relationship. Women could then take these examples back with them to their home institutions with an increased awareness to look for women such as those highlighted in the ELAM program. Zeldin and Pajares (2001) found that women in scientific/mathematical settings benefited most from vicarious experiences and verbal persuasions. Our findings support the usefulness of this source of self-efficacy as the Fellows indicated that collaborative experiences were highly beneficial.

Individual development. Although little research has been done on how people process multidimensional efficacy information, Bandura (1997) has noted that people must weigh and integrate diverse sources of efficacy information. Processing time for gradual development is essential for integrating information into existing schemas or developing entirely new schemas. We found that ELAM participants benefited from structured opportunities to process information in quiet reflection, as one Fellow noted:

> The introspective aspect of ELAM—the self-analysis [exercise], "What are your strengths and weaknesses," was extremely helpful to me. [So was t]he exercise where you had your peers evaluate you, the benchmarks. [It was equally] helpful to have the opportunity to sit and think about what I really wanted to do or didn't want to do.

Developing self-efficacy requires collaboration and involvement with others to gather information as well as time alone to re-collect and integrate one's learned skills. To strengthen self-efficacy relating to leadership development, we recommend that individuals be guided toward self-reflection experiences to enhance processing of new information.

The Importance of Informal and Formal Support Networks in Developing Self-Efficacy

Many interviewed Fellows spoke of the usefulness of formal and informal support networks. Formal networks included those in their institution as well as the individual mentors they had been involved with prior to, during, or subsequent to their ELAM experience. Informal networks included the personal friendships they had forged at ELAM as well as the general sense of sisterhood common among all ELAM alumnae. These support networks appeared to enhance their sense of self-efficacy and subsequent leadership development. Most importantly, they continued to provide a source for vicarious experiences and social models as well as a vital source of verbal persuasion. They also aided women with their leadership skill development and with the continued broadening of their horizons, as Fellows sought advice through their networks, gained professional development, and made the professional contacts necessary for leadership proficiency.

Other research has confirmed the importance of support networks for women's career advancement in academic medicine. Yedidia and Bickel's (2001) study of clinical department chairs revealed that success in developing the careers of junior faculty rested heavily on the obtainment of a good advisor who would serve as an effective mentor and guardian. Most significantly, the chairs interviewed in the study felt that mentors could help women in academic medicine navigate through the gender barriers they face in this male-dominated field.

Our data suggest that in academic medicine, women would do well to make a conscious effort to seek out other women to help reinforce and cultivate their own self-efficacy development as this relates to leadership. This can be achieved informally through social networks or more formally through programs, like ELAM, that foster mentor relationships and peer support.

Conclusion

The field of academic medicine has a low proportion of women in leadership positions. Although women enter medical schools at the same rates as those of men, they fail to rise to the top at comparable levels. One of the off-ramps that some women face is a lack of self-efficacy with regard to their leadership skills. We examined the ELAM program as a case study to understand how women extend self-efficacy associated with leadership development. While we concerned ourselves with academic medicine, our findings have relevance for the development of future women academic leaders in any field and perhaps to the development of women leaders in arenas outside academics.

A strong majority of interviewed ELAM Fellows (95%) indicated an increase in self-efficacy because of participation in the ELAM program. From our analysis, it was apparent that the ELAM program enhanced self-efficacy development along each of the four sources identified by Bandura (1997): mastery experiences, vicarious experiences/social models, verbal persuasion, and physiological and affective states. While women showed evidence of leadership skill building, growing confidence in their leadership skills, and, critically, a sense of agency that they might use those skills to reach desired and newfound leadership goals, the gradual nature of self-efficacy development became apparent to us and to them. We learned the importance of the collaborative and the independent process. In particular, interviewed Fellows revealed the benefits of mentors, role models, and informal and formal support networks. Fellows further revealed the value of structured opportunities for guided reflective work.

This study suggests the power of self-efficacy development as a foundation for increasing the numbers and validity of women academic leaders. We encourage individuals, departments, and leadership development programs to apply this knowledge in their ongoing quest to help women attain the recognition and advancement that is within their reach.

Note

1. *Concise Oxford English Dictionary*, 11th ed., s.v., "Confidence."

References

Association of American Medical Colleges. (1996). Increasing women's leadership in academic medicine. *Academic Medicine, 71,* 799–811.

Association of American Medical Colleges. (2002). Increasing women's leadership in academic medicine. *Academic Medicine, 77,* 101–119.

Association of American Medical Colleges. (2004). *Women in U.S. academic medicine: Statistics and medical school benchmarking, 2003–2004.* Washington, DC: Author.

Bandura, A. (1986). The explanation and predictive scope of self-efficacy theory. *Journal of Clinical and Social Psychology, 4,* 359–373.

Bandura, A. (1992). Psychological aspects of prognostic judgments. In R. W. Evans, D. S. Baskin, & F. M Yatsu (Eds.), *Prognosis of neurological disorders* (pp. 13–28). New York: Oxford University Press.

Bandura, A. (1993). Perceived self-efficacy in cognitive development and functioning. *Educational Psychologist, 28,* 117–148.

Bandura, A. (1994). Self-efficacy. In V. S. Ramachaudran (Ed.), *Encyclopedia of human behavior* (Vol. 4, pp. 71–81). New York: Academic Press.

Bandura, A. (1997). *Self-efficacy: The exercise of control.* New York: Freeman.

Benz, E. J., Jr., Clayton, C. P., & Costa, S. T. (1998, December). Increasing academic internal medicine's investment in female faculty. *American Journal of Medicine, 105,* 459–463.

Bickel, J. (2001). Women in medicine: The work that remains. *Journal of Women's Imaging, 3,* 1–2.

Birnbaum, R. (1988). *How colleges work.* San Francisco: Jossey-Bass.

Birnbaum, R. (1992). *How academic leadership works.* San Francisco: Jossey-Bass.

Buckley, L., Sanders, K., Shih, M., Kallar, S., & Hampton, C. (2000). Obstacles to promotion? Values of women faculty about career success and recognition. *Academic Medicine, 75,* 283–288.

Carr, P., Friedman, R., Moskowitz, M., & Kazis, L. (1993). Comparing the status of women and men in academic medicine. *Annals of Internal Medicine, 119*(9), 908–913.

Choi, J., Price, R. H., & Vinokur, A. D. (2003). Self-efficacy changes in groups: Effects of diversity, leadership, and group climate. *Journal of Organizational Behavior, 24,* 357–372.

Colletti, L., Mulholland, M., & Sonnad, S. (2000). Perceived obstacles to career success for women in academic surgery. *Archives of Surgery, 135,* 972–977.

De Angelis, C. D. (2000). Women in academic medicine: New insights, same sad news. *New England Journal of Medicine, 342,* 426–427.

Drexel University College of Medicine. (n.d.). *Welcome to ELAM.* Retrieved January 3, 2006, from http://www.drexel.edu/elam/AboutELAM/Application%20Brochure.pdf

Ely, R., & Meyerson, D. (2000). Advancing gender equity in organizations: The challenge and importance of maintaining a gender narrative. *Organization, 7*(4), 589–608.

Etzkowitz, H., Kernegor, M., & Neuschatt, M. (1994). The paradox of critical mass for women in science. *Science, 266,* 51–54.

Fried, L. P., Francomano, C. A., MacDonald, S. M., Wagner, E. M., Stokes, E. J., Carbone, K. M., et al. (1996). Career development for women in academic medicine. *Journal of the American Medical Association, 276,* 895–905.

Garman, K., Wingard, D., & Reznik, V. (2001, October). Development of junior faculty's self-efficacy: Outcomes of a national center of leadership in academic medicine. *Academic Medicine, 76*(10), S74–S76.

Hackett, G., & Betz, N. E. (1989). An exploration of the mathematics self-efficacy/mathematics performance correspondence. *Journal for Research in Mathematics Education, 20,* 261–273.

Heifetz, R. A. (1994). *Leadership without easy answers.* Cambridge, MA: Belknap Press/Harvard University Press.

Hewlett, S., & Luce, C. (2005, March). Off-ramps and on-ramps, keeping talented women on the road to success. *Harvard Business Review, 83*(3), 43–46, 48, 50–54.

Lenz, E., & Shortridge-Baggett, L. M. (2002). *Self-efficacy in nursing: Research and measurement perspectives.* New York: Springer.

Leyens, J., Desert, M., Croizet, J., & Darcis, C. (2000). Stereotype threat: Are lower status and history of stigmatization preconditions of stereotype threat? *Personality & Social Psychology Bulletin, 26,* 1189–1199.

McCormick, M. J., Tanguma, J., & Lopez-Forment, A. S. (2002). Extending self-efficacy theory to leadership: A review and empirical test. *Journal of Leadership Education, 1*(2), 2–15.

Morahan, P., Voytko, M. L., Abbhul, S., Means, L., Wara, D., Thorson, J., et al. (2001). Ensuring the success of women faculty at AMCs: Lessons learned from the National Centers of Excellence in Women's Health. *Academic Medicine, 76,* 19–31.

Murray, L. R. (2003). Sick and tired of being sick and tired: Implications for racial and ethnic disparities in occupational health. *American Journal of Public Health, 93,* 221–226.

Nonnemaker, L. (2000). Women physicians in academic medicine. *The New England Journal of Medicine, 342,* 399–405.

Pajares, F. (1996). Self-efficacy beliefs and mathematical problem solving of gifted students. *Contemporary Educational Psychology, 21,* 325–344.

Pajares, F. (2002). *Self-efficacy beliefs in academic contexts: An outline.* Retrieved January 22, 2005, from http://www.emory.edu/EDUCATION/mfp/efftalk.html

Richman, R. C., Morahan, P. S., Cohen, D. W., & McDade, S. M. (2001). Advancing women and closing the leadership gap: The Executive Leadership in Academic Medicine (ELAM) program experience. *Journal of Women's Health and Gender-Based Medicine, 10,* 271–277.

Ruderman, M., & Ohlott, P. (2002). *Standing at the crossroads: Next steps for high-achieving women.* San Francisco: Jossey-Bass.

Sandler, B. R., & Hall, R. M. (1986). *The campus climate revisited: Chilly for women faculty, administrators, and graduate students.* Washington, DC: Project on the Status of and Education of Women, Association of American Colleges and Universities.

Singer, M. (1991). The relationship between employee sex, length of service and leadership aspirations: A study of valence, self-efficacy, and attribution perspectives. *Applied Psychology: An International Review, 40,* 417–436.

Strauss, A. L. (1987). *Qualitative analysis for social scientists.* Cambridge, UK: Cambridge University Press.

Tom, S. C. (1997). Opening the doors to medical education: From the Victorian era to the present. *Initiatives, 58,* 23–37.

Valian, V. (1998). *Why so slow? The advancement of women.* Cambridge, MA: Harvard University Press.

Woods, R. (2004). *The effects of self-efficacy, transformational leadership and trust on leadership effectiveness of senior student affairs officers.* Unpublished doctoral dissertation, Regent University, Virginia Beach, VA.

Yedidia, M. J., & Bickel, J. (2001). Why aren't there more women leaders in academic medicine? The views of clinical department chairs. *Academic Medicine, 76,* 453–465.

Yin, R. K. (1994). *Case study research: Design and methods* (2nd ed.). Thousand Oaks, CA: Sage.

Zeldin, A., & Pajares, F. (2001). Against the odds: Self-efficacy beliefs of women in mathematical, scientific, and technological careers. *American Educational Research Journal, 37,* 215–246.

4

BARRIERS TO WOMEN'S LEADERSHIP IN FAITH-BASED COLLEGES AND UNIVERSITIES

Strategies for Change

Diane F. Wood

The phrase *glass ceiling* describes the barriers to women's upward mobility in the senior leadership of corporate America. It has become a metaphor to characterize how the policies and practices of all institutions, including colleges and universities, have embedded barriers that impede women's professional advancement (Nidiffer & Bashaw, 2001). Although they are relative latecomers to mass higher education, having entered academe in serious proportions only since the women's movement in the 1960s, women now surpass men as the majority of college students and have increased their proportions among college faculty and administrators. Yet they remain underrepresented in the leadership of colleges and universities (Chamberlain, 1988; Corrigan, 2002; Dean, 2004; Hersi, 1993; McCook, 1994; Scanlon, 1997). Even though they are highly competent, many women never advance that far. A glass ceiling caps their career ladders

I am indebted to Shawna Lafreniere, a doctoral student at Azusa Pacific University, for her detailed research on the history of the Women's Leadership Development Institute program; Karen Longman, vice president for academic affairs and dean of the faculty at Greenville College, creator and codirector of the Women's Leadership Development Institute, for her dedication to supporting my work; Laurie Schreiner, chair and professor of doctoral studies in education and Department of Higher Education and Organizational Leadership at Azusa Pacific University, for her time and support; and Kim Phipps, president of Messiah College, and Ron Mahurin, vice president for professional development and research at the Coalition for Christian Colleges and Universities, for their strong support. All were invaluable to the development of this chapter.

(Glass Ceiling Commission, 1995; Morrison, White, & Van Velsor, 1987; Scanlon, 1997).

Some institutional types and academic sectors do a better job of attaining gender diversity and equity in their academic leadership than others do. For example, community colleges and the academic disciplinary area of education have a greater proportion of women leaders than that found among research universities and the sciences. This chapter focuses on one institutional type where women remain underrepresented in academic leadership: faith-based colleges and universities. Focusing on institutions belonging to the Council for Christian Colleges and Universities (CCCU), this chapter explores unique barriers to women's advancement in such colleges as well as systemic and institutional equity change efforts under way. I build this scholarly chapter upon (a) document analysis gathered from CCCU and selected member institutions, (b) relevant literature elucidating gender equity issues in faith-based colleges and universities from higher education and church history perspectives, and (c) interviews with individuals at CCCU member institutions. Throughout, I infuse commentary on the organizational contexts and the interconnections between practice and espoused values. The chapter concludes with recommended strategies for creating more equitable environments in faith-based colleges and universities and for advancing women within them.

The CCCU

New England Puritans established the first Christian higher education institution in North America in 1636, naming it Harvard College. As American higher education developed, a considerable proportion of colleges were founded by or affiliated with religious denominations (Patterson, 2001). Over time the faith-based educational community refined and expanded its postsecondary enterprise at all levels. Today, over half (54%) of the nation's nonprofit private colleges and universities describe themselves as religiously affiliated, including those connected with Catholic, Jewish, and a wide range of Protestant faiths. This equates to over a quarter (27%) of all America's 3,000-plus nonprofit colleges and universities, a sizable proportion (Higher Education Publications, 2005). Therefore, when we think about gender equity within higher education, we need to concern ourselves with equity at faith-based institutions.

Within the realm of religiously affiliated institutions, this chapter focuses on the CCCU, an international organization formed in 1976. CCCU membership reflects great diversity in the location, curricular offerings, and resources of its members. Its 105 North American members are affiliated with or derived from the Evangelical segment of Protestant faiths and include such organizations as Assemblies of God, Baptists (American, Independent, Southern), Brethren, Christian and Missionary Alliance, Church of Christ, Church of God, Church of the Nazarene, Evangelical Covenant, Evangelical Free, Free Methodist, Friends, Mennonite (Brethren, General Conference, Independent), Missionary Church, Presbyterian (Independent, USA, Church of America), Reformed (Christian Reformed Church, Reformed Church in America), and Wesleyan Church (Garlett, 1997). Despite the broad scope of denominational and theological orientations represented, the CCCU has a common mission: "To advance the cause of Christ-centered higher education and to help our institutions transform lives by faithfully relating scholarship and service to biblical truth" (CCCU, n.d.). CCCU fervently supports colleges and universities that pursue this mission (Patterson, 2001) and plays an integral role in charting the course for faith-based higher education now and in the future.

Women and Academic Leadership in the CCCU

Research has implicated a glass ceiling for women aspiring to academic leadership in CCCU institutions (Cejda, Bush, & Rewey, 2002). In 1999, for example, Plotts, Lumsden, Newsom, and Wells (1999) studied the presidents of the 90 CCCU member institutions: All were men. Today there are only three women presidents out of CCCU's 105 member colleges and universities (R. Mahurin, personal communication, November 9, 2005).

Faith-based institutions, as with the majority of American colleges and universities, consider the chief academic officer position a significant step toward a presidency. In 2002, women represented only 14% of CCCU's chief academic officers (Cejda et al., 2002). Today, women hold about 19% of such positions (CCCU, 2005). The proportions of women in other academic leadership positions, such as deans and department chairs, are not known and remain an area for future study.

Looking at CCCU faculty, we can extrapolate from dated reports that women and men faculty differ significantly at the highest and lowest ranks of the professorial continuum. Women constitute only a third (33%) of all faculty (Baylis, 1995; CCCU, 2002). Among this small cadre, only a third are tenured (32%) and less than a fifth (18%) hold full professor rank (Baylis; CCCU). In comparison, half of men faculty are tenured (50%) and over two fifths (42%) hold full professor rank (Baylis; CCCU). At the other end of the continuum, 15% of women faculty are instructors—a proportion three times higher than that for men faculty (5%; CCCU). Aggregating all faculty ranks, women faculty are paid roughly 20% to 25% less than men faculty are (CCCU), even after controlling for experience (Schreiner, 2002).

The Impact of Gender Inequity

Gender inequity in the administration and faculty of CCCU institutions has deep repercussions on internal and external constituencies and on every level of an institution's organizational structure. Two critical repercussions include its effect on student populations and on institutional image.

Effect on student populations. The majority (67%) of students enrolled in CCCU institutions are women (National Center for Education Statistics, 2003). Research conducted as part of the Comprehensive Assessment Project, a major CCCU-wide undertaking to promote improvement and innovation among member institutions, has shown that women and men students differ in their perceptions of what is important in their college experience, how they spend their time, and what contributes to their satisfaction (Longman, 2002a; Schreiner, 2002). Critically, the college experience yields different perceptions for men and women concerning their skills and abilities. Men develop far greater confidence in their intellectual skills and academic abilities and rate themselves above average in leadership, public speaking, and general social skills (Longman-b; Schreiner). Women exhibit greater passivity and develop high levels of confidence only in their interpersonal understanding and writing skills (Longman-b; Schreiner).

Fueling these differences, gender inequity in faith-based culture conveys the perceived value of each individual's unique gifts and contributions to society. An inequitable environment inherently conveys that women and their contributions have low value.

Women college students need to discover their potential to reach great heights, no matter what avenue they pursue. Their college experience should result in greater confidence in their skills and abilities—not low confidence. They need to be supported by a culture that values women's abilities and talents. This includes having more women role models in the administration and faculty.

Men students equally need more women role models and a culture that values women. What men see modeled in the treatment of women classmates, faculty, and administrators will play a significant role in formulating their views and interactions with women in their homes, churches, communities, and workplaces.

Effect on institutional image. Gender inequity affects individual institutional images, as well as the collective image of faith-based colleges and universities. This critically has an impact on an institution's overall health and longevity, hampering its abilities to explore innovative ways to secure its position in the global marketplace, possibly affecting enrollment management, as well as generally dampening public relations. With so obviously few women in leadership positions in the senior administration and faculty, Christian institutions remain vulnerable to stereotypical labels, such as sexist, fundamentalist, right wing, and bigoted (Lumsden, Plotts, & Wells, 2000).

"As leaders of Christian colleges and universities," noted Kim Phipps (Phipps & Richardson, 2002), president of Messiah College, "we need to honestly examine the weaknesses and flaws of our institutions, particularly the inadequate level of institutional commitment to gender and racial justice" (p. 3). An engaged Christian university builds on the praxis between thought and action. Phipps challenges institutions to "nurture environments where the expectation goes beyond merely having discussions or forums, [creating] environments that will promote and sustain ongoing action that will lead toward gender and racial reconciliation" (p. 3).

A Need for Change

It is easy to detect issues of inequity in academe when women faculty have inadequate representation at every level of the salary scale (LeBlanc, 1993). I expand LeBlanc's observation to include the inadequate representation of women administrators. Data on women among CCCU institutions reflect a real need to address prevalent gender equity issues. The development and growth of faith-based higher education depends upon advancing, enhancing, and supporting gender equity. Phipps (Phipps & Richardson, 2002) calls this the right thing to do, "for the sake of our students, for the sake of our colleagues, for the sake of our institutions, and for the sake of our God whom we seek to honor and obey" (p. 12).

As a beginning, we must ask: Why is the proportion of women faculty and administrators so low? Why do women not attain higher faculty ranks in larger numbers or advance to academic leadership positions? What factors underlie these phenomena, and what will it take to foster real change?

Theological Beliefs Concerning Women's Leadership

Barriers to women's advancement in faith-based institutions emanate from theological foundations and denominational belief systems concerning women's role in the church and society. In the faith-based institutions that have kept strong ties with their affiliated denominations, these cultural norms become a part of institutional culture and lead to policies and practices that limit women's professional growth and contributions. Any effort toward fostering gender equity must begin with an understanding of these foundations.

Traditionalist Views

Glanville (2000), researching women's leadership development in Christian ministry, identified a two-part belief typology concerning women as leaders in the church. On one side, "traditionalists" and "complementarians" adhere to the conviction that "men and women were created differently for different roles that are meant to complement one another" (Glanville, p. 59). Traditionalists believe biblical scripture confirms a hierarchy between genders and among diverse roles assigned to each gender. At the root of this lies a belief that women should not have authority over men, including teaching or holding leadership positions over men.

Many traditionalists apply their hierarchical views only to contexts of spiritual authority and church roles. Some denominations take their views to an extreme and convey a decidedly nonwelcoming attitude toward women's leadership in the church (Garlett, 1997), prohibiting their service as congregational pastors, teaching pastors, and church board members or elders. The Southern Baptist Convention, for example, voted in June 2000 to limit its pastoral roles to men (Mead & Hill, 2001).

Ann Graham Lotz (2002), the daughter of well-known Evangelical pastor Rev. Billy Graham, described her experiences with a nonwelcoming traditionalist belief system when she was asked to speak to a group of 800 pastors and church leaders. As she entered the room and proceeded to the podium, to her amazement many of the members in the audience were moving their chairs. Once she reached the platform she was shocked to actually see that their backs were facing the front (Graham Lotz). Graham Lotz wondered, "How could godly men find what I was doing so offensive that they would stage such a demonstration, especially when their organization had invited me to speak?" (p. 7). Clearly, the pastors she encountered displayed hostile behavior. Those adhering to this form of traditionalism narrowly define their view of women's role in society at large, including the expectations that (a) women should not hold any kind of authority over a man, (b) women should be at home raising a family, and (c) women should be seen and not heard.

Other traditionalists take a more moderate approach, applying biblical scripture only to spiritual authority, not authority in general. Moderate complementarians believe that although women should not have authority in church situations they may in secular situations, that is, business, education, and so forth.

Egalitarian Views

On the other side of Glanville's (2000) typology, "egalitarians and biblical feminists" (p. 59) believe that God created men and women as equals. Subsequently, they support appointments to leadership positions based only on an individual's requisite gifts, talents, skills, or abilities—not gender. Thus, women can and do engage in the same types of positions in the church as men do, including pastoral, teaching, and all other leadership roles. Denominations with such welcoming views toward women include Quaker (Evangelical) and Free Methodist (Garlett, 1997).

Jack Willcuts (1984), who served in the Quaker church in a variety of capacities for many years, explains it from a more egalitarian view:

> In our church there is, of course, more than three centuries of Quaker history filled with examples of women used in ministry and missionary service. . . . Many issues have been raised in our nation's history, and resolved, such as women's suffrage, abolition of slavery, prison reforms, and other equal rights concerns, many from a Christian motivation; these are the outgrowth of God's wisdom in which Friends have had a part and at times were in leadership roles. There are also helpful insights relative to how the woman as pastor and preacher fills a role simultaneously of a mother and wife in church leadership responsibilities. Friends history is replete with heroic stories that must be read by each generation recounting the ways women (and men) have been used in specific ministries in public and church service. . . . This, as a denomination, is a rich heritage. There is no question for Quakers as to whether or not God uses women in the ministry. (p. 50)

Just as traditionalist views vary, the egalitarian or biblical feminist understanding also encompasses shades of beliefs about women as leaders. While the more liberal apply their egalitarian views to all aspects of human life— church and secular—others take a limited stand or accept various positions in between.

Complementarians and traditionalists concentrate on the divergence between men and women; egalitarians and biblical feminists converge on their resemblances. Interestingly, each perspective is based on biblical scripture. The difference lies in theological understanding and interpretations of the Bible. Traditionalists base their interpretations on I Timothy 2:11–13 (New International Version): "A woman should learn in quietness and full submission. I do not permit a woman to teach or to have authority over a man; she must be silent. For Adam was formed first, then Eve." Egalitarians base their views upon Galatians 3:28: "There is neither Jew nor Greek, slave nor free, male nor female, for you are all one in Christ Jesus."

Resulting Views on Women as Leaders in Academe

Interpretations of the Bible among various faith-based communities play a pivotal role in creating and sustaining organizational culture at these groups' affiliated college or university. What a denomination believes about women and their role in society will be evident at every level of their college or university and thus shape the campus climate for women.

Some campuses have made significant strides toward supporting gender equity and social justice while remaining consistent with the roots of their traditionalist denominational origins.

Occasionally the reverse happens: An institution affiliated with an egalitarian denomination develops an organizational culture inequitable for women. Such a disconnect results in organizational disequilibrium at many levels. Other campuses whose affiliated traditionalist denominations have a limited view of the role of women criticize the egalitarian perspective as a secular sociological approach that erodes, undermines, and rejects the very basis of Christian doctrine (Nathan, 2004).

Women who rise to academic leadership in faith-based institutions do so as a result of their diligent work ethic (Moreton & Newsom, 2004). They receive career advice not unlike that given to academic women across the country: Work twice as hard, don't complain, demonstrate the ability to get things done, find a mentor, and assert yourself at an appropriate time (Hopson, 1995; Moreton & Newsom, 2004). While such advice helps, it is not infallible. At many colleges and universities, attaining an administrative position may be almost impossible for women, especially where such positions require external experience as ministerial senior pastors. For example, CCCU presidents primarily come from a pastorate or another Christian ministry or organization (Plotts et al., 1999). Understandably, this requisite presents a problem for women who are shut out of church-leader roles in many denominations.

LeBlanc (1993) noted the importance for higher education to understand that gender inequality is no longer an acceptable professional norm. Phipps (2002) emphasized that faith-based institutions are called by God to value each individual equally. With their institutional missions of serving the greater community at all levels, faith-based colleges and universities need to evaluate their campuses to determine where social justice is not being followed within their own walls, thus opening opportunities for women. The emphasis on creating a global environment across all segments of society provides an even stronger impetus for advancing gender and social justice issues.

Systemic and Institutional Change Efforts

Clearly the Christian community disagrees at its very denominational roots concerning the role of women in society. CCCU, charting the course for faith-based higher education, faces the challenge of how to reconcile these beliefs and interpret the role of women in academic leadership and in society at large. Each CCCU member institution represents its own unique denomination or faith-based movement. This creates a prodigious task for CCCU, which must craft an inclusive organizational structure that represents an extensive range of biblical views and belief systems. The CCCU's interpretations affect students, faculty, administrators, and external constituencies. However, the primary role that exemplifies the CCCU organization as it works with each of its institutional members is pastoral and/or supportive in nature, not controlling or dictatorial (R. Mahurin, personal communication, November 9, 2005).

A definite effort to foster gender equity is evident at CCCU's systemic level. As part of its strategic planning, the CCCU developed an intercultural initiative to advance understanding in six areas considered vital to its members' future success: race/ethnicity, internationalization, world religions, human sexuality, gender equity, and disenfranchisement. CCCU (2004) committed to provide resources and support to member institutions seeking to advance these initiatives on their campuses.

To support its strategic objective in advancing gender equity, CCCU created the Women's Leadership Development Institute (WLDI) at the systemic level to assist in expanding opportunities for women who aspire to leadership positions within the member institutions.

The WLDI

CCCU initiated the Executive Leadership Development Institute in the mid-1990s. The Leadership Development Institute (LDI) grew out of this effort and offers professional development for emerging leaders in CCCU member organizations, including new presidents and chief academic officers. It has served about 265 participants since its inception (Lafreniere, 2005).

In 1998 the WLDI emerged from LDI as a distinct program. Instituted by Karen Longman, formerly CCCU's vice president for professional development and research, WLDI sprang from a concern over the lack of women at the executive leadership level in the CCCU institutions and represents a concerted effort to address this deficit.

Purpose and process. The institute provides aspiring women leaders with the opportunity to engage in leadership development and mentoring experiences. CCCU modeled the program on other national programs that develop men and women higher education leaders, including Harvard's Institute for Educational Management, Fuller Theological Seminary's DePree Leadership Center, Bryn-Mawr/Higher Education Research Services (HERS) Summer Institutes for Women in Higher Education, and various leadership programs sponsored by the American Council on Education (Lafreniere, 2005).

The institute itself is a 1-week long experience planned around topics relevant to senior-level management and unique to faith-based higher education. Selected topics include general management skills and knowledge areas such as governance, budgets, strategic planning, and conflict resolution, and campus culture knowledge areas such as politics, diversity, and knowing your constituency base. Participants, called Fellows, devote a significant amount of time to discussing leadership styles and issues facing women leaders. Each Fellow has the opportunity to identify her unique personal leadership strengths and develop a Professional Development Plan (PDP; Lafreniere, 2005).

The PDP includes designing a mentoring experience for the following academic school year, organized in collaboration with executive administrators among CCCU institutions who volunteer to serve as mentors (Lafreniere, 2005). The admission process includes an application, essays, and two nominations from senior-level college executives or academic leaders. WLDI admits about 20 Fellows for its biannual institutes and has hosted four institutes since its inception in 1998 (Lafreniere).

Program benefits. Going beyond providing content knowledge one might learn from books or other seminars, WLDI offers women several unique benefits. It gives Fellows the opportunity to hear firsthand from women administrators at CCCU institutions, providing role models and a realistic understanding of the role of an administrator. It creates an environment in which women can express, debate, and discuss questions and concerns about issues related to gender equity in faith-based institutions in an open and honest manner. It brings them in contact with other women colleagues from around the country who aspire to leadership positions, and it forges mentoring relationships with current CCCU leaders. The result is an automatic support network for further career exploration and advancement. The informal conversations and networking with other women, as well as the mentoring experience, greatly increase participants' confidence in their own leadership potential (Lafreniere, 2005).

Three former WLDI participants best articulate the program's benefits. Laurie Schreiner, chair and professor of doctoral studies in education in the Department of Higher Education and Organizational Leadership at Azusa Pacific University, described her WLDI experience as a supportive environment where she could explore the question, "What is God really calling me to do?" The initial week-long program provided her ample opportunity for informal conversations and to create a strong support network with other women. "The camaraderie," she said, "was phenomenal" (L. Schreiner, personal interview, November 22, 2005).

Andrea Cook, now vice president of institutional advancement at Goshen College, attended WLDI when she moved into a new administrative position and new institution. She described the program as validating the women involved. "They have the opportunity to hear from women who have experience navigating the waters of leadership in Christian higher education. I was encouraged by the questions, dialogue, and sense of calling expressed by the women involved in the leadership institute. . . . I think the program provides encouragement for women to pursue their calling to leadership roles. It creates networks of support and offers women the opportunity to receive counsel from those who have experienced the journey to roles of leadership. For me, the leadership institute provided a moment for reflection on the journey and to encourage others in theirs" (A. Cook, personal communication, August 7, 2004).

While the WLDI program provides valuable experiences for women interested in pursuing leadership positions, it also provides current leaders a chance to extend service outside their local college communities. The mentors understand that they play a vital role assisting in preparing future faith-based higher education leaders. Judy Fortune, provost emeritus at Simpson University, participated in WLDI as a presenter and as a mentor. Describing the mentoring program, she said, "It was the most rewarding experience in my professional life. It was extremely challenging; I learned as much as I gave out" (J. Fortune, personal communication, November 4, 2005).

The words of these participants and others like them underscore WLDI's important role in supporting the advancement of women to leadership in faith-based higher education. The institute provides a framework for reflection, networking, camaraderie, and mentoring for all involved. Recognizing that it fills a unique and momentous role in providing opportunities for women to explore and advance to administrative roles in faith-based institutions, CCCU has committed to continue supporting WLDI (R. Mahurin, personal communication, November 9, 2005).

However, no mandates require member institutions to align themselves to CCCU's gender-equity initiative or participate in the WLDI program. Each institution decides whether and how it will implement the six strategic objectives and whether to use any of CCCU's support and services. This poses inherent challenges given that each institution functions out of its own individual theological beliefs.

Institutional Efforts

Examples of colleges that have taken CCCU's gender equity objective to heart and action include Messiah College and Point Loma Nazarene College.

Messiah College

Messiah College has been at the forefront of pressing for institutional change. Through a Lilly Vocation Grant, Messiah plans to educate all students on the college's support for women's leadership in the ministry in addition to providing mentors and resources for women who aspire to such vocations (Phipps & Richardson, 2002).

Messiah has instituted a day care center to assist women and men faculty with young growing families and financially support faculty who are pursuing their doctorates, both tangible examples of its efforts to create a more supportive environment for women. Messiah's support is visible in symbolic ways, such as its recently founded award for women students in honor of Messiah's first woman academic dean (Phipps & Richardson, 2002).

President Kim Phipps (Phipps & Richardson, 2002) has played an integral role in the pursuit of gender equity and racial justice at all institutional levels. She articulates the challenge facing Messiah and other faith-based institutions:

> Every CCCU campus must perform the challenging task of discussing, writing, and publishing foundational statements concerning gender, racial justice and equality. These statements should be discussed, debated, and finally endorsed by the trustees, administration, faculty, staff, and students. The process of participative campus community input and involvement in developing these declarations is critical to educating campus constituents and to facilitating a sense of ownership. [However, the organizational] culture . . . will not change in meaningful ways unless institutional leaders . . . demonstrate steadfast commitment toward gender and racial equality [through] . . . consistent reinforcement of [gender and racially equitable] policies and protocols. (pp. 10, 14)

Point Loma Nazarene College

Other institutions have chosen their curriculum as the starting point for implementing CCCU intercultural initiatives. For the gender equity objective, this resulted in the creation of women's studies programs such as the one at Point Loma Nazarene College.

Linda Beail, director of the Margaret Stevenson Center for Women's Studies and professor of political science, described the grassroots beginnings of the women's studies program on the Point Loma campus. Ten years ago, before CCCU's intercultural initiative, a self-formed reading group of about 20–30 women and men faculty out of 140 faculty members began meeting on a regular basis. During these meetings, interesting and challenging discussions emerged around gendered issues, including faculty members' own experiences, intellectual analyses, and reflection. The members charged themselves with considering what action they could and should take beyond talking and theorizing about gender inequity. From this, the women's studies minor and the Center for Women's Studies were born (L. Beail, personal communication, November 2005).

At least nine CCCU member campuses have developed women's studies programs, including Azusa Pacific University, Goshen College, Messiah College, Seattle Pacific University, and Whitworth College (L. Beail, personal communication, November 2005). Several have been funded through Lilly Vocation Grants.

Shattering the Stained-Glass Ceiling

Although much can be done to transform an institution serious about addressing gender inequity, any change effort would benefit from five elements critical in strategic planning. As translated to the equity objective they are (a) strong, unified leadership committed to gender equity; (b) internal organizational assessment; (c) campuswide, honest dialogue; (d) a comprehensive plan for change that is responsive to institutional uniqueness; and (e) evaluation of equity initiatives.

Committed Leadership

Strong leadership committed to gender equity can advance change efforts, as seen at the systemic level through the WLDI program and at the institutional level through Messiah and Point Loma Nazarene colleges. However, strong leadership at the CCCU organizational level is not enough to advance broad-scale change, as shown by the fact that institutions have their choice of adopting or not adopting the CCCU's strategic gender equity objective.

Unified Leadership Is Required

CCCU institutions can look to Nine Presidents as a model of how they might unify their leadership and commit to transformative change. Nine Presidents includes the CEOs of the renowned institutions Harvard, Princeton, Stanford, and Yale; the University of California–Berkeley, the University of Michigan, and the University of Pennsylvania; and the California Institute of Technology and the Massachusetts Institute of Technology. These top-tier universities share a common thread with faith-based institutions: They are both built upon male-dominated traditions and struggle with overt gender inequity. In their efforts to foster gender equity, Nine Presidents has pledged to develop equitable academic personnel policies at its institutions, support those policies through institutional resources, and take steps to create more family-friendly and gender-equitable campus cultures (Felde, 2005).

Nine Presidents and University of California–Berkeley chancellor Robert Birgeneau called their unified leadership and initiatives "an historic moment for universities. I'm pleased that my colleagues share our commitment to . . . achieving gender equity in the academy" (Felde, 2005). A similar coalition formed among CCCU members would prove to be an equally historic moment for faith-based higher education. At the very least, individual institutional change efforts require strong, committed leadership among senior executives and major academic leaders, as well as support from the institution's trustees.

Organizational Assessment

Each institution committing to advance equity must begin with an in-depth organizational assessment, uncovering and acknowledging the extent and intensity of inequity on its campus in all its forms. What is hidden or ignored cannot be corrected. The WLDI program, for example, was born of the attention to gender inequity generated through CCCU's own Comprehensive Assessment Plan (CAP). CAP data, however, are aggregated and dated. Each individual campus needs current data.

Individual campuses could develop their own plans for assessment, or CCCU could develop a standard model that member organizations may use and compare results with one another. Data to be assessed include staffing; promotion and compensation data for faculty and administrators; and student grades, awards, and participation in programs and activities. An assessment should also include an examination of curricula, programs, and pedagogy used across campus to determine if there is gender bias, and an assessment of policies, practices, and procedures—including an inventory of benefits and their usage—to determine whether they are gender equitable and family friendly.

Wherever possible, comparative or benchmark data should be obtained for peer CCCU institutions and for U.S. private and public nonprofit post-secondary institutions.

Dialogue

On the heels of data should come dialogue. Shattering the stained-glass ceiling for women at faith-based colleges and universities will require a collaborative effort beginning with a series of open and honest campus discussions. This takes an administrative mandate that initiates bringing the appropriate individuals together to begin conversations around gender-related issues, including students, faculty, department chairs, deans, administrators, executives, and board members. Senior leadership endorsement and involvement will demonstrate that the issues are relevant to and valued by the institution. Without the commitment of senior leadership, campus conversations risk being viewed as superficial.

Knowing and understanding the theological views regarding women and their role within faith-based communities will be integral to the overall dialogue. Each institution's rich religious and cultural roots can provide a unique and significant viewpoint in examining how the university can better serve its women students, faculty, and staff, as well as women in its larger community and constituency bases.

Equally integral to the dialogue is a community evaluation of the institutional mission statement and existing goals to ensure that they reflect a strong commitment to all peoples represented and served by the institution.

Open, honest dialogue will raise awareness, reveal new qualitative information about the campus climate, reveal the level of commitment for pursuing a gender-equitable environment within all segments of the institution, facilitate a community prioritization of problems to be addressed, and generate ideas for crafting a plan for change.

Comprehensive Plan

Gathering data cannot initiate change nor can dialogue alone. Therefore, it is vitally important to have a plan for transformation in place that responds to and uses the data reported in order to institute effective change. A wide range of strategies may be designed to address gender equity issues. While individual institutions will need to select strategies that suit their campus needs best, CCCU might make best-practice examples available on its Web site's resource page, as it currently does for general information about gender equity (see http://www.cccu.org/migrate/resources_for_intercultural_compe tencies_gender_equity).

Whatever plan an institution develops, it must be accompanied with an appropriate timeline that accounts for and leaves time for necessary adjustments in the system to occur. For example, any plans involving curricular or pedagogical changes may require several semesters to implement. Some initiatives may require time to reallocate or obtain the resources needed to support them.

Transformational plans demand ultimate prioritization and focusing skills. They require the support of committed, strong leadership to ensure that the plans are developed and then initiated. They require campus dialogue to generate awareness and support.

Evaluation

All good planning processes include evaluation plans at the outset. Campuses serious about creating equitable environments should periodically evaluate their efforts. Evaluation plans will be contingent upon the types of problems uncovered during organizational assessment and campus dialogue. They might include regularly scheduled collection and reassessment of the original data collected, and periodic campus climate surveys.

CCCU as an organization can demonstrate its seriousness about creating equitable environments and intercultural understanding by developing plans to periodically evaluate efforts among member institutions. With regard to gender equity and women in academic leadership, the focus of this chapter, such an evaluation plan should include attention to the WLDI program.

An evaluation of the WLDI program would ensure a heightened awareness of the strengths and obstacles unique to the leadership institute and mentor phase of the program. For example, data on Fellows' career choices and attainment after their WLDI experience would reveal the program's efficacy for developing and advancing women leaders, and qualitative assessment of Fellows' experiences during and after the institute and mentoring phase would provide a basis for developing, refining, and expanding WLDI.

Evaluation can determine whether an institution achieves more equitable outcomes and has a more equitable environment than it did previously. As with organizational assessment, evaluation data should be compared with institutional baseline data (gathered during assessment and initial dialogues), as well as CCCU and national comparative data.

Strategies for Advancing Women in Academic Leadership

While the preceding recommendations will support the success of creating a more equitable environment generally, CCCU member institutions may take three specific strategies to advance women in academic leadership.

First, address policy barriers. Looking at employment and benefit policies, institutions should assess whether their policies are disadvantageous to single faculty, who are more likely to be women than men (CCCU, 2002), and whether they are disadvantageous to mothers, and then take steps to correct inequities. For example:

- Initiate a policy review and revisions to ensure a family-friendly environment, such as those undertaken by Nine Presidents.

Second, implement practices that develop women leaders. Institutions can implement programs to develop women's leadership as well as participate in those offered through CCCU and other national organizations. For example:

- Develop a strong mentoring program for women students, faculty, and administrators.
- Actively encourage women faculty who show interest and promise to apply for the WLDI, and support their applications through strong letters of nomination.
- Support women faculty pursuing their terminal degrees with the flexible time required for such an endeavor and also with financial support through revised tuition benefit policies. Increasing the proportions of faculty with terminal degrees would benefit students and the institution as a whole, as well as increase the pool of women who can advance to academic leadership ranks.

Third, address the imbalance of women faculty and academic leaders. Institutions can address their imbalances through external hiring as well as promoting from within. For example:

- When engaged in faculty or administrative searches, remind the search committee of the institution's commitment to gender equity, and train committee members how to conduct bias-free searches and interviews.
- When engaged in executive searches, use search firms to ensure a candidate pool equally representative of men and women.

- Diligently attend to gender equity when determining internal promotions of rank or when filling leadership positions from within, ensuring that promotion criteria and their application are bias-free.

Conclusion

This chapter presents data highlighting the inequitable advancement of women in faith-based colleges and universities and identifies barriers women face that are unique to faith-based higher education. Chiefly, these emanate from theological beliefs about women's roles in the church and society.

Gender inequity affects all institutional stakeholders and has an impact on men and women college students' development, institutional image, and overall institutional health—not to mention the individual development, satisfaction, and retention of women faculty and administrators. Inequity will have powerful repercussions in future generations. Faith-based institutions cannot afford to ignore these issues. Indeed, the board of directors of the CCCU has named gender equity among its six priority objectives for increasing intercultural understanding in member institutions.

Because faith-based college and university organizational cultures emanate from their theological roots, the acquisition of a mutually agreed-upon definition of biblical truth related to gender equity is essential for the long-term success of CCCU and its members. This unified definition must attend to equitable roles for men and women in all the main enterprises of a postsecondary institution—in teaching, research, service, and leadership—and it must drive the creation of new policies and practices that foster gender equity. Such community agreement and support can occur only if CCCU and member institutions facilitate an open and honest dialogue among stakeholders.

Undoubtedly, intensely traditionalist denominations and individuals will simply never align with gender-equitable views. They will interpret equity as a modern or worldly view, disobedient to their understanding of God's will. They will see secular and spiritual gender equity initiatives as a liberal culture's attempt to impose its agenda upon them. This must be handled carefully and with respect.

Fortunately, gender equity may be advanced among those Christian groups that differentiate between secular and spiritual leadership. Faith-based colleges and universities can begin by focusing on what is within their walls: women in their own academic leadership. This chapter provides examples of change—at the systemic level, such as through the WLDI, and at the institutional level, such as what two member colleges have done to advance a more equitable environment for women on their campuses. Building upon these examples, it offers general strategies for shattering the stained-glass ceiling and specifically for advancing women in academic leadership.

In conclusion, before faith-based colleges and universities can realize their mission of advancing Christ-centered higher education in a global society and its required underlying objectives of advancing intercultural understanding, they must take a stronger stand toward gender equity. They must acknowledge and identify gender inequity within their organizations and vigorously pursue a resolution. Transformation and equity are necessary if we are to educate and serve all constituencies with the respect and support they deserve.

References

Baylis, B. (1995). *Summary report of 1995 Faculty Survey.* Retrieved December 20, 2005, from http://www.cccu.org/filefolder/CAP_1995_faculty_survey_1.doc

Cejda, B. D., Bush, W. B., Jr., & Rewey, K. L. (2002). Profiling the chief academic officers of Christian colleges and universities: A comparative study. *Christian Higher Education, 1,* 3–15.

Chamberlain, M. K. (Ed.). (1988). *Women in academe: Progress and prospects.* New York: Russell Sage Foundation.

Corrigan, M. (2002). *The American college president: 2002 edition.* Washington, DC: American Council on Education.

Council for Christian Colleges and Universities. (2002, February). Gender issues in the CCCU faculty. *Towards excellence: Assessment and retention in the CCCU, February 2002,* 1. Washington DC: Author.

Council for Christian Colleges and Universities. (2004). *A significant initiative: Advancing intercultural competencies.* Retrieved on August 3, 2004, from http://www.cccu.org/professional_development/resource_library/a_significant_initia tive_advancing_intercultural_competencies2004

Council for Christian Colleges and Universities. (2005). *Members & affiliates.* Retrieved November 26, 2005, from http://www.cccu.org/members_and_affili ates

Council for Christian Colleges and Universities. (n.d.). *About CCCU.* Retrieved October 4, 2004, from http://www.cccu.org/about

Dean, D. R. (2004, November). *The presidential search experiences of America's women chief academic officers.* Paper presented at the annual meeting of the Association for the Study of Higher Education, Kansas City, MO.

Felde, M. (2005, December). *University leaders pledge to help women in academia.* Retrieved December 6, 2005, from http://berkeley.edu/news/media/releases/ 2005/12/06_pledge.shtml

Garlett, M. W. (1997). *Waiting in the wings: Women of God in the evangelical academy.* Unpublished doctoral dissertation, Claremont Graduate School, Claremont, CA.

Glanville, E. L. (2000). *Leadership development for women in Christian ministry.* Unpublished doctoral dissertation, Fuller Theological Seminary, Pasadena, CA.

Glass Ceiling Commission. (1995). *A solid investment: Making full use of the nation's human capital.* Washington, DC: U.S. Government Printing Office.

Graham Lotz, A. (2002). *My heart's cry.* Nashville, TN: Thomas Nelson.

Hersi, D. T. (1993). Factors contributing to job satisfaction for women. *CUPA Journal, 44*(2), 29–35.

Higher Education Publications. (2005). *2005 Higher Education Directory.* Falls Church, VA: Author.

Hopson, C. (1995). *Mentoring new administrators.* Paper presented at the annual meeting of the Southern States Communication Association, New Orleans, LA.

Lafreniere, S. (2005). *Council for Christian Colleges and Universities Women's Leadership Development Institute (WLDI) outcomes assessment.* Unpublished manuscript.

LeBlanc, D. S. (1993). Barriers to women's advancement into higher education administration. In P. T. Mitchell (Ed.), *Cracking the wall: Women in higher education administration* (pp. 40–49). Washington, DC: College and University Personnel Association.

Longman, K. (2002a, February). *Gender issues highlighted by CAP findings.* Retrieved July 1, 2004, from www.cccu.org/filefolder/Gender_Issues_Highlighted_eby _CAP_Findings.doc

Longman, K. (2002b, February). Gender issues in the CCCU faculty. *Towards Excellence: Assessment and Retention in the CCCU, 1.*

Lumsden, D. B., Plotts, J. G., & Wells, C. R. (2000). Profiling the presidents of Christian colleges and universities: A comparative study. *Journal of Research on Christian Education, 9*(1), 61–74.

McCook, D. (1994). Women in higher education administration. In M. N. Maack & J. Passet, *Aspirations and mentoring in an academic environment* (pp. 170–172). Westport, CT: Greenwood Press.

Mead, F. S., & Hill, S. S. (2001). *Handbook of denominations in the United States* (11th ed.). Nashville, TN: Abingdon Press.

Morrison, A. M., White, R. P., & Van Velsor, E. (1987). *Breaking the glass ceiling: Can women reach the top of America's largest corporations?* Reading, MA: Addison-Wesley.

Moreton, A. L., & Newsom, R. W. (2004). Personal and academic background of female chief academic officers in evangelical Christian colleges and universities: Part I. *Christian Higher Education, 3*, 79–89.

Nathan, R. (2004). *Recovering the scandal of liberalism: Disdaining the cross.* Retrieved January 15, 2005, from http://www.crossroad.to/articles2/04/scandal-cross.htm

National Center for Education Statistics. (2003). *The integrated postsecondary education data system* (IPEDS: 2003) [Data file]. Available from http://www.nces.ed .gov/ipeds/

Nidiffer, J., & Bashaw, C. T. (2001). *Women administrators in higher education.* Albany, NY: SUNY Press.

Patterson, J. (2001). *Shining lights: A history of the council for Christian colleges and universities.* Grand Rapids, MI: Baker Academic.

Phipps, K. S., & Richardson, B. D. (2002, March). *The challenge of being faithful to our calling.* Paper presented at the 2002 Annual Coalition of Christian Colleges and Universities Chief Academic Officers Conference, San Antonio, TX.

Plotts, J. G., Lumsden, E. B., Newsom, R. W., & Wells, C. R. (1999). Career paths of presidents of institutions belonging to the council for Christian colleges and universities. *Research on Christian Higher Education, 6,* 137–146.

Scanlon, K. C. (1997). Mentoring women administrators: Breaking through the glass ceiling. *Initiatives, 58*(2), 39–59.

Schreiner, L. A. (2002). *Closing the gender gap.* Paper presented at the Critical Issues for Christian Higher Education Conference, San Antonio, TX.

Willcuts, J. L. (1984). *Why friends are friends: Some Quaker core convictions.* Newberg, OR: Barclay Press.

5

INFORMAL LEARNING AMONG WOMEN COMMUNITY COLLEGE PRESIDENTS

Leila Gonzalez Sullivan

L eaders beginning new jobs often lack certain essential knowledge and skills to perform effectively even though they are well prepared for their position. For men and women across professional fields, each new position brings a new context, climate, and culture, as well as different problems, players, resources, and politics. What worked in a previous position may not be as effective in the new circumstances. Further, the leader may lack experience in a critical area and consequently need new skill sets to advance the organization successfully.

Women may feel a particular urgency to remedy any of their learning deficiencies and do so privately for a number of reasons. Proportionally women leaders remain a minority in most professions and work in organizational cultures where norms were set by White men. In such contexts, women executives are often high achievers who place great pressure on themselves to perform well and serve as role models for their underrepresented group. They have worked hard to overcome the continuing barriers—the glass ceiling—restricting entry to top organizational levels. Furthermore, White male-normed cultures often hold women (and minority) leaders to higher standards and are less forgiving of their mistakes. Thus, professional women may choose to do their learning quickly and privately without revealing any lack of knowledge or skill.

Very little research has investigated the ways professional women pursue on-the-job learning, the effectiveness of their learning strategies, and the ways organizational culture affects their learning processes and outcomes.

This chapter opens a new line of inquiry in this area. Specifically, it presents research addressing on-the-job learning needs and approaches used by women community college presidents (chief executive officers [CEOs]) in relation to current competencies needed for such positions. It concludes with implications and recommendations for the practice of developing women leaders and women community college CEOs in particular.

Theoretical Framework

The theoretical framework for this study draws from literature on the community college presidency, gender and organizational culture, and learning theory.

The Community College Presidency

Women have made considerable strides in attaining higher education presidencies over the past two decades. The number of women presidents more than doubled between 1986 and 2001, from 9.5% to 21.1%. In public community colleges, their proportions increased even more dramatically, from 5.8% to 27% during the same time span. Nevertheless, the proportion of women college and university presidents is not comparable to that of women faculty and executive administrators (40%) nor to women students (56.3%; *The Chronicle of Higher Education*, 2004).

In their latest survey of community college presidents, Vaughan and Weisman (2002) determined that the majority of presidents continue to be White/Caucasian (86%) and male (72%). Women presidents tend to be younger (average age 54) than their male peers (average age 57). Most of the survey respondents were in their first presidency (70%), and roughly 10% had been in office 1 year or less. The majority (79%) indicated that they intended to retire in the next 10 years, offering many opportunities for new leaders—particularly women and minorities—to step into these positions (Vaughan & Weisman; Shults, 2001).

Preparing for the presidency. The path to the presidency has remained substantially the same for many years. Most CEOs rose through the administrative ranks serving as chief academic officers (39%), in other vice presidencies with an academic overview (7%), or in positions responsible for academics and student services (6%). Holding a doctoral degree (88%), preferably in an educational field such as higher education administration, coupled with administrative experience in community colleges, has been the fundamental job requirement (Vaughan & Weisman, 2001). Various professional development programs, chiefly developed in response to the dearth of women and minority CEOs, have provided additional means of preparing for the presidential role. These include programs sponsored by the American Association of Community Colleges (AACC), its affiliated special interest councils, and the League for Innovation in the Community College (Duvall, 2003).

In addition to holding a terminal degree, McFarlin, Crittenden, and Ebbers (2000) identified four more commonalities in the preparation, qualities, and skills of community college presidents who had been judged outstanding by their peers: (a) study of higher education and community college leadership, (b) frequent publishing and presenting of scholarly work, (c) preparation as change agents, and (d) extensive involvement in peer networks and mentoring relationships.

Presidential competencies. The expected substantial turnover in leadership over the next 5 to 10 years has galvanized the community college field. In addition to the projected retirement of 79% of current presidents (Vaughan & Weisman, 2001), top administrators and senior faculty—the pipeline presidents often emerge from—will retire in similar numbers (Shults, 2002). Efforts to address this imminent leadership vacuum have led to much discussion concerning the competencies needed to perform effectively as head of a community college, now and in the future. Most scholars and practitioners agree that contemporary presidents are more akin to corporate CEOs than traditional scholarly leaders of faculty. The "first among equals" model simply does not reflect the current realities and demands of the job. Today's community college presidents are expected to be highly skilled in areas of general leadership, such as communication (listening, writing, and public speaking), development and management resources and people, conflict resolution and negotiation, political acumen and use of influence, and adaptive skills (change management and risk taking). They should also possess skills specific to community college/higher education, such as community awareness, understanding and promoting the community college mission, student centeredness and student development knowledge, creating a vision and leading the academic enterprise, creating a positive campus climate, forging and maintaining partnerships, fund-raising, and working with the board (Brown, Martinez, & Daniel, 2002; Burnham, 2002; Desjardins & Huff, 2001).

These skills are reflected in the core community college presidential competencies developed and endorsed by the AACC. In 2000 the AACC Board of Directors formed a Leadership Task Force charged with identifying the characteristics and professional skills needed by presidents so that these could be addressed through professional development activities. The resulting *Leadership 2020* report (AACC, 2002) led to the Leading Forward project, a 2-year, $1.9 million endeavor expanding the work of the task force to include input from the larger community college world through focus groups and surveys. The resulting six core competencies of community college leaders (Vincent, 2004) were endorsed by the AACC board in April 2005:

- Organizational Strategy: An effective community college leader strategically improves the quality of the institution, protects the long-term health of the organization, promotes the success of all students, and sustains the community college mission, based on knowledge of the organization, its environment, and future trends.
- Resource Management: An effective community college leader equitably and ethically sustains people, processes, and information as well as physical and financial assets to fulfill the mission, vision, and goals of the community college.
- Communication: An effective community college leader uses clear listening, speaking, and writing skills to engage in honest, open dialogue at all levels of the college and its surrounding community, to promote the success of all students, and to sustain the community college mission.
- Collaboration: An effective community college leader develops and maintains responsive, cooperative, mutually beneficial, and ethical internal and external relationships that nurture diversity, promote the success of all students, and sustain the community college mission.
- Community College Advocacy: An effective community college leader understands, commits to, and advocates for the mission, vision, and goals of the community college.
- Professionalism: An effective community college leader works ethically to set high standards for self and others, continuously improve self and surroundings, demonstrate accountability to and for the institution, and ensure the long-term viability of the college and community (AACC, 2004).

Gender and Organizational Culture

The impact of organizational culture on a leader's ability to move the organization forward and be successful cannot be underestimated. Organizational culture refers to the values and beliefs that members share regarding organizational activities and interpersonal relationships (Yukl, 2002). Managing and influencing organizational culture is the only thing of real importance leaders do (Schein, 2004). Leaders generally reinforce and transmit the existing culture through their reaction to incidents; allocations of assignments and resources; and the organizational structures, systems, and rituals they establish. However, this influence is bidirectional; while the leader attempts to affect the culture and bring about change, the culture exerts its own influence on the leader and may assist or hinder that leader's ability to succeed.

Because community college culture continues to be male oriented in terms of leadership styles, working relationships, and expectations (Amey, 2004)—as a result of having been created by males and its long tradition of male leadership (Cohen & Brawer, 2003; McFarlin et al., 2000)—women find themselves at a distinct disadvantage (Brown, Van Ummersen, & Sturnick, 2001; Buddemeier, 1998; DiCroce, 1995; Moore, 2000; Stout-Stewart, 2005; Townsend, 1995).

For example, to explore the types of problems women encounter and the steps women need for professional credibility and success as a president, the American Council on Education conducted a series of roundtables in 1998 with more than 130 women presidents of public and private 2- and 4-year institutions. Participants described many difficulties inherent to their gender (the "gender factor"), including having—or not having—a family, being single in a married world, sexuality and dating, judgments about appearance and attire, and being—or being seen as—trusting and nurturing (Brown et al., 2001).

Observing that boards of trustees are still male dominated and occasionally uncomfortable working with women presidents, participants cited power issues with their boards and the double-edged sword of being seen as either too tough or not tough enough (Brown et al., 2001). Some boards were reluctant to compensate women as they would men, and there were rapid and negative consequences when women presidents made a mistake.

Mentoring posed another dilemma, particularly in light of sexual harassment legislation. In a culture dominated by men, the good old boy network remains an influential force, and both current and prospective presidents are often advised to seek opportunities to be mentored by prominent members of that network. Mentoring relationships between a man and a woman, however, can lead to negative perceptions and even scandal regardless of the levels of each participant (Brown et al., 2001).

Not only have women in academe been denied opportunities to attain leadership positions and be evaluated fairly, but also, based on gender assumptions, they have been denied opportunities to learn leadership competencies.

Intersections of culture, knowing, and voice. Goldberger in Goldberger, Tarule, Clinchy, and Belenky (1996) explored more broadly the intersection of culture, knowing, and the individual's sense of personal efficacy and voice among people of color and women operating within cultures characterized by male dominance and political/social imperatives related to class, race, and ethnicity. She identified learning when not to speak—tactical or strategic silence—as essential for producing behavior appropriate to a particular situation and concluded that "constructed knowing is much more than the understanding that knowledge is contextual and situated and that the knower is always a part of the known. Such knowing also entails a *flexibility* [her emphasis] in approaches to knowing and *ability to assess the appropriateness and utility* of a particular way of knowing given the moment, situation, cultural and political imperatives, and relational and ethical ramifications" (Goldberger et al., p. 357). This understanding might then influence the individual's choice to speak or to remain silent and could be interpreted not as a lack of knowing but as a strategy for knowing in the particular context. In maneuvering through the community college culture, the use of strategic voice might be characteristic of women presidents and might also influence their decision to reveal or hide any lack of knowledge.

Women and Learning

Merriam and Caffarella (1998) noted that most adult learning takes place outside formal settings such as the classroom. In fact, adults engage in active learning and regularly undertake voluntary, systematic, and clearly focused learning activities in their own natural settings to acquire some knowledge, information, or skill (Merriam & Caffarella), although the process is not always recognized by adults or educators as "real" learning.

Experiential and situated learning. One form of active learning in informal settings is experiential or situated learning. Experiential learning, a holistic, integrative perspective, combines involvement in concrete experiences, reflective observation (perception), abstract conceptualization (cognition), and active experimentation (behavior; Kolb, 1983). The reflective phase further differentiates into reflection on action—or thinking about a situation *after* it has happened—and reflection in action—or thinking about what one is doing *while* doing it (Merriam & Caffarella, 1998).

Experiential learning focuses on the process of learning, on the "interplay between expectation and experience" (Kolb, 1983, p. 28) rather than on outcomes. The "educational process begins by bringing out the learner's beliefs and theories, examining and testing them, and then integrating the new, more refined ideas into the person's belief systems" (Kolb, p. 28). Because reflection—creating associations with previous knowledge, attending to associated feelings, and then integrating, validating, and appropriating the learning experience—is an essential part of the learning process, the unique past of the learner must be taken into account (Merriam & Caffarella, 1998).

The unique context of the learning environment must be taken into account as well (Merriam & Caffarella, 1998). Situated cognition, a perspective that builds upon experiential learning theory, inseparably intertwines learning and knowledge with the actual context or situation. For example, Hansman (2001) reflected on the importance of the social context for adult learning, where interactions with other people and the available tools for learning, such as computers and print materials, influence how and what learning takes place. She further noted that overtones of culture infuse the learning context as people bring their own prior knowledge, skills, beliefs, and values into the situation. Participation, collaboration, and interaction were all essential for adult learning.

Learning in the workplace. Building on the work of earlier researchers (LeGrand, Farmer, & Buckmaster, 1993; Rogoff, 1990), Johnson and Pratt (1998) considered learning from a cognitive psychological perspective and examined how situational learning in the workplace could be framed in terms of an intellectual apprenticeship. "Situated learning moves our focus from schemas (inside the heads of individuals) to the social contexts of participation and learning which are rich and complex with meaning" (p. 87). As people join a professional or trade community as novices and participate in that community's work, they develop schemas based on new meanings derived from their experiences and eventually gain enough knowledge and skill for mastery and full acceptance into the community (Johnson & Pratt; Lave & Wenger, 1991). This informal cognitive apprenticeship parallels professions and trades with formal apprenticeships to teach novices by working with seasoned practitioners.

Masters of any practice exhibit specific characteristics: deep knowledge or expertise in their professional area or trade, ability to apply that knowledge, strategies for acquiring new knowledge, and continued development of their professional identities. Further, they demonstrate "knowing-in-practice" (Johnson & Pratt, 1998, p. 93), an ability to act spontaneously without necessarily being able to describe the knowing on which their actions are based. Those who intentionally engage in a cognitive apprenticeship aspire to this level of mastery.

Wenger (1998) and Wenger and Snyder (2000) developed the concept of communities of practice, defining these as "groups of people informally bound together by shared expertise and passion for a joint enterprise" (Wenger & Snyder, p. 139). Such groups are self-organized, organic, spontaneous, free-flowing, and creative. They learn by examining work-related problems and may come together and disband at will. The energy and collective knowledge of a community of practice can yield great benefits for the organization or profession. As contexts for adult learning, cognitive apprenticeships and communities of practice could be tools to redesign the workplace (Hansman, 2001).

Gendered learning. Women have been excluded from knowledge construction in the male-dominated majority culture and from mainstream human development theories (Belenky, Clinchy, Goldberger, & Tarule, 1986). Examining women's learning modes, Belenky and her colleagues discerned five unique categories of women's learning: silence, received knowledge, subjective knowledge, procedural knowledge, and constructed knowledge. They further discerned that women preferred to learn in communal contexts where experiences could be examined and shared. It seemed that women felt that the best knowledge came from experience—their own and others'—and that collaborative explorations of what each knew (connected knowing) were of the most value for learning. The process of constructing knowledge followed the principles of situated cognition and empowered the learner.

In her exploration of voice as an aspect of knowing, Tarule (1996) asserted that conversation was the site for constructed knowledge and defined dialogue as "making knowledge in conversation" (p. 280). However, the thinking, learning, and resulting knowledge could be constrained or enhanced depending on the community (context). For example, when all community members feel a sense of equality, they freely contribute to the conversation and are not intimidated by differences in thinking or experience. Conversely, in communities marked by inequity—such as when experts or authority figures dominate the conversation—some members' voices might be silenced and the nature of the learning altered.

Tisdell (1993) addressed issues of inequitable contexts in her examination of the classroom where she observed women learners deferring to men. Power relationships in the learning setting were of great importance in terms of teacher-learner and intergender relations. She attributed this behavioral dynamic to the dominant culture, which reproduced white male privilege and denied women power and control. "Women seem to do best in learning environments where affective forms of knowledge or knowledge that comes from life experience are valued. In short, they do best in learning environments where there is an effort to relate theoretical concepts to real-life experience" (Tisdell, p. 98).

Hayes (2001) and later Hayes and Flannery (2002) drew together many of the themes discussed here in their discourse on women learners. Acknowledging the impact of context on learning, they discerned many contexts within our society as still very much male oriented with implicit messages and hidden curriculums that reinforce the dominant culture. These messages affected not just the content of the learning but women's identity construction and ability to give voice to their knowing. Hayes (2001) stressed women's preference for connection in learning, but cautioned that this description fits some—but not all—women. Such generalizations could only extend stereotypes of women as incapable of competition, self-direction, logic, and rational thought. She further suggested that researchers move beyond oppositional views of men's and women's learning and instead consider that differences in learning styles were greater within genders than between genders.

Focusing specifically on women's learning and professional development, Bierema (1999) conducted a qualitative study involving women corporate executives and identified a three-stage developmental model: Compliant Novices, Competence Seekers, and Change Agents. While the learning tactics of each stage differ, as do transitions between stages, relationships were of great importance in all stages, significantly paralleling other research on women's development (Belenky et al., 1986; Gilligan, 1983; Goldberger et al., 1996; Tisdell, 1993). She further identified the importance of mentoring as well as the difficulties of forming such relationships. Ironically, although relationships and mentoring were important to women's learning, the world of business remained a context in which "the majority of power holders . . . are white men, who have created an environment characterized by hierarchy, elitism, competition, male fraternity, and separate emotional ties between work and family" (Bierema, p. 108). Women executives identified sexism as their greatest obstacle in the workplace, affecting expectations for performance, opportunities for challenging assignments, and reward systems such as promotions.

Pursuing these themes in subsequent research, Bierema (2001) insisted that "women's learning at work is challenging because it happens in a context that has largely been created, maintained, and controlled by white men. Success for many women often means accepting and even emulating male-dominated organizational culture" (p. 53). Workplace learning frequently involved a hidden curriculum reinforcing existing power structures.

Research Questions

Women community college presidents stand at the intersection point of the preceding discussion. We have an urgent need for new community college leaders possessing specific competencies. The impending retirement wave offers many opportunities for women to advance to these positions (Shults, 2001; Vaughan & Weisman, 2002). We know that women community college leaders are high achievers, competent, confident, and capable of functioning effectively in the dominant culture of these institutions. Yet each successive step on the community college administrative hierarchy inevitably necessitates the acquisition of additional knowledge and skills in order to perform effectively at that new level. Inevitably, new community college presidents will engage in much on-the-job learning.

Women in academe, however, not only have been denied opportunities to attain leadership positions, they often have been denied opportunities to learn leadership competencies on the job. Furthermore, women often are unfairly evaluated and held to higher expectations, making it riskier to reveal their knowledge gaps. This, combined with a use of strategic voice (or tactical silence), might govern women's decisions about whether to reveal or hide any lack of knowledge and how they pursue necessary learning informally.

An interest in advancing women in community college leadership must be accompanied by an interest in improving the effectiveness of the inevitable on-the-job learning that will be required. Much can be learned from examining women community college presidents and their informal learning experiences. At this intersection then, a number of questions arise:

- What did women community college presidents feel they needed to learn at the beginning of their tenure?
- How public were/are they regarding their lack of knowledge?
- What learning strategies do they choose and why?
- How do their chosen learning strategies relate to theories of adult and gendered learning?
- In what ways might community college culture influence their informal learning?

Methodology

In spring 2005, I conducted a qualitative study to explore the on-the-job learning needs and strategies of six purposefully sampled women community college presidents, two each from the West, Southwest, and Northeast. Half of the women were in their first presidency and half were in their second presidency. Their time in the current presidency ranged from 7 months to 9 years. For those who were in their second CEO position, the time in their previous presidency ranged from 5 to 8 years.

The administrative positions these women held immediately prior to their first presidency included campus dean or provost, executive vice president, vice president, and special assistant to a president. They started their career paths in positions such as faculty, counselor, director, or assistant director of a program, and their paths showed steady and rapid progression upward. Most had experience in academics and student services, and some had assignments in planning, institutional advancement, and similar positions. Two of the women had extensive experience at universities, one had corporate experience, and two had taught in high schools. All held advanced degrees: half had PhDs and half had EdDs.

Two of the women were African American, two were Hispanic, and two were White/Caucasian. Their ages ranged from 40 to 60-plus years.

Data Collection

I used guided interview techniques, with follow-up questions emerging from the conversations. Although semistructured, each interview was a joint product of what the participants and I talked about together, how we talked together, and our shared understanding of the meanings of questions and answers (Mischler, 1986). In several ways I functioned as a "participant observer" (Bogdan & Biklen, 2003), although I attempted to control for this presence to the extent possible. For example, my perspectives and personal experiences as a Latina and former community college president influenced my research and interview questions. My knowledge of the community college field, including its culture and the structure of the institutions where the respondents serve as presidents, may have helped to capture metamessages and nuances that another researcher might have missed. Further, my standing as a former president may have influenced participants toward greater self-disclosure.

Data Analysis

All recorded interviews were transcribed. I analyzed data through a coding system (Table 5.1) derived from the theoretical framework presented earlier in this chapter. Codes for the presidents' learning needs were based on the six competencies identified in the Leading Forward project (AACC, 2004). Two of the competencies (organizational management, professionalism) were further subdivided to reflect more accurately the presidents' comments. Codes for their learning strategies were based on theories of adult and gendered learning in the workplace. Codes for possible community college cultural influences were derived from research on organizational culture.

TABLE 5.1
Characteristics of Informal Learning Among Women Community College Presidents

Learning Needs	Learning Strategies	Community College Cultural Influences on Learning
Organizational strategy	Apprenticeship	Culturally derived
Resource management	Colleague informant	expectations of self
Facilities	Consultant/expert	Culturally derived
Fiscal	Formal institute	expectations others have
Fund-raising	Graduate courses	for self (perceived)
Human resources	Meeting—Specific to topic	Traditional male areas
Planning	Mentoring	Power issues
Technology/information	Reading—general	
management	Reading—specific to topic	
Communication	Workshop/conference	
Collaboration	Other	
Advocacy		
Professionalism		
Authenticity/ethics		
Community college		
mission		
Contribution to		
profession		
Learning/reflection		
Stress management		
Vision		

Research is "always strongly autobiographical. Our research interests come out of our own narratives of experience and shape our narrative inquiry plotlines" (Clandinin & Connelly, 2000, p. 121). As the data collection and analysis proceeded, my own unprocessed memories of informal learning as a newly appointed president surfaced and led to personal reflection and new learning on my part. While not included as findings, my own experiences provided an added lens for analyzing and finding patterns shown by the data (McCracken, 1988) as well as interpreting findings.

Findings

I present research findings according to learning needs, public/private stance toward lack of knowledge, learning strategies, and community college cultural influences. Respondents are identified by code (AA through FF).

While these women leaders reported on their learning needs and strategies, their positions in the organizational power structure (their authority as the head of the college) inevitably affected relationships developed around their learning experiences. Placing this power factor in the context of Bierema's (1999) model for executive women's learning, the women presidents were Competence Seekers (or even Compliant Novices under some circumstances) with regard to their specific learning needs. However, from their overall position in the institution they could expect to be treated as equals with or even superiors to some whom they selected to help them learn. This aspect of the study will be more fully developed through the discussion that follows.

Learning Needs

Using AACC's (2004) six core competencies for community college leaders, what did women community college presidents feel they needed to learn at the beginning of their tenure? Two participants chose to speak about their learning needs when they assumed second presidencies while the other four spoke about their first CEO positions. Most added information about the learning needs they still had.

Organizational strategy. Three presidents (BB, EE, FF) had initial learning needs related to organizational strategy. Specifically, they needed to learn the culture of their new institution and key internal and external players. One respondent came from a university and did not feel fully informed about the mission and culture of community colleges, while the other two had moved from one part of the country to another and found their new communities quite different from their previous environments.

With regard to learning needs the presidents still had at the time of the study, AA's new focus was another element of organizational strategy: learning how to create a compelling vision and inspire her campus to work collectively toward it.

As data analysis proceeded, it became apparent that organizational strategy encompassed the other five competencies identified in the Leading Forward project. Thus, further discussion of organizational strategy–related learning needs occurs under subsequent competencies.

Resource management. All six presidents stated that one or more resource management subcategories (fiscal resources, human resources, facilities management and construction, technology, planning, and fund-raising) were urgent learning needs as they assumed their positions. For example, although AA and EE managed large budgets in their previous positions, responsibility for the total college budget was a new experience, particularly when it involved capital funds. As AA observed, "I had managed budgets before, actually fairly substantial ones but . . . it is one thing to understand a budget on a page, piece of paper, and it is another thing to understand again, what is the culture around the budget . . . what parts of the budget do you really control and what parts you don't." EE recalled feeling intimidated at the idea of managing the total budget in her first presidency even though she previously had served on a university budget committee and several community boards. Eventually, she came to understand that "it's all zeroes": Many decisions were the same regardless of budget size.

Two presidents inherited large facility construction projects and felt considerable urgency to learn about this area. For BB, a swimming pool and theater were under construction and three new buildings were to be built relatively soon after her arrival. DD reported: "I was responsible for building a new building, [and the] renovation of buildings, when the hot water things blew up or the air conditioning went down, or the pipes and the drainage. . . . There was so much that had to do with the facilities and . . . the OSHA rules. . . . That is not something you learn in . . . leadership classes."

Although DD now felt confident about her knowledge of capital construction, she still needed to learn about contracts and legal issues associated with such projects. FF had not needed to learn about construction up to the present but now needed to become competent in this area since her college anticipated constructing a new building in the near future.

Four presidents expressed learning needs concerning human resource management. Although all were confident about their ability to interact productively with others, they acknowledged the CEO's special responsibility to manage the institution's human capital. BB, AA, and DD all spoke of the complexities of grievances, union contracts, and conflict resolution. As DD commented: "There's always a learning curve on personnel issues. When you think that you understand and have it down, something completely different will come up where you are not sure how to deal with it."

Particularly with changes in legislation and collective bargaining agreements, presidents were constantly learning in this area. FF stated that even after much experience in two presidencies her current learning activities focused on a particular aspect of human resource management: recruiting and nurturing exceptional faculty.

Although technology resource management might be expected among presidents' learning needs given the speed and complexity of technology changes, interestingly, only one president cited this as an initial learning need. For CC, this was in fact her greatest need, as her new college had botched the introduction of a new administrative software system and was in crisis. Thus, she needed to understand what had gone wrong with the implementation process and how to rectify the situation. Some of her learning needs in this regard also touched on human resource management, since she had to determine whether staff were incompetent, sabotaging the effort, or simply could not make the transition without further assistance.

While only one president identified fund-raising among her initial needs when assuming the presidency, this essential skill in the current environment of reduced resources for public higher education was now a learning focus for three CEOs. CC stated, "The next area I am going to tackle is fund-raising. I understand the preliminary pieces . . . but there is an art to that and I would like to be better at it." FF had a particular emphasis in mind: "how to go after the big gifts, how to develop capital campaigns." EE also intended to learn about capital campaigns.

Finally, one president (CC) took a blanket approach to resource management, indicating that she knew "the theoretical piece" of managing the business aspects of an institution but wanted to learn the practicalities: "budget management I have always had a handle on. It's the ins and outs of the details of running the business [that I need to learn], if that makes sense. It's how does financial aid connect with the business office connect with the programs . . . the billing of students, the insurance. . . . Do I know as much as a chief business officer? I don't think so, but my goal is to be as knowledgeable [as a chief business officer] because I think that is where presidents get into trouble."

Communication. Communication refers to listening, speaking, and writing skills and "honest, open dialogue at all levels of the college and its surrounding community" (AACC, 2004). Three presidents cited learning needs in this area as they began their presidencies. FF, for example, needed to learn how to communicate with the external community—city leaders, legislators, and other power figures—as she assumed her second presidency at a large urban college.

For EE, her learning needs centered on the considerable public speaking her new role would involve, which she found daunting. Although she had been in the classroom and had written speeches for others, the idea of speaking before an audience made her "fearful and nervous." She spoke word for word from scripts for several years before becoming more confident in her speaking skills.

AA, on the other hand, realized she had to strengthen her communication and collaboration skills after an action she took on her new campus created problems with the unions. In retrospect, AA understood that her inexperience caused the problem and that she should have developed a working relationship with the union leaders before issuing a gentle but official reminder about work obligations. She reflected on the importance of opening communication lines: "If I had to do it all over again . . . I would put on my list in that first week or two of getting to a college, along with meeting all the deans and leadership and department heads, meet your local union leaders that people will turn to even though they may not have titles." Because AA failed to learn about her college's culture before attempting to enforce regulations, her learning experience could also be tied to organizational strategy. Her continuing learning needs involved communication skills, as she was now working on how to communicate a compelling vision for her college that all constituencies could endorse and work toward enthusiastically.

Collaboration. The competency of collaboration—working "effectively and diplomatically with unique constituent groups" (AACC, 2004), both internal and external to the college—builds on communication skills. For example, AA's failed communication experience with the unions was equally a need to develop collaborative relations with the collective bargaining units and with the staff in her system's office in order to effectively manage labor relations on her campus.

Two presidents, although seemingly seasoned and skilled communicators, expressed a need to build collaborative skills. FF, for example, cited initial learning needs in this area. She worked in a sophisticated urban environment characterized by close scrutiny of public figures such as herself: "I just felt I did not have the social skills to deal with the broader community. . . . I was just not ready for that spotlight that [city] puts you in." During the first 2 years of her second presidency she attended every social event and public meeting. "I forced myself out into the broader community," she said, to thoroughly understand her environment and develop connections that would benefit her institution.

President BB had a current specific collaborative skill need: "I am doing some quick learning on public/private partnerships, capital development and how to manage the swimming pool with a private partner." Her current learning also involved win-win management and shared governance to help her build collaborative and productive relationships inside her college.

Community college advocacy. Community college advocacy aligns with organizational strategy, communication, and collaboration. Two presidents had needed to learn a specific aspect of advocacy—interactions with legislators. As part of her overall need to connect with a new community at the beginning of her second presidency, FF had to identify and implement effective means to work with city and state officials on behalf of her campus, while also working in concert with other college presidents. Similarly, CC acknowledged a need to build her skills in this area. Although there was an advocacy organization for community colleges in her state, she found early that her small college was not being represented effectively by that organization and she would have to work directly with legislators to be sure her institution was not at a disadvantage. As she explained, "The power base right now is the good old boys." Her previous jobs had not given her much exposure to working with legislators, so it now became a priority learning need.

Professionalism. Professionalism includes demonstrating transformational leadership with authenticity, ethics, high standards, and vision; self-assessing performance; managing stress; exhibiting courage; using power and influence wisely; respecting people and their unique viewpoints; and contributing to the profession (AACC, 2004). Although each president was already well respected for her leadership and professionalism, three cited further learning needs in this area. EE, for example, needed to learn more about the community college mission and culture at the beginning of her first presidency. AA currently needed to build her visioning skills. DD, reflecting on how stressful a presidency can be, stated, "One area . . . I myself am pursuing . . . is . . . quality of life in the leadership role . . . and what I am coming to terms with is not only the quality of life but [also] when is it time to leave, when is it time to do something different. . . . I am doing some soul searching, I'm doing some praying, I'm doing some spiritual work." She regretted that in "giving [her] heart and soul to the college," she had neglected her family relations and was determined to regain a healthy balance between her personal and professional lives.

Self-assessment and identifying learning needs. In the course of the interviews, I asked each president why she had felt an urgent need to learn in the specified areas. Their responses clustered around two themes. First, all six stated firmly that to do their jobs effectively they needed a certain level of knowledge and skill in particular areas so they could ask and answer questions. Their ability to question was directly tied to their sense of competence and control. As FF remarked: "I want to be able to find the questions so I can get the kind of information I need." BB's approach to keeping construction projects on track was learning what was working and where glitches were so that she could formulate questions. Three presidents (BB, CC, and EE) wanted to learn operational details to become more effective CEOs and avoid trouble. While EE wanted simply to appear more competent and capable, CC specifically felt her institution was in crisis and she needed to be able to move the college out of this mode.

Second, all six were motivated by the sheer joy of learning. They characterized themselves as "lifelong learner[s]" (BB, EE), "virtual student[s]" (AA), "good student[s]" (DD), "continuous student[s]" (FF), and regularly engaging in professional development (CC).

Stance Toward Lack of Knowledge

New presidents might be reluctant to reveal their perceived weaknesses. The process of selecting presidents is an arduous one, and candidates must demonstrate extensive experience and skills applicable to a complex and demanding job. In a male-oriented community college culture where women presidents are still in the minority and may be judged more stringently (Brown et al., 2001), women candidates and newly appointed women presidents might wish to keep their inexperience or ignorance of certain areas private until they can obtain the needed learning and achieve competence.

So how public were these presidents regarding their lack of knowledge? Rather than concealing their ignorance, the opposite seemed true for most respondents. Five of the six women were completely open about their lack of knowledge in certain areas. AA actually told the search committee what she needed to learn during her interview. "I told them those were my two areas [of weakness], so that was kind of like if you didn't want those weaknesses, then please don't hire me." BB used her learning needs as a means of connecting with her new staff. "I make it clear that I don't have all of the answers . . . and that I need to be educated as well as they do. . . . I need to have them know that I don't know everything." DD commented, "I think people know when you don't know. In terms of facilities and capital projects I always said that my background is not architecture. . . . So, sure, I shared it with them and said 'I hired you, you are the experts. You work with me and tell me what is going on.'" FF and CC revealed their areas of ignorance but also exhibited overall self-confidence and competence that mitigated their lack of knowledge. Only one president (EE) chose to keep her areas of weakness private because she wanted to be seen as capable and competent as she took on this strenuous new role.

Learning Strategies

What learning strategies did the women presidents choose, and how do those strategies relate to current theories of adult and gendered learning?

Chosen strategies. All women presidents employed combinations of strategies rather than taking a single approach to learning. They reported using many of the adult learning strategies discussed earlier in this chapter, including mentoring, apprenticeships, the use of expert consultants, and discussions with colleagues (informants) who had more experience. They also attended meetings/briefings specific to the topic (e.g., budget sessions or construction updates) and read associated reports. Five of the six reported seeking out sessions specific to the area of interest whenever they attended conferences. As DD remarked, "I actually was a person that if I went to conferences, I went to the workshops."

Two presidents (CC, EE) were avid readers on all topics related to community colleges and also read extensively in the target learning area. In contrast, several of the others noted they seldom had time for much reading unless it was directly related to the topic they were learning. Interestingly, none of the women mentioned using the Internet or reading research reports as part of their learning.

Formal studies were not the preferred mode for five of the six presidents, most likely because all six hold doctorates. CC was the only president to enroll in a formal institute on higher education business management sponsored by a national association of business officers and a state university; the institute involves intensive study over three summers and results in certification.

All were very intentional about their learning, recognizing a lack of knowledge, determining how best to address the lack, carrying out the learning strategies in a planned way, assessing their performance, and eventually expressing satisfaction with their achieved competence. Their reported time to competence ranged from 6 months to 7 years depending on the learning need, with an average time of 3 to 4 years.

Finally, as noted earlier, these women held positions of power as president, which undoubtedly affected the relationships they formed to facilitate their learning and which must be considered when evaluating the links between their learning strategies and learning theory. Nevertheless, clear linkages were evident with experiential contextual learning, connected learning, mentoring and apprenticeships, consultants and experts, communities of practice, colleague informants, and reflection.

Experiential contextual learning. Congruent with descriptions of adult learning (Belenky et al., 1986; Hansman, 2001; Hayes, 2001; Hayes & Flannery, 2002; Kolb, 1983; Merriam & Caffarella, 1998), these six women leaders preferred informal, contextual, and experiential learning formats corresponding directly to perceived needs for job-related knowledge or skills. For example, AA decided that the best way to learn about her new institution's budget was to experience an entire fiscal year with guidance from her dean of administration and the financial experts at her system's central office. "During the budget process I really worked hand in hand with the dean of administration. . . . In the process I learned more and more about the budget and the wiggle room that might be in the various places . . . just to be a student of it, and I was very much that in my first couple of years." BB described her first contact with facilities construction as "just being thrown into the situation and learning quickly." FF recalled, "I forced myself out into the broader community. . . . I spent the first two years at every gala, at every public meeting, you know, really getting to know the [city] community." EE acknowledged her fears of public speaking but then "just went ahead and did it." In effect, these women chose total experiential immersion for their learning.

Connected learning. All the women presidents selected learning strategies that involved other people and demonstrated a clear preference for connected learning, a mode typical of women (Belenky et al., 1986; Bierema, 1999, 2001; Goldberger et al., 1996; Hayes, 2001; Hayes & Flannery, 2002). As DD commented, "I just surrounded myself with people who knew it. . . . I watched them and asked them and I was open to their input and learning from them and open to take their recommendations." Similarly, CC began to deal with the software implementation crisis at her new college by involving experts. "I picked people that I knew I could trust that they would tell me the truth and were knowledgeable and could come, assess things quickly, and then level with me on how you would address the problem. And in doing all of that, they were in essence educating me first hand—on-the-job training."

Mentoring and apprenticeships. Their engagement with people who had greater knowledge and skills took several forms. One strategy involved finding a mentor, as AA, EE, and FF did. AA actually was assigned a mentor, another woman president in her system who provided inside information and orientation to that system's culture. Notably, she spoke of interacting as an equal with her mentor and other system officials. "I think I am going to resolve it or take this action, what do you think? So that they were more in the position of giving advice rather than, you know, kind of instructing me what to do." FF selected as her mentor another president in her system she felt comfortable with. "[Mentor name] got here a year before me but he had grown up in [name of city] and the other presidents were all men and much older." AA, CC, and EE used former colleagues to assist them with learning about fiscal matters, a kind of targeted mentorship rather than the broader relationships described by AA and FF.

Brown et al. (2001) stressed the importance of mentoring women leaders in academe. Bierema (2001) acknowledged the importance of mentoring in relation to workplace learning, particularly for certain types of knowers: "Constructivists are likely to seek mentors in all guises, role models, and consultants regardless of age, race, gender, or appearance. Informal mentoring works best for constructivists" (p. 59). Constructivist knowers see truth as contextual, value multiple approaches to knowing, and acknowledge their selves and personal commitments as part of defining truths (Goldberger et al., 1996).

Clearly, the presidents in this study understood the value of mentoring and sought out this type of guidance when it seemed appropriate for their purposes. The intellectual or cognitive apprenticeships described by Johnson and Pratt (1998) and others (Hansman, 2001; LeGrand, Farmer, & Buckmaster, 1993) bear similarities with such mentorships, as they both involve establishing a teacher-learner relationship with another person who has greater knowledge and/or skill. Although it would be difficult to sort out the distinctions between the two types of relationships, the important point is that both apprenticeships and mentoring are connected learning strategies where personal interactions facilitate the learning. Three of the presidents described what might be considered apprenticeships, although they did not use that term—AA working with her dean of administration on budget, FF working with the system public relations staff to orchestrate her entry into the community, and BB learning about facilities construction and bond referendums from other officials in her district.

Consultants and experts. Some presidents hired consultants who could help the president learn—another form of connected learning—and bring a sense of authority and objectivity to the process that would be respected by the campus. CC and DD used such experts. In DD's case, the hired expertise was clearly necessary, because she worked with a team of architects and design experts on her new construction project. In CC's case, she lacked trust in several key people on her new campus and even feared sabotage. Consultants provided CC with trustworthy information to aid her difficult decisions about the personnel and administrative structure of the college. Based on this learning, CC developed an action plan to put the software implementation program back on track. As she launched her efforts to learn about fund-raising, CC used experts she met while at a business management institute and planned to hire a community leader as a consultant.

Communities of practice. Communities of practice (Wenger, 1998; Wenger & Snyder, 2000) seem particularly applicable to the community college presidency. Wenger and Snyder's (2000) description of such groups as bound together by shared passion and shared expertise certainly applies to contemporary community college CEOs who meet periodically to share experiences and expertise. AA, for example, attended sessions on collective bargaining at the AACC convention and other conferences. "Anything I went to professionally, one of the first things I would do would be to go through the program and see what, if anything, was there on collective bargaining."

Further, almost all states have a community college presidents' association that meets on a regular basis to formulate joint strategies and policies, manage fiscal resources received from the state, and consider issues affecting their colleges. Such groups are local communities of practice and they welcome any newly appointed CEO, particularly one moving into a first presidency. Through one such association, AA was assigned a formal mentor from among the other presidents in her system. CC connected with her state presidents' association to lobby the legislature for resources. BB, EE, and FF relied on the other campus/college CEOs in their system for important information, and DD noted, "I would talk to other colleagues who built buildings and . . . I would go to other colleges to see their building or their landscape or their architect or whatever. I would get ideas and I would go look at what they had."

Colleague informants from communities of practice. Besides their presidential community of practice, the women in this study built relationships with their internal college communities and thus tapped into their colleagues' communities of practice. All six recognized that they needed access to the knowledge and skills of people at lower levels of power and subsequently placed themselves in positions of dependence on these other "experts" for the purpose of learning. AA, for example, learned through painful experience that she needed working relationships with union leaders on her campus and at the state level if she expected to successfully manage her college's collective bargaining agreements. BB envisioned a "web of communication" among and between those people on her campus and those at the district level who had direct responsibility for construction. CC had to determine who was trustworthy at her college and form alliances with them in order to carry out her action plan for software implementation. BB and DD relied heavily on their deans of administrative services for guidance on capital projects, as did AA and EE for indoctrination into the intricacies of the total campus budget.

EE spent her first few months on the job talking to faculty, staff, and community leaders to learn as much as she could about the world of community colleges so she could become an effective advocate. Finally, FF counted on the district and college public relations staff to assist with her acculturation into her city's social and political scene.

Such dependence could be viewed as legitimate peripheral participation in a community of practice (Johnson & Pratt, 1998; Lave & Wenger, 1991). In this process, "novices enter a community of practice (a workplace, institution, or association), and work alongside more seasoned practitioners. . . . In this way they acquire situated knowledge" (Johnson & Pratt, p. 89). Paradoxically, although these women already held full community membership as presidents with associated powers, they were also novices who by necessity selected people of lesser power but greater expertise to teach them. As novices or apprentices, they were active learners, cooperative and social in their participation and willing to subjugate themselves until they were deemed competent subject "masters" who merited full roles in the community. As presidents, they could step out of the learner role and back into the role of superior at any moment, making decisions about budget or construction or personnel relations regardless of their current level of knowledge. Without a doubt, their status as college heads also influenced the behavior of their master teachers, who either reported to the president learner on campus or held lower rank as external district officials.

Reflection. Reflection, a key component of adult learning, allows adults to integrate new knowledge into an existing network of ideas, values, and beliefs (Belenky et al., 1986; Kolb, 1983; Merriam & Caffarella, 1999). Three stages of the reflective process support experiential learning: replaying the experience, being aware of feelings attached to the experience, and reevaluating the experience. In this process, according to Boud, Keogh, and Walker, the learner connects new data with what is already known, integrates the data, validates the authenticity of ideas, and finally appropriates or makes the knowledge one's own (as cited in Merriam & Caffarella, 1998).

Amey (2004) stressed the importance of reflection specifically in the context of community college leadership, urging that the new generation of leaders become "active inquirers into one's own and others' practices . . . (and) recognize the value and limitations of our own expertise and knowledge bases" (p. 8). Fulton-Calkins and Milling (2005) proposed that new leaders needed nine essential skills, including learning from the past while embracing the future, enriching the inward journey, and values-based leadership. Finally, AACC (2004) included self-assessment of performance and reflection among the professional competencies desirable in a leader.

The presidents in this study often exhibited reflective behavior, particularly when connecting experience to prior knowledge and when understanding consequences of their actions. They also offered numerous reflective personal insights as they addressed the interview questions. One (DD) spoke candidly about a difficult period in her tenure as a CEO: "There are bad things that happen to good presidents, or good deans or good VPs, and you are good but you start to question yourself. . . . Your self-confidence starts to waver. . . . How do you regain your confidence? How do you know that what you are doing is the right thing?" BB commented, "I think about . . . what were the prevailing patterns in my life, people who were effective and ineffective as leaders. . . . I tend to be creative, a strong alternative learner, fluid. I can jump to conclusions very quickly, but you know that's not the way you can do it. So I have done some self learning in growing up in the ranks and that has helped me, hopefully, to be effective in working with management teams." These and similar comments indicate that presidents were processing their experiences, linking them to prior knowledge, and assessing their performance in light of what they knew about themselves as persons and professionals. At the same time, they projected a sense of confidence and potency based on experience and a fully developed set of values. As FF concluded, "I have always been just who I am and have a great deal of confidence in who I am. And in most arenas, you know, what you see is what is. I think I have an awful lot of strengths but I also have some weaknesses. However, I don't get too uptight about those."

To summarize, in terms of adult and gendered learning theories, these six women presidents clearly reflected the theories in their professional lives. They operated from a position of power yet were willing to disclose their lack of knowledge in certain areas they deemed important for effective performance in their jobs. They sought out experiential and contextual learning opportunities and employed strategies that emphasized connectedness and collaborative exploration. Finally, they reflected often on their experiences, good and bad, and were eager to share what they had learned with future generations of leaders.

Community College Culture's Influence on Learning

Social context is a critical factor in learning—with people, tools, and setting all interacting to determine what is learned and how learning occurs (Hansman, 2001). In the workplace, "a highly political space" (Fenwick, 2001, p. 5), the organizational culture and its dominant social networks essentially dictate learning.

While greater numbers of women have assumed positions of increasing responsibility in recent years, the culture of American higher education continues to reflect male values (Brown et al., 2001). Community college culture is no exception. Male oriented from its inception (Cohen & Brawer, 2003), the community college workplace is often hierarchical, male dominated, and elitist (Amey, 2004). Women presidents referenced elements of community college culture that appeared to influence their opportunities for learning as well as the content of their learning along four themes: traditional male areas, power issues, culturally derived expectations of self, and culturally derived expectations others have for self.

Traditional male areas. Bierema (1999, 2001) found that the White male-dominated corporate culture dramatically affected women executives' learning strategies, access, and success. While operationalization of gender stereotypes was the women's greatest obstacle, male fraternity often excluded them. Women's "actions and thoughts functioned to reproduce and adapt to the existing culture, not challenge it" (Bierema, 1999, p. 113). Indeed, the workplace has a hidden curriculum reinforcing the prevailing power structure (Bierema, 2001), perhaps a curriculum that extends to gender cultures within the broader society (Harding, 1996; Hayes, 2001).

The respondents in this study offered their perspectives on the male-oriented community college culture and how it affected their learning. BB observed, "I think a guy has to do . . . things the way the men do it and, because there perhaps have been more of them in the field for a longer period of time with more collegiality and connectivity, that it is still a challenge for women to . . . have a strong place at the table. . . . You end up *intruding* [emphasis added] yourself into that conversation all the time." FF described the other presidents in her system as "far more savvy than me with the quick lines and the glib, you know, the spotlight." These other leaders were all men and older than she, so she felt little affinity for them as mentors. Her women peers were more willing to ask for and share advice, while her male counterparts were willing to share information but less willing to seek out advice.

CC stated, "My general observation is that [campus business officers] don't share a lot of information and I think part of it, now that I understand more how things operate in that arena [business affairs], it's quite complex and for you to try to explain a very complex process and structure to someone who doesn't have a background in that can be quite overwhelming. . . . It has more to do with the fact that they don't think we could comprehend it." While she tried to be generous in her interpretation, CC was describing a stereotype-based situation where she was being shut out of areas traditionally viewed as male domains because she didn't have the background and would not understand it anyway. She also discovered to her chagrin that the male-dominated presidents' organization in her state was not acting on behalf of small colleges such as hers, in spite of an agreement to approach the legislature as a block—another experience of exclusion from male networks.

The matter of male domains—traditional male areas—bears relevance to the community college context of this study. When closely examining the initial and current learning needs expressed by the women presidents, many originate in male domains. These include budget and fiscal management, facilities management and construction, fund-raising, technology, and collective bargaining. DD, for example, stated: "I think that the men administrators have been more exposed to budgets than we have on a larger scale. They have been involved in the kind of meetings, or have been mentored by other men about budget issues . . . so that they have had more experience and background." At least for these women there seem to have been insufficient opportunities to gain knowledge and skills in these areas as they moved upward in their careers. Whether through intentional or inadvertent exclusion, they lacked important experiences and skills in relation to the AACC's (2004) core competencies of community college leaders.

Power issues. Tisdell (1993) addressed power issues in learning, positing that White male privilege is reinforced and reproduced in workplace learning. She asserted that knowledge gave power over others, and male leaders in an organization often chose to deny others access to knowledge and information as a means of retaining their power. These powerful people also tended to value qualities and behaviors similar to their own and to devalue qualities that were not similar. For example, women's ways of learning through shared experience and collaborative discourse might be devalued by men who preferred to present themselves as all-knowing and would hide any lack of knowledge. Another means of exerting power was to patronize the out group, thus establishing superiority and controlling access.

Women presidents in this study reported a number of instances where power issues entered the picture. FF, for example, explained that in her first presidency, "I'm not sure how independent I really was there because [chancellor's name] had always been a mentor and recruited me to [college's name]. . . . There was kind of a little protectiveness that I probably didn't feel that I needed, but he felt that he had to give me." This protectiveness resulted in her not gaining experience in some essential areas. CC realized that among the community college presidents in her state "the powerbase right now is the good old boys." She continued, "I don't think that I have as extensive a network that I observe my male colleagues to have. . . . I see them more as competition than as people who would want to help me."

Culturally derived expectations of self. Women leaders who finally break into the executive levels can be extraordinarily demanding of themselves, perhaps because they are aware that the slightest error might push them back out of the power circle (Brown et al., 2001). Bierema (1999) noted that the Competence Seekers among her study's participants "had a near obsession with being highly competent and accepted. Competence was often described as the key to gaining access to and acceptance in the male-dominated culture" (p. 113). By the time her participants became Change Agents, they began to understand that competence and adaptation were not necessarily sufficient and that the culture itself was the problem.

The presidents I interviewed placed great pressure on themselves in their jobs, much like the Competence Seekers. EE felt a sense of urgency. "I was passionate about community colleges and . . . knew I had to learn about this new sector and do this quickly . . . to be an effective advocate and interact with others around [a] common cause." BB went even further. "As a leader, I need to be visionary. I can't be visionary if I don't understand and value the context." In terms of her learning, she stated, "I have to be up on my feet very quickly." BB also acknowledged that this effort had taken its toll. "I am a single woman who has managed to successfully lead nine years at a community college in [state]. . . . And in a month, six weeks, you know, I sold my condo, drove cross-country, bought a home and started at [name of new college]. . . . It has been very hectic and mostly because I want to live here happily, I don't want to be dying on the job, but it is difficult." DD described herself as giving her heart and soul to her college. "I have always been Type A and I have always been very stubborn and I have always been in it to the end." She too recognized that such dedication took its toll, particularly on her family, and she was beginning to seek a better balance in her life. It is possible that these high expectations of self arose from the culture in the sense that the women felt they had to overachieve in order to be successful in a field dominated by men. As CC concluded, "We may have to work a little bit harder or possibly take on the bigger challenges to get to the presidency; in other words, the really plum jobs may not be available to us."

Culturally derived expectations that others have for self. In addition to their own self-expectations, women presidents were influenced by what they perceived as the expectations that others held for them. The presidents understood that they were under constant scrutiny from others and that some of this scrutiny was colored by gender relations in society and in the field of community colleges. Wanting to be seen as effective presidents, they worked even harder. EE put it succinctly: "I wanted to appear competent and capable." CC felt great pressure to resolve the crisis at her college. "A lot of the people that were here thought that I would only be here a year or two and then I would move on and it was just a matter of waiting for me to leave so that things could continue the way they were. And I am not leaving, I'm not leaving until I get this college turned around because I see it now as a challenge to me." In this instance, people saw her as a rising star who would only use this college as a stepping-stone, while she viewed the situation as an opportunity to apply her many skills to make the institution better. Both of these women internalized others' perceptions and pushed themselves to perform at even higher levels.

Others' perceptions concerning women presidents' personal demographics add pressures as well. For example, AA commented that people made judgments based on her marital status as well as gender. "If you are female and single or female and recently divorced . . . sometimes that can become a kind of an issue . . . [and] can sometimes influence how quickly [women presidents] can get up to speed, depending on how people are embracing or not embracing who they are when they walk in the door." FF noted her ethnicity as another pressure. "I never hold too much on the fact that I was the only woman president, but I was also the only African American president so, you know, I also felt the responsibility . . . to carry the banner for those who may come after us and those who look like us. So that, too, added to the pressure, if you will, which is self-imposed probably to measure up."

Changing the culture. Bierema (1999) found that 11 executive women in her study were in a category of learner she called Change Agents. These women had discovered that simply being competent was not enough; culture continued to be a barrier. They had begun shifting their learning activities toward self-exploration and personal development, and were willing to take significant risks in their careers. They also used whatever power they possessed to change the organizational culture and make it more hospitable to people of both sexes. In particular, these participants stressed the importance of relationships and interconnectedness.

An unanticipated finding of the current study was that several of the women community college presidents were Change Agents who used their learning process to influence the culture of their institutions. BB, an excellent example of this, said, "I am trying to educate my people . . . the college has been in somewhat of a transition and their systems and processes were very relaxed when I got here. . . . I am trying to help the place and the people work effectively with me and me with them." Similarly, FF expressed a need to learn how to recruit and retain good instructors and was working closely with her faculty to develop a welcoming and nurturing environment. "The more we include others in a participatory sense or fashion, the more value we get." AA's intention to learn more about crafting a compelling vision, particularly as the college faced an accreditation visit, also involved teaching and inspiring the campus community by "combining those things into motivators for perpetual growth and change and forward momentum."

These efforts to alter and improve their campus cultures signaled a high degree of professionalism, an AACC (2004) core competency. As learners, the women had achieved the level of Change Agents. As presidents, they demonstrated transformational leadership, authenticity, and integrity in their interactions with the campus community and beyond. Above all, they set high standards for themselves, continuously reflecting on their performance, expanding their skills, and seeking balance in their lives.

Implications and Recommendations for Practice

This study provided considerable insight into the learning activities of one group of women community college leaders. While further research along these lines is necessary to explore these findings with men community college leaders, with specific ethnicities, and with leadership roles other than the presidency, we may draw from the findings five implications for the practice of developing community college leaders.

First, the various learning needs expressed by the presidents matched the leadership competencies developed by the AACC (2004) Leading Forward project. None of the women named a learning need that was not included in that competency list. In a sense, then, the study validates the Leading Forward list and suggests that graduate programs and professional development events should concentrate on these competency areas, particularly the resource management subcategories that were frequently cited as a priority learning need. Likewise, those who aspire to leadership positions in community colleges might incorporate these competency areas in their personal learning plans.

Second, women presidents' clear preference for contextual learning involving interactions with other people supported much of the research on adult and women's learning. This suggests that degree and training programs should incorporate components such as mentoring, apprenticeships, real-life applications, and case studies, all of which encourage collaborative learning. Such collaborative learning strategies would benefit both men and women who aspire to higher education leadership.

Third, the presidents were well aware of their membership in a community of practice, although they did not use that terminology. This concept could be applied to the world of higher education in a more overt and intentional way. The term *community of practice* could bring a new understanding to graduate programs where professors are seen as subject or skill masters, and students engage in legitimate peripheral participation as learners and apprentices. The same would be true of professional development programs, such as those in which veteran community college leaders are masters who provide training to deans and vice presidents (apprentices) who follow in their footsteps.

Fourth, the women spoke of the challenges they faced in navigating the community college culture where male norms still prevail. The findings suggest that the dominant culture poses a barrier to learning and performance in this field, at least for some professional skill or knowledge areas. All community college leaders—women and men alike—must commit to eliminating vestiges of gender and other stereotypes that limit access and opportunity for any previously excluded groups if they truly want to realize the mission of community colleges.

Finally, the richness of the data obtained from this study gives rise to numerous other questions. Would a larger sample of presidents representing both genders and different ethnic backgrounds show differences within and among groups with regard to leadership learning opportunities and needs? Do men and women exhibit differences in learning styles, choice of learning strategies, and willingness to disclose lack of knowledge? What differences, if any, are experienced by men and women who engage in mentoring relationships? How might the concepts of intellectual apprenticeships and communities of practice be applied in higher education? Do the prevailing culture and power relationships of community colleges affect women and men leaders differently? How effective are training programs for future leaders? Is there value in programs targeted specifically to women and various minority groups?

While we wait for the research that will deepen our understanding of these issues, the current study provides a road map for the near future in terms of steps that can be taken to prepare new leaders. It also reassures us that today's community college leaders—if these women presidents can be seen as representative—are highly competent, reflective practitioners who are dedicated to their own continuous professional growth and the preparation of their successors. Their true legacy may well be their modeling of adult learning principles in their roles as leader educators.

References

American Association of Community Colleges. (2002). *Leadership 2020: Recruitment, preparation and support.* Retrieved June 2, 2005, from http://www.ccleadership.org/leading_forward/Leadership2020.htm

American Association of Community Colleges. (2004). *Leading Forward competencies.* Retrieved June 2, 2005, from http://www.ccleadership.org/resource_center/competencies.htm

Amey, M. (2004, February–March). Learning leadership in today's community colleges. *Community College Journal, 74*(4), 6–9.

Belenky, M., Clinchy, B., Goldberger, N., & Tarule, J. (1986). *Women's ways of knowing: The development of self, voice, and mind.* New York: Basic Books.

Bierema, L. L. (1999). A model of executive women's learning and development. *Adult Education Quarterly, 49*(2), 107–121.

Bierema, L. L. (2001). Women, work, and learning. *New Directions for Adult and Continuing Education, 92,* 53–62.

Bogdan, R. C., & Biklen, S. K. (2003). *Qualitative research for education: An introduction to theories and methods* (4th ed.). Boston: Allyn & Bacon.

Brown, G., Van Ummersen, C., & Sturnick, J. (2001). *From where we sit: Women's perspectives on the presidency.* Washington, DC: American Council on Education.

Brown, L., Martinez, M., & Daniel. D. (2002). Community college leadership preparation: Needs, perceptions and recommendations. *Community College Review, 30*(1), 45–65.

Buddemeier, S. (1998). *Female community college presidents: Career paths, experiences, and perceptions of the presidency.* Unpublished doctoral dissertation, North Carolina State University, Raleigh.

Burnham, P. F. (2002, Winter). Twenty-first century leadership paradigm: Defining the elements of community college leadership. *Academic Leadership, 9*(1), 16–18.

The Chronicle of Higher Education. Almanac 2004–2005. (2004). *The Chronicle of Higher Education, 51*(1), p. 3.

Clandinin, D. J., & Connelly, F. M. (2000). *Narrative inquiry: Experience and story in qualitative research.* San Francisco: Jossey-Bass.

Cohen, A. M., & Brawer, F. B. (2003). *The American community college* (4th ed.). San Francisco: Jossey-Bass.

Desjardins, C., & Huff, S. (2001). *The leading edge: Competencies for community college leaders in the new millennium.* Phoenix, AZ: National Institute for Leadership Development and League for Innovation in the Community College.

DiCroce, D. (1995). Women and the community college presidency: Challenges and possibilities. *New Directions for Community Colleges* (89), 79–84.

Duvall, B. (2003). The role of universities in leadership development. *New Direction for Community Colleges* (123), 63–72.

Fenwick, T. (2001). *Socio-cultural perspectives on learning through work.* San Francisco: Jossey-Bass.

Fulton-Calkins, P., & Milling, C. (2005). Community college leadership: An art to be practiced: 2010 and beyond. *Community College Journal of Research and Practice, 29*(3), 233–250.

Gilligan, C. (1983). *In a different voice: Psychological theory and women's development.* Cambridge, MA: Harvard University Press.

Goldberger, N., Tarule, J., Clinchy, B., & Belenky, M. (1996). *Knowledge, difference and power.* New York: Basic Books.

Hansman, C. A. (2001). Context-based adult learning. *New Directions for Adult and Continuing Education, 89,* 43–51.

Harding, S. (1996). Gendered ways of knowing and the epistemological crisis of the West. In N. R. Goldberger, J. M. Tarule, B. M. Clinchy, & M. F. Belenky (Eds.), *Knowledge, difference, and power: Essays inspired by "Women's Ways of Knowing."* New York: Basic Books.

Hayes, E. R. (2001, Spring). A new look at women's learning. *New Directions for Adult and Continuing Education, 8,* 35–42.

Hayes, E. R., & Flannery, D. D. (2002). *Women as learners: The significance of gender in adult learning.* San Francisco: Jossey-Bass.

Johnson, J., & Pratt, D. D. (1998). The apprenticeship perspective: Modeling ways of being. In D. Pratt & Associates, *Five perspectives on teaching in adult and higher education* (pp. 83–103). Malabar, FL: Krieger.

Kolb, D. (1983). *Experiential learning: Experience as the source of learning and development.* Upper Saddle River, NJ: Prentice Hall.

Lave, J., & Wenger, E. C. (1991). Situated learning: Legitimate peripheral participation. *Educational Researcher, 18*(1), 32–42.

LeGrand, B. B., Farmer, J. A., & Buckmaster, A. (1993). Cognitive apprenticeships approach to help adults to learn. *New Directions for Adult and Continuing Education* (59), 69–72.

McCracken, G. D. (1988). *The long interview.* Newbury Park, CA: Sage.

McFarlin, C. H., Crittenden, B. J., & Ebbers, L. H. (2000). Background factors common among community college presidents. *Community College Review, 27*(3), 19–32.

Merriam, S. B., & Caffarella, R. S. (1998). *Learning in adulthood: A comprehensive guide* (2nd ed.) San Francisco: Jossey-Bass.

Mischler, E. (1986). *Research interviewing: Context and narrative.* Cambridge, MA: Harvard University Press.

Moore, T. (2000). *Female presidents of independent colleges: Career paths, profiles, and experiences.* Unpublished doctoral dissertation, North Carolina State University, Raleigh.

Rogoff, B. (1990). *Apprenticeship in thinking: Cognitive development in social context.* New York: Oxford University Press.

Schein, E. H. (2004). *Organizational culture and leadership* (4th ed.). San Francisco: Jossey-Bass.

Shults, C. (2001). *The critical impact of impending retirements on community college leadership: Executive summary.* Washington, DC: American Association of Community Colleges.

Stout-Stewart, S. (2005). Female community-college presidents: Effective leadership patterns and behaviors. *Community College Journal of Research and Practice, 29*(3), 303–315.

Tarule, J. M. (1996). Voices in dialogue: Collaborative ways of knowing. In N. Goldberger, J. Tarule, B. Clinchy, & M. Belenky (Eds.), *Knowledge, difference, and power: Essays inspired by "Women's Ways of Knowing"* (pp. 274–304). New York: Basic Books.

Tisdell, E. J. (1993, Spring). Feminism in adult learning: Power, pedagogy and praxis. *New Directions for Adult and Continuing Education, 57,* 91–103.

Townsend, B. (Ed.). (1995, Spring). Gender and power in the community colleges. *New Directions in Community Colleges* (89).

Vaughan, G. B., & Weisman, I. M. (2002). *The community college presidency 2001: Research brief.* Leadership Series no. 3. Washington, DC: American Association of Community Colleges.

Vincent, E. T. (2004). *A qualitative analysis of community college leadership from the Leading Forward summits: Final report prepared for the American Association of Community Colleges.* Iowa City, IA: ACT.

Wenger, E. (1998). *Communities of practice: Learning, meaning, and identity.* Cambridge, UK: Cambridge University Press.

Wenger, E. C., & Snyder, W. M. (2000, January–February). Communities of practice: The organizational frontier. *Harvard Business Review,* pp. 139–145.

Yukl, G. (2002). *Leadership in organizations* (5th ed.). Upper Saddle River, NJ: Prentice Hall.

6

RESOURCES, ROLE MODELS, AND OPPORTUNITY MAKERS

Mentoring Women in Academic Leadership

Diane R. Dean

omen are no rarity on college campuses. Most college students are women, making up 55% of all undergraduate and 60% of all graduate students across the nation (*The Chronicle of Higher Education*, 2005b) and earning a respectable proportion (45%) of all doctorate degrees awarded (*The Chronicle of Higher Education*, 2005a). Women also represent a majority (64.3%) of all full- and part-time nonprofessional staff, half (50.7%) of all full- and part-time professional staff, and a respectable proportion (43.4%) of all full- and part-time faculty combined (*The Chronicle of Higher Education*, 2005c).

Yet despite the ethos of equity and opportunity, women remain underrepresented in top college and university leadership positions. Consider the curious imbalance: Although women hold the majority of nonprofessional positions and half of all professional positions (*The Chronicle of Higher Education*, 2005c), they hold only 23% of all presidencies (American Council on Education, 2007) and only a little over 18% of all chief academic officer (CAO) positions (Dean, 2003) in nonprofit colleges and universities. Among academic positions, although women compose nearly half (46%) of all instructional and research assistant positions, and a respectable proportion (43%) of all full- and part-time faculty combined (*The Chronicle of Higher Education*, 2005c), that figure drops to 39% when looking only at full-time faculty positions. Within the full-time faculty career trajectory, women hold more than half of the lower positions (52% of all full-time lecturers and 51% of all full-time instructors), and their proportions steadily decrease moving up the tenure track from assistant (45%) to associate (33%) to full professor (24%; *The Chronicle of Higher Education*, 2005d).

From analyzing the numbers above and the longitudinal data presented in the introduction to this volume, the cold truth emerges. Women do not advance to top leadership positions in academe in proportions expected from the demographics in feeder positions. The growth of women in leadership positions has been considerably slow and has not taken place consistently among different types of institutions (American Council on Education, 2007; Corrigan, 2002; Ross & Green, 2000). Thus, the pipeline to the top dwindles to a trickle.

What forces underlie this phenomenon? Countless qualified women desire to advance their careers and yet do not reach their goals. Those who make it must overcome many barriers as women in a professional culture based on White male norms. They must overcome assumptions in American society concerning what constitutes leadership behavior and what leaders should look like, as well as expectations concerning how professional women should behave. In fact, the gender imbalance in academe merely extends what is pervasive through American society. The U.S. Department of Labor reports that women hold nearly half (47%) of all jobs in the American workforce (U.S. Bureau of Labor Statistics, 2008), yet women hold only 15% of corporate officer positions in Fortune 500 companies (Catalyst, 2008), and head only a scant 2% of Fortune 500 companies (Women CEOs, 2008).

Researchers attempting to understand why some women climbed to the top of their career ladder while others reached a plateau have identified a cluster of professional assets that seem to accelerate promotion. Among these is mentoring. To further our understanding of the phenomena contributing to the low numbers of women in academic leadership, this chapter examines the current and total career mentoring experiences of women in academic leadership. Specifically, it focuses on CAOs, those women who report directly to the president of a college or university and have responsibility for the oversight of the institution's academic programs and faculty. Considering differences in mentoring experiences according to personal and professional demographics, it draws implications for increasing the proportion of women who lead American colleges and universities.

Theoretical Framework

The framework for this study draws upon literature elucidating the significance of mentoring for women's career advancement.

The Significance of Mentoring

The word *mentor* dates from 3,000 years ago to Homer's *The Odyssey*, when Odysseus gave his friend Mentor full charge of his household and the responsibility to look after his son, Telemachus, while he journeyed 20 years during the Trojan War and his long voyage home. Mentor advises, aids, and protects Telemachus during his formative years between youth and manhood. His counseling influences the boy's intellectual, social, and emotional development.

In the workplace, mentoring implies an active relationship (Buddemeier, 1998) in which the mentor takes a personal and vested interest in the development of the protégé. Mentors, among their many functions,

- professionally socialize protégés in the customs, demands, and expectations of organizational and professional cultures;
- increase protégés' understanding by sharing wisdom and professional knowledge;
- develop and refine protégés by providing encouragement and comments on their work; and
- facilitate protégés' career advancement through offering opportunities for leadership roles, encouraging career progression, and writing recommendations and nominations (Durnovo, 1990; Lagakis, 2001; Merriam & Thomas, 1986; Moore & Amey, 1988; Shakeshaft, 1987; Simeone, 1987).

Essential for success. For nearly 30 years, research has recognized mentoring as essential to women's success in corporate careers. Among the earliest studies, Hennig and Jardim (1977) studied women executives' mentoring relationships with their male bosses and discerned the importance of those relationships in providing support, encouragement, professional development, and even strength within the organization. Women's mentors, in fact, gained or increased their protégés' respect and professional standing in the organization by cloaking their protégés within their own aura of respect. Similarly, Kanter (1977) studied men and women and determined that while men executives needed mentoring, women needed it more so to overcome the gender inequities and unequal opportunities. Decades later, Bierema (2001), Catalyst (1996), and Morrison, White, and Van Velsor (1987), also studying women in corporate America, confirmed the importance of mentoring for women's professional development and advancement.

Academe, while very unlike corporate America in many regards, shares its male-dominated history. American higher education's peculiar history is a story of paradox: the great catalyst of opportunity for multitudes while harboring inequity within. When organizational structures are not equally permeable for all members within them, people and networks become the critical conduits for career mobility. Thus, as with their counterparts in corporate America, higher education leaders who were successful repeatedly point to the impact of a mentor who recognized their potential for leadership, encouraged them to develop that potential, and guided them toward achieving promotion (Bower, 1993). For women in academe, scholars and researchers consider mentoring a decided and perhaps critical career advantage (Bower; Brown, Van Ummersen, & Sturnick, 2001; Buddemeier, 1998; Glazer-Raymo, 1999; Lagakis, 2001; Leach, 2000; LeBlanc, 1993; McDade & Walton, 2001; Moore & Salimbene, 1981; Morrissey, 1997; Reed-Taylor, 1998; Salimbene, 1982; Shakeshaft, 1987; Simeone, 1987; Trujillo-Sanchez, 1992; Vaughan, 1989, 1990).

Conversely, while a lack of mentoring does not spell failure, research has cited it as a barrier to women's advancement in higher education (LeBlanc, 1993).

Effects of mentoring. The numerous effects of mentoring are divided into two types: professional and psychosocial (Kram, 1985), and link to increased job satisfaction (Godshalk & Sosik, 2003; Scandura, 1997).

As professional developers, mentors expand their protégés' knowledge and resource base, offer role models, and provide opportunities for feedback and assistance on career and job challenges. They help shape their protégés' career goals and guide them toward developing skills based upon their own wealth of career knowledge and expertise (Bennis & Nanus, 1985; Kram, 1985; Zey, 1984).

As career advancement aides, mentors provide sources of information about position openings and support their protégés' efforts at seeking promotions through providing nominations and references. Equally important, mentors teach their protégés how to get such information for themselves— how to network and with whom—and often serve as gateways to the experts and resources the protégé will need. Occasionally, a mentor may directly hire or place a protégé in an advanced position.

Mentors also often promote the external visibility of their protégés, making their talents known to those responsible for nominating, recruiting, or hiring decisions (Kram, 1985). This includes facilitating and endorsing their protégés' entrance into professional networks and cliques, helping them gain acceptance among other experienced professionals, acceptance that might take years—if ever—to develop alone, as America's male-dominated professional networks often intentionally or unintentionally deny access to women.

Mentors might also encourage their protégés to pursue traditional vehicles for attaining high external visibility, such as publishing; giving presentations and speeches; and serving on commissions, accreditation teams, and corporate and nonprofit boards. Additionally, a mentor may facilitate or broker these opportunities. Visibility and networking foster career growth in higher education administration, where career advancement typically occurs through external moves (McNeer, 1983).

Psychosocial benefits of mentoring include professional and personal counseling, emotional support, and friendship (Kram, 1985; Zey, 1984). Mentors build confidence through role modeling, encouragement, personal feedback, respect, validation, and ultimately acceptance and confirmation (Kram). Thus, they contribute to their protégés' self-acknowledgment of their own capacity and growing sense of self-efficacy.

As both professional and psychosocial developers, mentors support and challenge their protégés, providing vision (Daloz, 1999) and shaping their emerging professional philosophies and identities (Bennis & Nanus, 1985).

Hard sought but rarely gained. Researchers have noted the difficulties professional women face in forming mentoring relationships (Anderson, 2005; Bierema, 2001; Wellington & Spence, 2001). The challenge of finding a mentor includes the general limited availability of mentors, women's lack of access to mentors, difficulties for women and men to identify with each other as part of the mentoring process, and the limited availability of women mentors in particular.

Women who are excluded from informal networks and at a disadvantage in organizational power structures (Anderson, 2005; Burke, 2002; Hennig & Jardim, 1977; Kanter, 1977; Mattis, 2002) often lack visibility or access to those who might mentor them. Often, mentoring relationships begin when a would-be mentor personally identifies with his or her would-be protégé (Hall & Sandler, 1983; Kanter). Mentors making such selections intentionally or unintentionally overlook those who are unlike themselves (Hall & Sandler, 1983). This includes the tendency for male mentors to have difficulty identifying with women as their protégés (Anderson; Armstrong, Allinson, & Hayes, 2002; Catalyst, 1996; Eby, McManus, Simon, & Russell, 2000; Kanter). Hall and Sandler (1983) and Burke (2002) refer to this as the "old boys' network," in which male-dominated leadership selects and grooms male protégés. Unfortunately, the "old girls' network" remains small in membership, scope, and depth of influence. Thus, women may lack female mentors because of their rarity.

Certainly, women in academe may obtain some of these assets through other means. Networking and participation in professional development programs and associations, for example, can provide similar cognitive and affective benefits. Executive recruitment firms and hired career coaches can shape careers and aid advancement. Yet mentoring remains a special asset for two reasons. First, it can accelerate career advancement by providing access to the distillation of a mentor's experience without having to learn those same lessons through years of trial and error. Second, mentoring is a career asset in which the relationship is intimate. Mentors identify with their protégés, care about their growth and success, and thus open the doors to their wealth of knowledge and influence.

Rationale for Studying Women CAOs

The proportions of women in academic leadership drop off sharply as rank increases. The thinnest ranks include women CAOs and presidents. I chose to focus on CAOs because they have reached the top rungs of their career ladder and yet still have a rung of opportunity for advancement—the presidency. Women presidents agree that mentoring played an important role in their own careers and that more and better mentoring would help more women advance in the presidential pipeline (Brown et al., 2001; Vaughan, 1990).

I think of mentoring as important to women academic leaders for at least three reasons: (a) aiding their advancement to their current position, (b) helping them excel at what they currently do, and (c) moving them even farther along their career path to future positions. Although we recognize mentoring as an asset in higher education careers, we know little about the mentoring experiences of those at the top of the academic career ladder who are directly in line for the presidency.

What are women CAOs' experiences with mentoring? What can we learn from their experiences? Are there any differences in experience according to their personal or professional demographics?

Methodology

To answer these questions, I draw upon data from a national study of women CAOs in U.S. colleges and universities that I conducted in 2003–2004, which included all the 657 women CAOs in U.S. public and private, non-profit, nonspecialized colleges and universities at the 2-year, 4-year, and graduate levels, as identified through the *2002 Higher Education Directory*. A majority (57%), of women CAOs responded, with nearly even proportions from among institutional types (public 57%, private 58%, associate's 58%, baccalaureate 55%, master's 59%, and doctoral/research 50%.).

The complete survey included 93 qualitative and quantitative questions, pilot tested through a panel of nine women identified as having particular knowledge or experience regarding women's career advancement in higher education. While the complete survey addressed a range of research issues concerning women CAOs and their professional development and advancement, this chapter builds on three subsets of survey questions.

Mentoring experiences. I asked participants about their mentoring experiences, seeking information regarding how many mentors each woman has had, if any, over the course of her career and how many she had currently. I asked participants to describe the mentors' roles in or connections to their lives and the nature of the mentoring relationship.

Personal characteristics. I collected information about personal characteristics that the literature suggests affect career progression. While the full demographic survey was quite extensive, the characteristics examined for the purposes of comparing women's experiences in this chapter include age, marriage and family, and ethnicity/race.

Professional characteristics. I also collected a wide range of professional characteristics, including the three used for this chapter: length of service in higher education, length of service in the current job as CAO, and the Carnegie Classification of the current institution.

I analyzed quantitative data in SPSS 16.0 using standard strategies for descriptive research, evaluated the findings against expectations suggested by the literature, and drew out resulting patterns and relationships. I applied appropriate methods of statistical analysis for ordinal data to evaluate the significance of any suspected relationships between variables.

I managed qualitative data analysis through NVivo 7, coding qualitative data for language describing the nature of the mentoring relationship and benefits derived from the experience. To support category validation for qualitative data, I discussed findings with peer reviewers.

Results: Mentoring Experiences of Women CAOs

Mentoring Rates

Across the board, the majority of women CAOs in the study have had some level of mentoring throughout their careers (82%; see Table 6.1). While the levels of current mentoring trail the levels of total career mentoring, nearly half of women CAOs still have a mentor (47%), but typically only one mentor (25%).

TABLE 6.1

Mentoring Experiences Among Women CAOs by Institutional Type

	Mentoring Rates Among Women CAOs (%)						
	Associate	Baccalaureate	Master's	Doctoral	Public	Private	All
Mentoring Throughout Career							
No	13	36	19	11	14	25	18
Yes	87	64	81	89	86	75	82
Total	100	100	100	100	100	100	100
Mentoring at the Time of the Study							
No	49	60	52	61	48	60	53
Yes	51	40	48	39	52	40	47
Total	100	100	100	100	100	100	100

Note. $N = 370$. Figures rounded to nearest whole percent; 370 out of 375 participants responded.

Mentoring rates by institutional type. Several professional and personal characteristics related to the likelihood of having a mentor. In general, more CAOs at public institutions received mentoring over the course of their careers (86%) and had current mentors (52%) than their counterparts at private universities (75% mentoring throughout career; 40% current mentors).

The rates dropped below average for CAOs at baccalaureate colleges, only 68% of whom had mentors at any point in their careers (versus the overall frequency of 82%). Rates rose slightly above average for those at associate's colleges and doctoral universities (87% and 89% respectively).

Because research has shown that academics tend to build and restrict their careers within one particular institutional type without a great degree of mobility between institutional types, we may reasonably assume that a majority of women CAOs have largely led their careers at institutions similar to the one where they worked at the time of the study. My analyses of other data from the national study have supported this assumption (Dean, 2003). Thus, the differences in mentoring experiences by institutional type emerged as a point of concern.

When looking at mentoring over the course of women CAOs' careers, we can extrapolate the findings to suggest two things. First, women in academic administration at public institutions receive more mentoring than their private college and university counterparts. Second, among institutional types, those at associate's colleges and doctoral universities receive more mentoring than their baccalaureate college and master's university counterparts.

Mentoring rates by age and years of service. The number of women CAOs' current mentors dropped significantly as their age increased (see Figure 6.1).[1]

FIGURE 6.1

Current Mentoring Rates Among Women CAOs by Age Range

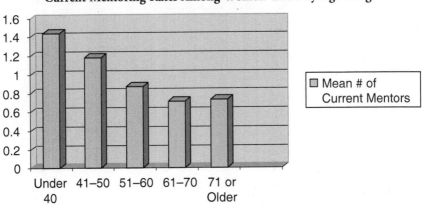

While the common assumption that mentors must be older than their protégés might partly explain this pattern (as one participant noted, "people expect *me* to be their mentor now" [emphasis in original]), older women CAOs also had received significantly less mentoring over the course of their total careers.[2] This means that as younger women they received less mentoring than younger women are receiving today.

Similarly, and perhaps because age and years of service correlated, I found that as the length of CAOs' service in their current jobs increased, their rates of current mentoring and mentoring throughout their total careers decreased.[3] This means that newer CAOs were more likely to have mentors (currently and throughout their career) than CAOs with long-term service.

We can interpret this in several ways. The good news: Perhaps academe does a better job of mentoring newer/younger professionals and professors (the academic administrators and faculty who are on the career rungs to the CAO position). The bad news: Older professionals seem shortchanged in mentoring experiences. Although the typical mentoring relationship involves an older, more experienced mentor and a younger, less experienced protégé (Daloz, 1999; Kram, 1983; Levinson, Darrow, Klein, Levinson, & McKee, 1978; Mullen, 1994; Phillip-Jones, 2001), it need not always be so. Mentoring can also occur in age-inversed relationships and among peer-to-peer relationships (Kadar, 2005; Kram, 1983). Women CAOs may overlook such opportunities.

Mentoring rates by race/ethnicity. Looking at race and ethnicity, women of color experienced higher rates of mentoring throughout their careers and in their current positions than Caucasian women (see Table 6.2). In fact, while the majority of all participants had received mentoring over the course of their careers (82%), only the majority of women CAOs of color had current mentors (African American, 62%; Hispanic/Latina, 75%; all other ethnicities of color combined, 60%.)[4] This was not true for their Caucasian peers. Although a strong majority of Caucasian women CAOs had received mentoring (80%) during their careers, less than half (45%) of them had current mentors at the time of the study.

However, we should consider the mentoring rates of women CAOs by race/ethnicity against data showing the proportions of women CAOs by race/ethnicity. The vast majority (87%) of the 375 women CAOs who participated in this study were Caucasian (Dean, 2003). Although well mentored, women CAOs of color are relatively scarce (13%).

Mentoring rates by other personal characteristics. While researchers commonly suggest that marriage, children, and lesbianism constrain women's careers, I found no salient differences for mentoring rates according to sexuality, marriage, or number of children.

TABLE 6.2
Mentoring Experiences Among Women CAOs by Race/Ethnicity

	Mentoring Rates Among Women CAOs (%)			
	African American/Black	*Hispanic/Latina*	*All Other Races/Ethnicities*[a]	Caucasian
Mentoring Throughout Career				
No	7	0	10	20
Yes	93	100	90	80
Total	100	100	100	100
Mentoring at the Time of the Study				
No	38	25	40	55
Yes	62	75	60	45
Total	100	100	100	100

Note. $N = 365$. Figures rounded to nearest whole percent; 365 out of 375 participants responded.

[a] The numbers of women of other ethnicities were not sufficient to present each classification separately.

Profile of the Mentors

Who were the mentors? What were these relationships like? Collectively, the women in this study named 250 men and women past and current mentors. These mentors may have been older, younger, or the same age as their protégés, and the CAOs had met them through a wide range of relationships within their current institutions and at other colleges and universities, including graduate school. They included former professors and advisors, current and former colleagues, and current and former bosses (Figure 6.2).

Sitting or retired presidents (57%) were the largest group. Among these, half were the CAOs' current bosses and one sixth were their former bosses. Senior higher education administrators (23%) made up the next largest group, including their peer CAOs and various other vice presidents and vice chancellors. The remaining three groups were faculty colleagues (11%; half of whom were the CAOs' professors or advisors while in graduate school); other higher education administrators in a variety of positions (6%); and assorted people in the higher education community (3%), such as consultants, state and federal education administrators, and college or university board members.

FIGURE 6.2
Positions Held by the Mentors of Women CAOs

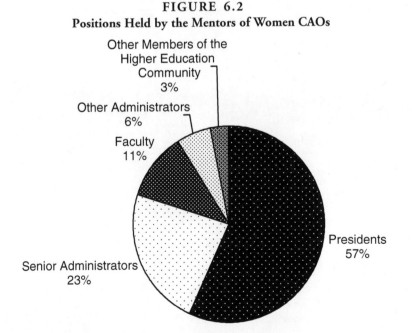

Although the survey inquired about their mentors' gender, participants aggregated their answers so that it was not possible to discern the gender of each of these types of mentors, nor the gender of current versus past career mentors. The question will need redesign in future reiterations of this study. Yet, while the research linking mentoring to career advancement identifies the influence of a higher proportion of male mentors, no research to date has assessed any qualitative differences in the mentoring provided by men or women, although research has suggested that women prefer women mentors (Burke & McKeen, 1995).

The Mentoring Relationship

Women CAOs described their experiences in ways that echo the literature. They said their mentors served as resources, guides and advisors, supporters, role models, and opportunity makers.

To delve further into these five aspects of mentoring relationships, participants reported that their mentors served as resources by increasing participants' understanding about higher education issues and the day-to-day business of managing and leading a college or university. Mentors willingly shared insights gained from their own years of experience. Specifically, they served as resources concerning academic programs, higher education finance, and general administrative skills and best practices. "[My mentor] helps me troubleshoot," reported one participant. "[My mentor] directs me to various resources and policies when I need clarification," reported another. Another said that her mentor had "taught [her] everything [she knew] about leadership."

As advisors, mentors socialized their protégés in the customs, demands, and expectations of higher education cultures. They were typically politically connected and known in a variety of environments. Participants repeatedly used the adjectives "intuitive" and "politically astute" to describe their mentors, and described their willingness to share this special type of knowledge base. Political socialization takes on a special importance in light of research that shows women's lack of experience in organizational politics is a distinct disadvantage in their careers (Perrewe & Anthony, 2000).

As guides, mentors help their protégés navigate these cultures and serve as sounding boards. For example, one participant wrote, "I can talk with my mentors about anything on any level and know they will give me objective advice." Another said her mentor "always discusses her decisions and strategies with [her] regarding organizational challenges." Another defined her mentor as "wise, warm, experienced and empathetic regarding all the battles and joys of higher education and being a woman in higher education."

Beyond being willing to share one's knowledge base and insights on the world of higher education, mentoring involves an active, intimate relationship in which the mentor takes an interest in guiding and facilitating his or her protégé's development and advancement (Buddemeier, 1998). As supporters, mentors developed and refined their protégés. "He cares about my aspirations," wrote one CAO. My mentors "care about me and my professional growth," wrote another. "He always sees the best in me," reported a participant. "She is strong and loyal to me," another said of her mentor. Others said that their mentor "always encourages me to stretch and grow," and "constantly urg[es] me to push myself for advancement."

The combination of behaviors yielded mentors who became shareholders in their protégé's successes or failures. They demonstrated their interest through a commitment of time, and often friendship. Participants described their mentors with adjectives such as "accessible," and "always available." One CAO said her mentor "wants me to succeed and spends much time and energy mentoring me." About a third of participants also described their mentors as "good friends" or "personal friends." The telephone and e-mail provided means for continued contact when mentors and their protégés worked on separate campuses.

Such investments of time, caring, loyalty, consistency, and sincere friendship in mentoring relationships can help women gain a sense of empowerment and self-worth.

In addition to furthering their protégés' growth and development, mentors served as role models. This was especially true of mentors who were sitting or former presidents. The words of admiration participants used to describe their mentor may reflect the types of leaders they aspire to become themselves. Admired skills typically included strong leadership; vision, excellent delegation; shared decision making; and wonderful interpersonal and communication skills. Admired affective areas included integrity, honesty, friendliness, creativity, enthusiasm, professionalism, and passion.

The literature says that women's movement into top leadership positions is not accidental and that career planning aids their advancement (LeBlanc, 1993; McDade, 1990; Morrissey, 1997; Touchton, Shavlik, & Davis, 1993; Winship, 1992). Many of women CAOs' mentors either were facilitating (for current mentors) or had facilitated (for past mentors) their protégés' career advancement by serving as opportunity makers for them in three critical ways.

First, mentors created opportunities for professional development. "My mentor," wrote one participant, "provided me with wonderful learning opportunities and the chance to try some things outside of my current role."

Others listed specific areas in which their mentors had involved them. Second, mentors served as career catalysts for vertical or lateral promotion. Participants said their mentors shared information about career openings and nominated and wrote recommendations for them. Third, sometimes mentors directly facilitated advancement. Most commonly this occurred when a president promoted a CAO from the faculty. "To provide the mentoring functions that enhance protégé's careers, mentors must have power and influence within the organization" (Anderson, 2005, p. 67).

However, not all power for facilitating career advancement came downward through the hierarchy. The power to create opportunity could come from other sources as well. "My mentor is a classified employee in a significantly lower position," wrote one participant, "the leader of the campus shadow government. He arranged to place me in this interim position and counseled me into serving when I was reluctant to do so."

Summary

So what does all of this mean? The good news: Women CAOs, for the most part, were receiving mentoring. The majority had mentors at some point in their careers (82%) and many still had current mentors (47%). They perceived their mentors as incredible professional assets, as resources, guides, and role models who supported and facilitated their professional development and advancement opportunities. Their mentoring relationships exhibited caring, loyalty, and constant encouragement, a powerful combination yielding a mentor who holds a share in the protégé's successes and failures. Yet despite this good news, we have room for improvement.

Discussion

Four important implications in addressing the problem of the low numbers of women in academic leadership emerge.

Mentoring Women Leaders at All Types of Institution

CAOs at private institutions and at baccalaureate and master's colleges and universities received less mentoring than their counterparts at public institutions and at associate's colleges and doctoral universities. The primary implications of this disparity are twofold. First, institutions who wish to demonstrate their professed commitment to equity and opportunity should create mentoring cultures. Private institutions in particular, as well as baccalaureate and master's colleges and universities (both public and private), should examine the extent to which their organizational cultures and structures formally and informally promote and support mentoring.

Second, women aspiring to academic leadership should consider these findings when charting their career path and evaluating job opportunities. They might increase their odds for success by consciously choosing institutional types that have demonstrated higher levels of mentoring for women and by carefully investigating the formal and informal mentoring culture of an individual college or university when evaluating job opportunities.

What is a mentoring culture? Zachary (2000) offers 10 signs of a mentoring culture.

1. Accountability for mentoring, including program coordination and evaluation, are serious matters.
2. Mentoring aligns with a culture that places a high priority on individual and organizational learning.
3. People want to become protégés and are eager to participate as mentors.
4. Adequate human and financial resources are in place to support mentoring, and people respect and dedicate time for mentoring.
5. People speak positively about mentoring across the organization at all levels.
6. Mentoring occurs in multiple ways, such as individual, group, and long-distance mentoring.
7. Rewards and recognition for participation are built into the culture.
8. Mentoring excellence is visible, publicized, and role modeled for participants.
9. Support is available to the mentors and protégés when relationships work out poorly.
10. Periodic briefings remind people about mentoring and its availability.

A scan of a college's formal mentoring culture might include checking the available professional development programs and opportunities for students, faculty, and administrators. A scan of the informal mentoring culture might include artful questions asked during the interview process and campus visits. A true mentoring culture, one conducive for enhancing the overall quality of academic leadership, would manifest itself along the entire career path of academic leadership from undergraduate to graduate students, from graduate students to new faculty, and from faculty to academic administration. The creation or improvement of such a culture would benefit women and men, and could help develop succeeding generations of academic leaders as well as contribute to overall student/faculty/staff satisfaction and retention.

Mentoring Women Leaders at All Ages and Stages of Their Career

Mentoring experiences (current and throughout their career) among women CAOs dropped significantly as their age and years of service in their current jobs increased. While academe may do a better job of mentoring newer/younger professionals and professors, we should not shortchange older CAOs or those who have been in their positions long term. A lack of mentoring not only hinders women's advancement, it equates to the loss of a basic and significant form of professional development. Even for those who do not seek career advancement, the rapidly changing external and internal environments in which colleges and universities operate necessitate continual professional development and growth. Leadership must keep pace with the demands placed upon it. Any institution concerned with maintaining a vibrant, effective, and creative cadre of leaders should provide professional development to its staff regardless of age or length of service.

Mentoring, as noted previously, can occur in age-inversed relationships and among peer-to-peer relationships. The mentors of participants in this study hailed from a variety of positions and a variety of ages—older than, younger than, and the same age as their protégés. Potential mentors should not overlook the value they can bring to an older CAO or one with many years of experience in her position. Nor should women refrain from seeking mentors at any age or stage of their career.

Mentoring Women of Color Leaders and Increasing Diversity in Academic Leadership

The findings for mentoring among women CAOs of color invoked the "glass half full, half empty" paradox. While the high mentoring rates among women CAOs of color gave a positive outlook, the findings were dampened by the very low proportions of women CAOs of color overall (Dean, 2003).

The implications are several. First, we should celebrate this high rate of mentoring among women CAOs of color—to enhance their retention, success in their positions, and advancement to top academic positions. Second, we should focus on increasing the proportions of women CAOs of color, which would inherently necessitate a focus on increasing diversity in all positions along the path to academic leadership. Third, similar to the recommendation to create or improve mentoring cultures, we should attend to the formal and informal cultures for mentoring women (and men) of color throughout the entire career path of academic leadership, including students, faculty, and academic administration.

Conclusion: Advancing Women to Academic Leadership

Women remain vastly underrepresented in academic leadership. Increasing their proportion among academic leaders necessitates focusing on their professional development. Yet less than half of the nation's colleges and universities have leadership development programs for women and people of color (Corrigan, 2002). Among public colleges and universities, only 45% offer such programs specifically for women and 40% for people of color. Among private institutions, only 32% offer programs for women and 28% offer programs for people of color (Corrigan).

Although half of women CAOs were receiving mentoring, this might not adequately address the problem of women's underrepresentation in academic leadership. Furthermore, vast swaths of the women CAO population were receiving below average levels of such development. The study evidenced disparity by institutional type, by age and length of service, and by race and ethnicity.

Mentoring matters. It provides cognitive and affective benefits. It prepares protégés for advancement and can be instrumental in moving them forward (identifying and creating opportunities, increasing visibility, making recommendations and nominations). Women considering or seeking to enter academic leadership should recognize mentoring as essential to their success and take the initiative to develop such relationships inside or outside their institution among peers, with individuals in higher positions, or with anyone who can offer beneficial knowledge, support, or opportunities. The data for this chapter suggest where to begin: among presidents, senior administrators, and faculty.

Those concerned with or involved in the preparation, recruitment, selection, and development of higher education leadership should seek to understand and address the steep dropoff in mentoring among women CAOs (from 82% over the career span to 47% currently). Efforts could range from the informal, such as peer CAOs, presidents, and trustees reaching out to mentor women CAOs to their full career potential, to the formal, such as higher education institutions or associations creating or expanding their mentoring programs for women and people of color with attention to those in the academic leadership pipeline.

Mentoring matters not only for the professional and personal development of those who seek to do their very best in the jobs they currently hold; it matters for assuring succeeding generations of committed, capable, creative leaders. *Those having torches will pass them on to others* (Plato, *The Republic*).

Notes

1. Significant at $p < .01$ (two-tailed), using Kendall's τ-b coefficient, with value of $-.205$, $N = 359$.

2. Significant at $p < .01$ (two-tailed), using Kendall's τ-b coefficient, with value of $-.130$, $N = 359$.

3. Current mentoring $=$ significant at $p < .01$ (two-tailed) with value of $-.150$, and mentoring throughout one's career $=$ significant at $p < .05$ (two-tailed) with a value of $-.085$, using Kendall's τ-b coefficient. $N = 362$.

4. The numbers of women of other ethnicities were not sufficient to present each classification separately.

References

American Council on Education. (2007). *The American college president: 2007 edition*. Washington, DC: Author.

Anderson, D. R. (2005). The importance of mentoring programs to women's career advancement in biotechnology. *Journal of Career Development, 32*(1), 60–73.

Armstrong, S. J., Allinson, C. W., & Hayes, J. (2002). Formal mentoring systems: An examination of the effects of mentor/protégé cognitive styles on the mentoring process. *Journal of Management Studies, 39*(8), 1111–1137.

Bennis, W. G., & Nanus, B. (1985). *Leaders: Strategies for taking charge*. New York: Harper & Row.

Bierema, L. L. (2001, Winter). Women, work, and learning. *New Directions for Adult and Continuing Education, 92,* 53–62.

Bower, D. F. L. (1993). Women and mentoring in higher education. In P. T. Mitchell (Ed.), *Cracking the wall: Women in higher education administration* (pp. 89–97). Washington, DC: College and University Personnel Association.

Brown, G., Van Ummersen, C., & Sturnick, J. (2001). *From where we sit: Women's perspectives on the presidency*. Washington, DC: American Council on Education.

Buddemeier, S. D. (1998). *Female community college presidents: Career paths, experience and perceptions of the presidency*. Unpublished doctoral dissertation, North Carolina State University, Raleigh.

Burke, R. J. (2002). Career development of managerial women. In R. J. Burke & D. L. Nelson (Eds.), *Advancing women in management: Progress and prospects* (pp. 139–160). Malden, MA: Blackwell Publishers.

Burke, R. J., & McKeen, C. A. (1995). Do managerial women prefer women mentors? *Psychological Reports, 76*(2), 688–690.

Catalyst. (1996). *Women in corporate leadership: Progress and prospects*. New York: Author.

Catalyst. (2008). *2008 Catalyst census of women corporate officers and top earners of the Fortune 500*. Retrieved March 11, 2009, from http://www.catalyst.org/publica

tion/283/2008-catalyst-census-of-women-corporate-officers-and-top-earners-of-the-fortune-500

The Chronicle of Higher Education. (2005a, September). Characteristics of recipients of earned doctorates, 2003. *Almanac 2005–06, 52*(1), 19.

The Chronicle of Higher Education. (2005b, September). College enrollment by age of students, Fall 2003. *Almanac 2005–06, 52*(1), 15.

The Chronicle of Higher Education. (2005c, September). Employees in colleges and universities by racial and ethnic group, Fall 2003. *Almanac 2005–06, 52*(1), 26.

The Chronicle of Higher Education. (2005d, September). Number of full-time faculty members by sex, rank, and racial and ethnic group, 2003. *Almanac 2005–06,* 52(1), 26.

Corrigan, M. (2002). *The American college president: 2002 edition.* Washington, DC: American Council on Education.

Daloz, L. A. (1999). *Mentor: Guiding the journey of adult learners* (2nd ed.). San Francisco: Jossey-Bass.

Dean, D. R. (2003, November). *America's women chief academic officers and their presidential aspirations.* Paper presented at the meeting of the Association for the Study of Higher Education, Portland, OR.

Durnovo, M. (1990). Emerging characteristics of women administrators in Texas public community and junior colleges. In L. B. Welch (Ed.), *Women in higher education: Changes and challenges* (pp. 147–160). New York: Praeger.

Eby, L. T., McManus, S. E., Simon, S. A., & Russell, J. E. (2000). The protégé's perspective regarding negative mentoring experiences: The development of a taxonomy. *Journal of Vocational Behavior, 57*(1), 1–21.

Glazer-Raymo, J. (1999). *Shattering the myths: Women in academe.* Baltimore: Johns Hopkins University Press.

Godshalk, V. M., & Sosik, J. J. (2003). Aiming for career success: The role of learning goal orientation in mentoring relationships. *Journal of Vocational Behavior, 63*(3), 417–437.

Hall, R. M., & Sandler, B. R. (1983). *Academic mentoring for women students and faculty: A new look at an old way to get ahead.* East Lansing, MI: National Center for Research on Teacher Learning. (ERIC Document Reproduction Service No. ED240891)

Hennig, M., & Jardim, A. (1977). *The managerial woman.* Garden City, NY: Anchor/Doubleday.

Kadar, R. S. (2005, November). *Peer-mentoring relationships: Toward a non-hierarchical mentoring approach for women faculty.* Paper presented at the annual conference of the Association for the Study of Higher Education, Philadelphia.

Kanter, R. M. (1977). *Men and women of the corporation.* New York: Basic Books.

Kram, K. E. (1983). Phases of the mentoring relationship. *Academy of Management Journal, 26*(4), 608–625.

Kram, K. E. (1985). *Mentoring at work: Developmental relationships in organizational life.* Glenview, IL: Scott, Foresman.

Lagakis, V. (2001). *Female chief executive officers: A national study of the profile and career progression of female presidents/chancellors in public master's colleges and universities 1 and 2 in the United States.* Unpublished doctoral dissertation, Teachers College, Columbia University, New York.

Leach, M. T. (2000). *Career path profiles of female administrators in the University of North Carolina System.* Unpublished doctoral dissertation, North Carolina State University, Raleigh.

LeBlanc, D. (1993). Barriers to women's advancement into higher education administration. In P. T. Mitchell (Ed.), *Cracking the wall: Women in higher education administration* (pp. 41–49). Washington, DC: College and University Personnel Association.

Levinson, D. J., Darrow, C. N., Klein, E. B., Levinson, M. H., & McKee, B. (1978). *The seasons of a man's life.* New York: Ballantine.

Mattis, M. C. (2002). Best practices for retaining and advancing women professionals and managers. In R. J. Burke & D. L. Nelson (Eds.), *Advancing women in management: Progress and prospects* (pp. 309–332). Oxford, UK: Blackwell.

McDade, S. A. (1990). Planning for career improvement. In K. M. Moore & S. B. Twombly (Eds.), *Administrative careers and the marketplace* (pp. 47–55). San Francisco: Jossey-Bass.

McDade, S. A., & Walton, K. D. (2001). At the top of the faculty: Women as chief academic officers. In J. Niddifer & C. T. Bashaw (Eds.), *Women administrators in higher education: Historical and contemporary perspectives* (pp. 85–100). Albany, NY: SUNY Press.

McNeer, E. J. (1983). Two opportunities for mentoring: A study of women's career development in higher education administration. *Journal of the National Association for Women Deans, Administrators and Counselors, 47*(1), 8–13.

Merriam, S., & Thomas, T. (1986). The role of mentoring in the career development of community college presidents. *Community/Junior College Quarterly, 10,* 177–191.

Moore, K. M., & Amey, M. J. (1988). Some faculty leaders are born women. *New Directions for Student Services, 44,* 39–44.

Moore, K. M., & Salimbene, A. M. (1981). The dynamics of the mentor-protégé relationship in developing women as academic leaders. *Journal of Educational Equity and Leadership, 2,* 51–64.

Morrison, A. M., White, R. P., & Van Velsor, E. (1987). *Breaking the glass ceiling: Can women reach the top of America's largest corporations?* Reading, MA: Addison-Wesley.

Morrissey, M. M. (1997). *A qualitative study of the factors that influence the career advancement of female higher education administrators.* Unpublished doctoral dissertation, Seton Hall University, South Orange, NJ.

Mullen, E. J. (1994). Framing the mentoring relationship as an information exchange. *Human Resource Management Review, 4*(3), 257–281.

Perrewe, P. L., & Anthony, W. P. (2000). Political skill at work. *Organizational Dynamics, 28*(4), 25–37.

Phillip-Jones, L. L. (2001). *The new mentors and protégés.* Grass Valley, CA: Coalition of Counseling Centers/The Mentoring Group.

Reed-Taylor, J. (1998). *Career paths, mobility patterns, and experiences of two-year college women presidents of color.* Unpublished doctoral dissertation, University of Minnesota, Twin Cities.

Ross, M., & Green, M. F. (2000). *The American college president.* Washington, DC: American Council on Education.

Salimbene, A. M. (1982). *Pathways to the presidency: An examination of the careers of current college and university chief executives.* Unpublished doctoral dissertation, Pennsylvania State University, University Park.

Scandura, T. A. (1997). Mentoring and organizational justice: An empirical investigation. *Journal of Vocational Behavior, 51*(1), 58–69.

Shakeshaft, C. (1987). *Women in educational administration.* Newbury Park, CA: Sage.

Simeone, A. (1987). *Academic women working towards equality.* South Hadley, MA: Bergin & Garvey.

Touchton, J., Shavlik, D., & Davis, L. (1993). *Women in presidencies: A descriptive study of women college and university presidents.* Washington, DC: Office of Women in Higher Education/American Council on Education.

Trujillo-Sanchez, G. C. (1992). *The twenty-first century female academician: Beyond the glass ceiling.* Unpublished doctoral dissertation, Union Institute, Cincinnati, Ohio.

U.S. Bureau of Labor Statistics. (2008). *Employed persons by occupation, sex and age.* Retrieved March 11, 2009, from http://www.bls.gov/cps/cpsaat9.pdf

Vaughan, G. B. (1989). *Leadership in transition: The community college presidency.* New York: American Council on Education/Macmillan.

Vaughan, G. B. (1990). *Pathway to the presidency.* Washington, DC: Community College Press.

Wellington, S., & Spence, B. (2001). *Be your own mentor: Strategies from top women in business on the secrets of success.* New York: Random House.

Winship, S. P. (1992). *An analysis of gender differences in position paths of community college presidents.* Unpublished doctoral dissertation, University of Kansas, Lawrence.

Women CEOs. (2008). Retrieved March 11, 2009, from http://money.cnn.com/magazines/fortune/fortune500/2008/womenceos/

Zachary, Lois J. (2000). *The mentor's guide to facilitating effective learning relationships.* San Francisco: Jossey-Bass.

Zey, M. G. (1984). *The mentor connection.* Homewood, IL: Dow Jones-Irwin.

7

PREPARING WOMEN OF COLOR FOR LEADERSHIP

Perspectives on the American Council on Education Fellows Program

Caroline Sotello Viernes Turner and Janelle Kappes

P rofessional development opportunities in higher education are critical, especially for women seeking leadership positions in the field. According to *The Chronicle of Higher Education* (2005), 21.1% of college and university presidents in 2001 were women. Further, less than 13% of college presidents were members of underrepresented populations.

Despite the fact that women make up the majority of higher education students, women are underrepresented in all senior positions in higher education (Walton & McDade, 2001). Figures 7.1 and 7.2 compare college presidents by gender and racial/ethnic group, revealing that the overwhelming majority are White males. Further, women in chief academic officer positions remain anomalies, and most who rise to this critical position are the first of their gender in that role at their institution.

Women from underrepresented populations face barriers because of historical, cultural, and social factors that have shaped their experience and development in American society (Allen et al., 1991). Pervasive racist and sexist attitudes continue to limit educational opportunities for women of color. Moreover, women faculty may encounter obstacles that constrain their ability to move up the academic hierarchy.

The authors would like to express appreciation to all who took the time from their busy schedules to provide their perspectives and share information used in this study.

FIGURE 7.1
College and University Presidents by Race/Ethnicity, 2001

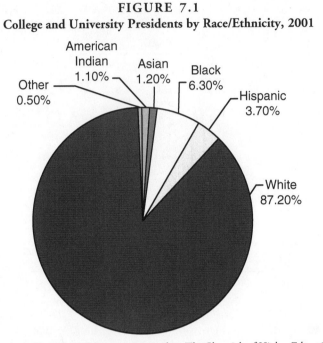

Source: American Council on Education, as cited in *The Chronicle of Higher Education* (2005). Characteristics of college presidents, 2001. *Almanac Edition, 2005–06, 52*(1), 25.

FIGURE 7.2
College and University Presidents by Race/Ethnicity and Gender, 2004

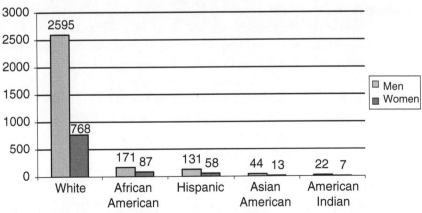

Source: Harvey, W. B. & Anderson, E. L. (2005). *Minorities in higher education: Twenty-first annual status report, 2003–2004.* Washington, DC: American Council on Education.

The number of women of color administrators pales in comparison with the rising number of underrepresented students entering higher education. Demographers indicate that the increasing number of minorities, especially Hispanics, are preparing for and going to college (Haro & Lara, 2003). High school graduates in Texas and California, two of the most populous states, are 50% Hispanic. Given the increasing number of Hispanic and other underrepresented students gaining access to colleges and universities, it is essential to employ minority staff to assist in attracting, socializing, and helping students matriculate (Haro & Lara).

This chapter examines one of several professional development and training programs, specifically the American Council on Education's ([ACE], n.d.) Fellows Program. We were particularly interested in examining the Fellows Program from the perspectives provided by women of color who were/are ACE Fellows. First, we provide an overview of several development programs for professionals seeking leadership opportunities in higher education.[1] Some programs are designed to provide leadership training for women, others focus on the development of racial/ethnic minorities, while still others provide opportunities for men and women of all racial/ethnic groups. The ACE Fellows Program fits into the latter category. The study's methodology, purpose, and results will also be presented, and we conclude with our interpretation of the results.

Professional Development and Training Programs in Higher Education

In 2005 Michael Coray (personal communication, November 18, 2005) disseminated a survey to determine the best training and development opportunities for women interested in leadership positions in higher education. He surveyed women via the Campus Women Lead Listserve[2] and posed the following question: What are the best training/development opportunities for women who want to become executive employees in higher education (i.e., deans and above)? Of the programs mentioned by respondents to his question, Bryn Mawr's Higher Education Resource Services ([HERS], n.d.), the ACE Fellows Program (ACE, n.d.), and the Harvard Graduate School of Education's ([HGSE], n.d.) Management Development Program (MDP) were noted most frequently.

Also included in our discussion is the American Association of State Colleges and Universities' ([AASCU], n.d.) Millennium Leadership Initiative (MLI) program. The MLI program was included because it focuses on leadership development training for men and women from underrepresented populations. The other programs noted in Coray's survey were not mentioned as frequently as the four above and thus will not be the focus of this chapter. Nonetheless, while examining the four programs noted above, it is useful to present some of the most common characteristics of several programs listed by Coray's survey respondents as well as other programs found in the literature.

Comparison of Leadership Programs and Institutes

Based on a review of program and institute Web sites, conversations with program representatives, and information from Coray's survey, the researchers examined 9 leadership program documents (Appendix 7.B) and created a data table to compare the programs (Appendix 7.C). Based on our information, 5 programs are identified that focus on leadership development for women; 1 is specific for women of color, 5 are for racial/ethnic minorities and/or to develop leadership for minority-serving institutions, and 10 do not specify programming for particular racial/ethnic or gender populations. Included in Appendix 7.C, not included in Coray's survey results, are the Kellogg Minority-Serving Institutions Leadership Fellows Program (KMFLP), the Leadership Education for Asian Pacifics and Asian Pacific Americans in Higher Education (LEAP/APAHE), the Leadership Development Program for Higher Education (LDPHE), and Virginia's Higher Ground Women's Leadership Development Program. The KMFLP is an important initiative focused on leadership development for tribal colleges, historically Black colleges and universities, and Hispanic-serving institutions. The LEAP/APAHE leadership program provides development opportunities for Asian Pacific Americans in higher education. As we describe and briefly discuss the most frequently cited programs (as identified by women participating in Coray's survey), we will highlight the competitiveness and cost of entering as well as participating in the programs. A longer discussion of the ACE Fellows Program (ACE, n.d.), the focus of this chapter, concludes this section.

Bryn Mawr's HERS

The HERS (n.d.) program is held for 4 weeks each summer at the Bryn Mawr campus in Bryn Mawr, Pennsylvania. Begun in 1976, this residential program focuses on improving the status of women in middle and executive levels of higher education administration. Each summer 75–80 women faculty and administrators are engaged in a rigorous program focused on the development of skills in educational administration. A primary program goal is to foster a network of peers and mentors who provide information, support, contacts, and resources. Women also receive training and instruction regarding institutional environments; budgeting and finance; strategic planning; and political, social, and economic trends in higher education.

The HERS program has an extensive application process. Interested participants must complete an application form, submit a current résumé, and provide an organizational chart from their home institution that indicates their position. The application form asks applicants to provide a profile of their institution, information about their professional careers, accomplishments, service to their institution, and awards and honors received; applicants must also provide the amount of funding their institution will provide for the program. Additionally, two references, including one from the president or chief executive officer of the institution must be completed on the participant's behalf. Finally, interested participants are required to write a letter describing their strengths and why attending the HERS program will help them achieve their professional goals.

The 2009 fee of $7,900 for the HERS program includes a $75 nonrefundable application fee and includes room, board, tuition, and instructional materials. For women who choose not to live on the Bryn Mawr campus, the cost of the program is $4,900. Applicants are encouraged to request financial support from their institutions, and nearly all of the participants are funded in full or in part by their home institution.

Harvard Graduate School of Education's MDP

The Harvard MDP, founded in 1986, targets male and female higher education professionals in the early years of their professional careers (HGSE, n.d.). This 2-week program is described as preparing its participants to become more effective managers as well as to develop a more forward-thinking, reflective leadership style. The program is designed for deans, directors, and other administrators who head units and want to become better at managing their department. The MDP believes it is critical for administrators to master seven key topics: leadership, fostering innovation and change, planning, diversity and community, financial management, institutional value and integrity, and professional renewal.

The application process for the MDP is also quite extensive. Interested participants must complete the MDP application form, which includes several essay questions pertaining to the applicants' professional goals and their objectives for the program. The key to admission to the MDP is a personal statement from each applicant that clearly indicates what the applicant would gain from the MDP and why the program is appropriate at this stage of the applicant's professional career. Applicants are also responsible for securing two recommendations, one from an immediate supervisor and a second from a colleague who can comment on professional accomplishments and future potential. The 2009 comprehensive program fee for the MDP is $6,885, which covers tuition, room, meals, and instructional materials.

The MLI Program

Of the four programs reviewed in this section, the MLI, founded in 1998 by the AASCU (n.d.), is designed specifically to strengthen the preparation and eligibility of people who are traditionally underrepresented in the roles of president and chancellor. This leadership initiative consists of a 4-day institute each summer followed by a year-long mentoring program. During the institute, the program exposes protégés to a variety of issues essential to the presidential career path, such as search process strategies and skills and assessment of career path options.

The mentoring program component formally links graduates with presidents and chancellors who serve as a resource and provide counsel throughout the search process and the days of their first presidency. The goal of MLI is to serve higher education by preparing the next generation of campus chief executive officers in the public and private sectors. MLI does not just prepare one for the presidency but helps candidates succeed once in the position. In order to be considered for the program, applicants must receive a nomination from an AASCU member president or an endorsement from an AASCU member president (if the applicant is nominated by someone other than an AASCU president). A presidential participant selection subcommittee consisting of campus presidents on the Executive Planning Committee makes decisions about the applicants for this program.

The coordinators of this program invite nationally recognized faculty to participate in the 4-day institute. One of the hallmarks of the program is that it strives to maintain a one-to-one ratio between participants and faculty. The program involves an intense, targeted curriculum focusing on job-searching skills, effective communication, financial skills, and career planning. Most importantly, the program fosters a network of peers and mentors for each participant. Finally, the participants are provided with an advisor-guided professional development plan and interactive counseling sessions.

The 2009 registration fee for MLI is $1,800 for individuals from AASCU member institutions and $2,800 for individuals from AASCU nonmember institutions. The registration fee includes four nights' accommodation and meals and instructional materials.

Only 5 years after MLI was founded to tackle the issue of the shrinking numbers of people of color in the college presidential pipeline, the institute has helped 20 men and women—19 from underrepresented minorities—rise to the presidency. Another 26 MLI protégés have attained the rank of provost or vice president. And 18 others have reached the rank of associate provost, assistant vice president, dean—or left academia entirely to take senior leadership posts in the private sector, according to Marvalene Hughes, one of the founders of MLI (Hamilton, 2004).

The ACE Fellows Program

History. Founded in 1918, ACE is the nation's largest higher education association, representing more than 1,600 college and university presidents and more than 200 related associations nationwide. It seeks to provide leadership and a unifying voice on key higher education issues and influence public policy through advocacy, research, and program initiatives. The ACE Fellows Program began in 1965.

According to Marlene Ross, program director, the 2005–2006 class was heralded as the most diverse in ACE history because it included 10 African Americans, 6 Hispanics, 7 from community colleges, 4 from baccalaureate institutions, 11 from master's institutions, and 15 from doctorate degree–granting institutions. Of those who have participated in the first 40 years of the program, more than 300 Fellows have gone on to serve as chief executive officers of more than 350 colleges and universities (M. Ross, personal communication, February 1, 2006). In addition, more than 1,100 have served as provosts or vice presidents and more than 1,100 have served as deans (ACE, 2005).

Overview. The ACE Fellows Program is the only national, individualized, long-term professional development program in higher education that provides on-the-job learning.

The Fellows Program enables participants to immerse themselves in the culture, policies, and decision-making processes of another institution. ACE Fellows spend an extended period of time on another campus, working directly with presidents and other senior leaders observing how they address strategic planning, resource allocation, development, policy, and other issues. As a result, the ACE Fellows Program is described as one of the most comprehensive leadership development programs in American higher education today.

Program description. ACE Fellows design an individualized learning plan for the year, based on issues jointly identified by the nominating institution and the Fellow. When Fellows work on site at their host campuses, they pursue various projects that coincide with their own interests as well as those of their home and host institutions. The host institutions also keep the Fellows informed of issues and projects on their institutional agendas. The plan includes immersing oneself in the off-campus experience, working on issues identified with the nominating institution, reading professional literature, visiting colleges and universities throughout the country and abroad, attending national meetings, and other activities.

Fellows work with their nominating institutions to design their off-campus learning experience at the host institutions. This aspect of the program is intentionally designed to help Fellows achieve concrete skills that they can then take back to their nominating institution upon their return. This experience enables Fellows to observe firsthand how another institution and its senior administrators lead the institution and deal with change. The Fellows are mentored by a team of experienced administrators—usually presidents and vice presidents. Regular progress reports serve as checkpoints to assess the Fellows' experiences based on the Learning Plan and to revise the plan as necessary.

In addition to placement at an off-campus site, the program staff organizes three required seminars in August (Opening Seminar), January (Midyear Seminar), and June (Closing Seminar) at various locations throughout the United States. These week-long sessions incorporate active-learning pedagogy (e.g., case studies, simulations, problem-solving workshops, role playing, lectures/small-group discussions, and preseminar readings) to address critical leadership issues in higher education. The free-flowing dialogues among Fellows, national leaders, and other experts enrich the unique learning experiences at the seminars. The Fellows' mentors from their host campuses are invited to attend and participate in the seminars.

Application process. The process for acceptance into the ACE Fellows Program is one of the most rigorous and challenging. Interested applicants must complete application forms that require responses to essay questions asking potential Fellows to assess their experiences and readiness for leadership, as well as submission of an analysis of a critical issues case provided in the application materials. Further, applicants cannot directly apply but must receive a nomination from their campus president or chief academic officer. Campuses can nominate up to two individuals each year. Along with a résumé, interested applicants must provide letters from four professional references and an official transcript. According to one of the respondents in this study, the rigor and competitiveness of the application process continues after the paperwork has been completed. Once the required items are submitted, selected applicants are invited to Washington, DC, for several rounds of required and intensive face-to-face interviews with sitting campus presidents, vice presidents, and ACE staff. Questions are posed to determine the nominated applicant's understanding of the basic organizational structure of higher education and critical issues facing the field. In addition, interviewees must verbally articulate their readiness for leadership and commitment to their development as leaders in higher education.

Program fees. Program costs vary, depending on the placement option selected: year-long placement, semester-long placement, and periodic visits to other campuses. In the year-long and semester-long placements, the participant spends a year or semester at a host campus. Periodic visits involve several month-long visits to one other campus throughout the year. However, one stipulation applies to all placements: The nominating institution funds the Fellow's salary and benefits for the duration of the fellowship (year or semester) and covers all interview and placement process expenses.

In 2009–2010, for year-long placements, the host institution pays the $7,500 program fee and provides the Fellow with a professional development budget of up to $14,000 to attend seminars and national meetings and to visit other campuses. For semester-long placements, the nominating and host institutions each pay $3,750 toward the $7,500 program fee, and each institution contributes one half of the professional development budget ($7,000 per institution), which enables Fellows to attend seminars and national meetings and to visit other campuses. And for periodic visits, the nominating institution pays the $7,500 program fee and provides the Fellow with a professional development budget of up to $14,000 to attend seminars and national meetings and to visit other campuses.

Women of Color and Their Perspectives on the ACE Fellows Program

Purpose and Methodology

As exemplified by the 2005–2006 class, progress is being made toward racial/ethnic diversity within fellowship cohorts. Nonetheless, program representatives and study participants indicate that more must be done to address the lack of women of color served by ACE and other leadership development programs. Since the inception of the ACE Fellows Program, based on the data received for this study from the ACE Fellows office, less than 5% of the participants have been identified as women of color. Further research will yield a higher percentage as the data set identifying women of color participants is being updated (M. Ross, personal communication, January 31, 2006).

The purpose of this study was to examine the experiences of this small cadre of current or past women of color participants in the ACE Fellows Program. In November 2005, we disseminated a survey via e-mail to the 71 alumnae and current participants in the ACE Fellows Program who were identified as women of color. The names of the participants were provided by the ACE Fellows Program office. Participants were asked to respond to questions concerning their experiences in and as a result of the ACE Fellows Program (Appendix 7.A). Participants were given about 2 weeks to respond to the survey questionnaire.

We asked study participants to respond to the questions via e-mail. As we received questionnaires, we immediately copied the responses into new coded documents to protect respondents' confidentiality. In order to clarify some responses, we made follow-up phone calls to those who said we could contact them. The women who chose to participate in the study were each assigned an alphabetic character (A–Q) as a code for their questionnaire responses. In total, we received 17 completed questionnaires, representing about 25% of the invited participants.

Survey Results

Initial survey questions asked respondents to provide the year they participated in the ACE Fellows Program and to indicate their racial/ethnic identification.

As evident from Figure 7.3, the majority of the respondents were within 5 years of their ACE Fellows experience.

Several women indicated more than one racial/ethnic background. For instance, Respondent J indicated that she was African American with Hispanic heritage. In these cases, the researchers assigned the respondents to both ethnic groups: Hispanic/Latina and African American.

As indicated by Figure 7.4, over 60% (13) of those who responded gave African American for their racial or ethnic background. About 24% (4) of the respondents gave a Hispanic/Latina background for their ethnicity, with 12% (2) saying they were Asian American.

FIGURE 7.3
Survey Participants by ACE Cohort Year

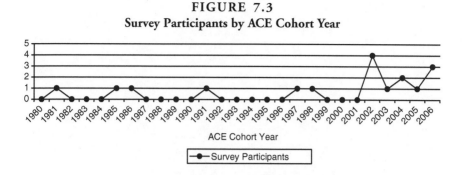

Figure 7.5 provides the current professional positions of respondents. While one respondent said she was a president, the majority of respondents were vice presidents/provosts, associate vice presidents/provosts, or deans on their campuses. Two of the participants gave professor as their current title.

Trend Analysis

As part of this survey, the respondents described their perceptions of the ACE Fellows Program in terms of its strengths, challenges, and impact on their professional careers.

ACE Fellows Program strengths. Nearly all of the respondents noted that networking opportunities and interaction with senior leaders in higher education were the greatest benefits of the ACE Fellows Program. Respondent C stated, "Meeting many presidents and other leaders who gave me time

FIGURE 7.4
Survey Participants by Race

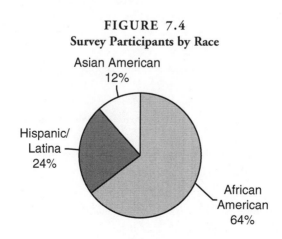

FIGURE 7.5
Survey Participants by Current Professional Title

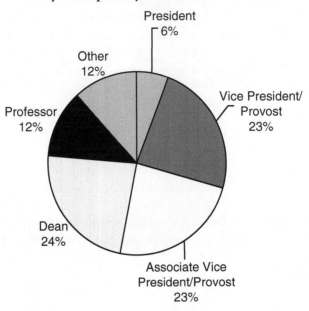

because I was a Fellow" was the most positive aspect of the Fellows Program. Respondent B concurred and added, "The ACE network/friendships were a direct connection to my present position."

The second most positive experience for these women of color were the workshops and seminars provided during the program. Respondent H noted, "I thoroughly enjoyed the workshops on strategic planning." Nearly as important as the seminars were the discussions generated by them; Respondent D remarked, "The discussions made me aware of issues that I had not explored before (budgets, system issues, articulation issues, etc.)." Respondents noted that the diversity in their Fellows classes led to rich discussions about a variety of postsecondary systems and methods. Nonetheless, two respondents stated they felt the seminars were too narrowly focused on 4-year institutions.

ACE Fellows Program challenges and recommendations. With regard to Fellows Program challenges, the site selection process was mentioned numerous times. As noted earlier, one component of the ACE Fellows Program involves spending an extended period of time at another institution working with senior administrators and becoming immersed in that institution's culture. Thus, for women with families, this tended to be extremely challenging. Respondent F noted, "I limited myself to basically [one region], while there were colleges further [away] I would have enjoyed." For those who chose to stay close to their home institution, common issues often arose. As Respondent H candidly observed, "The decision to remain at home and in the same city for my fellowship [was the most challenging experience for me]. It was difficult trying to separate from my home institution for the year and I regret not going away further even though it would have been a major sacrifice for my family."

Thus, participation in the ACE Fellows Program requires commitment of significant resources—fiscal and time—from the host and home institutions and from the individual. Many women in the study mentioned that the placement options were the most challenging aspect of the program because of familial obligations. For instance, Respondent C stated that while the Fellowship was a great experience, there should be other less time-intensive opportunities for professional development for women of color.

Further, women of color may hesitate to ask their home institution for such a large financial commitment. In addition to the costs we have already described, nominating institutions may have to cover an ACE Fellow's position responsibilities while he or she is away from campus. Some institutions with an unsupportive environment for women of color and/or because of a lack of financial resources may not consider providing such an opportunity for them. According to Canul (2003), while it may be acceptable in the dominant culture to ask for additional resources, some women of color, particularly Latinas with strong cultural values, may experience a sense of discomfort in asking for resources and risking the shame of receiving a negative response to their request.

Another common challenge mentioned by the respondents was their perception that issues specifically related to women of color were minimized. Respondent B frankly observed that there was "a trivialization of key areas related to race and equality during seminars, discussions, conferences, and activities." Further, Respondent O received an indication that she would need to subdue her ethnicity in order to succeed as a leader in higher education. This challenge, the minimization of issues related to women of color, led to a recommendation for the Fellows Program to invite more women of color to facilitate workshop and seminar presentations.

This recommendation also addresses a concern by many of the respondents that women of color have different needs and issues that should be addressed throughout the ACE Fellows experience. Respondent J emphatically stated, "I do think separate sessions for them [women of color] on women and leadership in higher education as part of the ACE fellowship Program should be part of the Program." Echoing Respondent J's comments, Respondent P stated that the single most important way to improve the Fellows Program would be to bring in women of color to facilitate workshops and sessions throughout the year.

Respondents mentioned the importance of the two women of color summits (not part of the ACE Fellows Program but jointly sponsored by the ACE Office of Women in Higher Education and the Center for Advancement of Racial and Ethnic Equity as programs that provided the type of exposure they needed to gain a further understanding of the issues they may face in the academy while providing inspirational stories from women of color who had attained the presidency. Respondent K noted that the summit was the most transformative professional development experience that she had ever experienced.

Mentoring and the ACE Fellows Program. Mentoring relationships have played a significant role for most of the Fellows. Respondent K stated, "Being mentored by a VP for Academic Affairs while a Fellow at my host institution built my knowledge, skills, and abilities, making me more competitive for my current position in Academic Affairs." Further, those who received great mentorship often reflected that they felt compelled to mentor others. Respondent K noted, "The Fellows Program has amplified my ability to mentor and I have continued to mentor a number of individuals in one form or another." Other respondents noted that because the Fellows Program is widely known, they had been sought after as mentors. Respondent O noted, "I do receive calls from those who know I've participated in ACE and need a mentor. I also have mentored several individuals interested in the ACE Fellowship."

Relevant to the Fellows Program, one recommendation mentioned several times by the respondents was that ACE should formalize a mentoring program for women of color during and after the Fellows experience. When asked what would improve the Fellows Program, Respondent A noted, "More mentors that are women of color as part of the Program." Respondent H stated, "Solicit the support of more women of color mentors," and Respondent L echoed, "Establish a more formal mentoring program with former Fellows of color."

However, there were also several comments regarding mentoring after the Fellows experience. Respondent I observed, "The Fellows Program was wonderful and quite timely for me personally and professionally. More assistance is needed 'post-Fellowship' with mentoring, coaching, and career ascension." And Respondent I was not alone; other respondents also noted a "post-Fellowship experience" when returning to their home campuses that was described by some as "alienation" and others as "just plain strange." Even though Fellows are expected to return to their home campuses, colleagues are surprised to see them back in their former position. Many feel that the Fellow would return to, or leave for, a higher-level administrative position.

According to most of the respondents, mentors for women of color seeking leadership positions in higher education are generally lacking, which serves as a major obstacle to their upward mobility. When asked about the outlook for women of color in the coming decade, Respondent L noted, "Increased opportunities may be on the horizon; much will depend on women in leadership positions and mentors supporting continued nomination and hiring of women of color." Respondent D simply summarized, "I hope more senior women of color give back to help those in the pipeline."

Perceived outlook for women of color in the coming decade. Despite lack of mentors and other obstacles for women of color seeking leadership positions in higher education, the majority of the respondents indicated they were cautiously optimistic when asked about the future for women of color leaders in the next decade. Respondent K observed, "I think it is promising as long as there continue to be programs like the Fellows Program and related ACE programs. First, however, women of color must have opportunities to come up successfully through the ranks across all disciplines of the professoriate." Other respondents were not so optimistic and listed the "chilly climate" and male-dominated field as reasons for their views. One interesting note is that the Hispanic women seemed to express a less-optimistic outlook than African American women respondents when assessing the future for women of color and leadership in the coming decade. Two of the three Hispanic respondents noted that the outlook for women of color in the coming decade was "not positive" and "not encouraging."

Relevance of the ACE Fellows Program to future women of color. Overall, all but one of the respondents indicated that they would recommend this program to other women of color. Most noted the prestige of the program and the networking opportunities as reasons for recommending this program. Three of the respondents also stated that despite any shortcomings, the ACE Fellows Program is the best training and development program that exists. Respondent J summed up respondent opinions when she stated, "I think it is still the most comprehensive program of higher education administrative leadership. I think being associated with ACE still brings clout and a powerful network. I also feel that the alumni network is a resource for women of color." The one respondent, O, who indicated that she would not recommend this program, stated there are simply better training opportunities for women of color than the Fellows Program. According to Respondent O, "ACE seems tailored to producing the same types of leaders we've had in the past that fit the system; not new leaders to address the latest issues. This Program best prepares young, white males to fit into a male-dominated system." Several women also commented on the lack of representation of women of color in their Fellows cohort. For example, Respondent C stated, "Of course we are not there yet with African American women, but there were no Latinas in my class, no Native women, no Asian women."

Interpretation of Results

As in some of the literature describing the status of women of color in higher education, results of this examination of the ACE Fellows Program through the experiences of women of color yield concerns/themes also discussed in the literature: the importance of effective mentorship, the lack of emphasis on women of color issues in leadership development programs, the potential ramifications with regard to a potential leader's outspokenness on racial and ethnic issues, and the prevalent theme that the ACE Fellows Program as well as other such programs continue to be important in the professional development of women and people of color.

The Importance of Effective Mentorship

The importance of a mentor relationship was a constant theme for nearly all the participants in this study. Participants noted the critical role played by mentors with regard to imparting informal and formal knowledge. One participant noted that she learned not only budgeting, management, and leadership skills, but also how to navigate through delicate political situations through her mentor. Other participants stated that the lack of an available and willing mentor at their host institution was detrimental to their overall ACE Fellowship experience. Likewise, the literature review revealed a similar theme. Judson (1999) keenly observed, "I earned my experience the hard way, without a mentor" (p. 91). As McDemmond (1999) noted, "We [senior administrators who are of color] . . . must take it upon ourselves to help each other achieve and to increase our numbers. We must be willing to go the extra mile and assist other minorities in obtaining, retaining, and advancing in administrative positions in higher education" (p. 80).

The Lack of Emphasis on Women of Color Issues Throughout Leadership Programs

While opportunities such as the ACE Fellowship can play important roles in leadership development, especially for people of color, new efforts may be required to establish programs that identify and develop minorities for leadership positions in higher education (Haro & Lara, 2003). Judson (1999) observed, "There [is] an added dimension of difficulty and complexity for a minority administrator" (p. 89). There are many reasons that women of color experience multiple challenges as they attempt to move up in academe (Ideta & Cooper, 1998; Rains, 1998; Turner, 2002), and women of color, judged by the response of the participants in this study, need a leadership program that addresses these issues. One criticism echoed by study participants was the lack of emphasis on issues that directly pertain to the experience of women of color in academe. Respondents indicate that topics related to equality, diversity, and social justice in higher education can be given a more prominent place in the curriculum for the three required seminars as well as the yearly Council of Fellows meetings and the ACE annual meeting. They also noted the lack of women of color who serve as ACE workshop/seminar leaders and mentors. As part of the ACE Fellows Program, the establishment of a more formal mentoring program for all Fellows of color in addition to seminars and workshops addressing concerns for women of color in academe was recommended. One respondent articulates the idea of the program as merely cloning the existing White male and female leadership styles that will only produce that same result: few women of color at the helm.

Given these respondent perceptions, interestingly enough, the ACE Fellows Program office reports that "more than half of the evaluations each year indicate that we spend too much time on diversity issues" (M. Ross, personal communication, January 30, 2006). Furthermore, a review of selected 2004–2006 ACE Fellows Program seminar agendas, provided by the ACE Fellows office in Washington, DC, reveals 18 individual women of color (some participated more than once) as featured speakers, panelists, focus group leaders, case study team members, and a commencement speaker. We did not review ACE Fellows Program documents thoroughly or systematically, but this information demonstrates efforts by the ACE Fellows Program to diversify its curricular offerings as well as its speakers. There is a disconnection between study respondent perceptions and these efforts by the ACE Fellows Program. On one hand, some respondents participating in the ACE Fellows Program prior to 2004 underscored the lack of women of color as workshop speakers. On the other hand, several 2004–2006 respondents state there is a continued need for sessions to discuss issues specific to women of color. Research needs to be done to further explicate these findings.

Potential Ramifications With Regard to Outspokenness on Racial and Ethnic Issues

Speaking out regarding racial/ethnic matters, whether formally or informally, can have negative repercussions, especially for women of color. Three women in the study stated their perception that they would need to "tone down" or focus less on issues central to people of color in order to move through the ranks of academe. Similarly, McDemmond (1999) observed that her outspokenness and involvement in minority professional organizations may have led to misperceptions that all her actions and decisions were racially motivated when in reality her decisions were based on her belief systems. The women in the study who commented on this theme were quick to note that issues for people of color, such as affirmative action and immigration, affect *everyone* in higher education, not just individuals from underrepresented groups.

The Importance of the ACE Fellows Program

Overwhelmingly, the participants in the study rated the ACE Fellows Program as beneficial; all but one of the participants stated they would recommend this program to other women of color. According to Walton and McDade's (2001) survey of women in the role of chief academic officers, nearly 10% of the participants in their survey said they had participated in the ACE Fellows Program. The benefits of the ACE Fellows Program, particularly the mentorship and networking opportunities, the seminars, and the intensive, extended period on another campus are repeatedly noted by study participants. Further, according to them, the ACE Fellows Program's reputation has led to promotions, job nominations, and an extended network of friends and colleagues across the country.

Additional Themes From the Study Participants

There were two additional themes reflected by the participants in this study: the hopefulness for future women of color in senior-level administrative positions and the importance of the ACE Fellows network. Despite the challenges and barriers facing women of color, the majority of the participants remained cautiously optimistic regarding the future of women of color in senior-level administrative positions. Several participants went on to mention the importance of mentoring with regard to increasing the number of women of color in the pipeline.

Networking, and specifically the ACE Fellows network, was noted several times throughout the study. It provided personal and professional benefits to all of the women in the study. The ACE network led directly to job promotions and nominations for some of the participants. Other participants noted that connections formed through the network assisted with research, job searches, and created mentoring opportunities.

Lack of Women of Color Represented Across Professorial Ranks

An important point noted time and again in the literature is the lack of women of color ascending through the professorial ranks of academe. One study participant observed that this is a major barrier contributing to the lack of women of color in academic leadership positions. In other words, the pathway to the presidency for most campus leaders includes the successful navigation up through the faculty ranks. When asked about the future of women of color in higher education, Participant K stated, "I think it is promising. . . . First, however, women of color must have opportunities to come up successfully through the ranks across all disciplines of the professoriate. Then they and their institutions must see that they have opportunities for line experience leading faculty in academic departments on up. It will take an enlightened system for all of this to happen." The underrepresentation of women of color in assistant, associate, and full professor ranks is well documented (*The Chronicle of Higher Education*, 2005; Harvey & Anderson, 2005), and there is a body of literature citing the myriad of barriers women of color must overcome to succeed in academe (McDemmond, 1999; Rains, 1998; Turner, 2002).

Conclusion

Women of color responding to this survey overwhelmingly support the ACE Fellows Program and express the value of their experience with regard to its mentoring and networking components. However, many criticize the program for not addressing issues they face just by being women of color in leadership roles.

Notwithstanding the critical role leadership development programs play in the preparation of future campus leaders, furthering leadership opportunities for women of color does not fall solely on the shoulders of such programs. Respondent statements and literature cited in this chapter point to the important role higher education institutions must play in the education, hiring, and development of women of color leaders. Women of color need the support of their home institutions as they progress toward full professor and senior-level academic administration. For example, several of the programs noted in this study, including the ACE Fellows Program, require a nomination from senior leadership at their home institution to even be considered for the program. If women of color with requisite academic rank and prior leadership experiences are not nominated, then they are unavailable to be selected.

The ACE Fellows Program has been in existence for 41 years. Our study respondents underscore the critical importance of this program in preparing leaders for the 21st century. We believe that the strengths and challenges as well as recommendations identified here point to ways in which the ACE Fellows Program as well as other such programs can ensure their continued and growing role in the preparation of the next generation of women of color for leadership in academe.

Notes

1. The researchers acknowledge that this discussion does not include all leadership development programs.

2. The results of Coray's survey were sent to one of the authors through the Campus Women Lead Listserve (campuswomenlead@list.aacu.org). Campus Women Lead is the Web site of the National Initiative for Women in Higher Education (NIWHE), a unique grassroots alliance promoting a multicultural women-led agenda for the sustained transformation of higher education for the 21st century. The American Association of Colleges and Universities (AACU) is the administrative home for the National Initiative. This Web site seeks to capture the range of institutional changes that promote gender equity in higher education. It features sections on leadership, teaching/learning/research, work/life, campus/community connections, and women's networks.

References

Allen, W., Epps, E., Guillory, E., Suh, S., Bonus-Hammarth, M., & Stassen, M. (1991). Outsiders within: Race, gender, and faculty status in U.S. higher education. In P. Altbah & K. Lomotey (Eds.), *The racial crisis in American higher education* (pp. 189–220). Albany, NY: SUNY Press.

American Association of State Colleges and Universities. (n.d.). *The Millennium Leadership Institute: Preparing the next generation of leaders.* Retrieved November 15, 2005, from http://www.aascu.org/programs/mli/2009/

American Council on Education. (2005). *Forty college faculty and administrators named to ACE Fellows Program.* Retrieved December 14, 2005, from http://www.acenet.edu/AM/Template.cfm?Section=Home&CONTENTID=7027&TEMPLATE=/CM/ContentDisplay.cfm

American Council on Education. (n.d.). *ACE Fellows Program.* Retrieved November 1, 2005, from http://www.acenet.edu/Content/NavigationMenu/ProgramsSer vices/FellowsProgram/index.htm

Canul, K. (2003). Latina/o cultural values and the academy: Latinas navigating through the administrative role. In J. Castellanos & L. Jones (Eds.), *The majority in the minority: Expanding the representation of Latina/o faculty, administrators and students in higher education* (pp. 167–175). Sterling, VA: Stylus.

The Chronicle of Higher Education. (2005, August). The nation: Faculty and staff. *Almanac 2005–06, 52*(1), 26.

Hamilton, K. (2004, August). Cracking the "cement wall" to the college presidency: Millennium Leadership Initiative prepares minority higher education profession- als for the administrative ranks. *Black Issues in Higher Education, 21,* 7–22.

Haro, R., & Lara, J. F. (2003). Latinos and administrative positions in American higher education. In J. Castellanos & L. Jones (Eds.), *The majority in the minor- ity: Expanding the representation of Latina/o faculty, administrators and students in higher education* (pp. 153–165). Sterling, VA: Stylus.

Harvard Graduate School of Education. (n.d.). *Programs in professional education.* Retrieved March 11, 2009, from http://www.gse.harvard.edu/~ppe/highered/ programs/mdp.html

Harvey, W. B., & Anderson, E. L. (2005). *Minorities in higher education: Twenty- first annual status report 2003–2004.* Washington, DC: American Council on Edu- cation.

Higher Education Resource Services. (n.d.). *HERS Bryn Mawr Summer Institute.* Retrieved March 11, 2009, from http://www.hersnet.org/Institutes.asp

Ideta, L., & Cooper, J. (1998). Asian women leaders of higher education: Stories of strength and self discovery. In L. Christian-Smith & K. Kellor (Eds.), *Everyday knowledge and uncommon truths: Women of the academy* (pp. 129–146). Boulder, CO: Westview Press.

Judson, H. (1999). A meaningful contribution. In W. Harvey (Ed.), *Grass roots and glass ceilings: African American administrators in predominantly white colleges and universities* (pp. 83–112). Albany, NY: SUNY Press.

McDemmond, M. (1999). On the outside looking in. In W. B. Harvey (Ed.), *Grass roots and glass ceilings: African American administrators in predominantly white col- leges and universities* (pp. 71–82). Albany, NY: SUNY Press.

Rains, F. (1998). Dancing on the sharp edge of the sword: Women faculty of color in white academe. In L. Christian-Smith & K. Kellor (Eds.), *Everyday knowledge and uncommon truths: Women of the academy* (pp. 147–173). Boulder, CO: Westview Press.

Turner, C. S. (2002). Women of color in academe: Living with multiple marginality. *Journal of Higher Education, 73*(1), 74–93.

Walton, K. D., & McDade, S. A. (2001). At the top of the faculty: Women as chief academic officers. In J. Nidiffer & C. T. Bashaw (Eds.), *Women administrators in higher education* (pp. 85–100). Albany, NY: SUNY Press.

ACE Fellows Survey Questionnaire

1. In what year did you participate in the ACE Fellows Program?
2. How do you self-identify in terms of your racial/ethnic background? Please specify.
3. What is your current position (Faculty, Department Chair, Dean, Vice President, etc.)?
4. How has the ACE Fellows Program led to subsequent professional career opportunities for you?
5. Briefly describe your most positive experience(s) in the ACE Fellows Programs.
6. Briefly describe your most challenging experience(s) in the ACE Fellows Program.
7. How has the ACE Fellows Program helped you gain the skills and knowledge required to lead a college or university (i.e., informal knowledge vs. formal knowledge)?
8. How has your participation in the ACE Fellows Program helped you to establish mentoring relationships?
9. What do you see as the outlook for women of color as leaders in the coming decade?
10. How could the ACE Fellows Program improve to better engage women of color and assist them with their progression?
11. Would you recommend this Program to other women of color? Why or why not?
12. In what ways has your ACE Fellows experience contributed to (or failed to contribute to) your legitimacy as an academic leader?
13. How did your ACE Fellows experience contribute to your sense of self-efficacy as a leader?
14. Please add anything else about your ACE Fellowship experience that you would like to include.
15. If you feel comfortable, please share your name and e-mail address so that I can contact you if I have additional questions.

Leadership Program Documents Reviewed

American Council on Education (2004, June 5–11). ACE Fellows Program, Closing Seminar Agenda: The Business of Higher Education.

American Council on Education (2004, August 27–September 4). ACE Fellows Program, Opening Seminar Agenda.

American Council on Education (2005, January 7–13). ACE Fellows Program Agenda, Mid-Year Seminar.

American Council on Education (2005, June 4–10). ACE Fellows Program, Closing Seminar Agenda.

American Council on Education (2005, August 24–30). ACE Fellows Program, Opening Seminar Agenda.

American Council on Education (2006, January 6–12). ACE Fellows Program, Mid-Year Seminar Agenda.

American Council on Education (n.d.). *The American Council on Education's Fellows Program*. Retrieved March 12, 2009, from http://www.acenet.edu/Content/NavigationMenu/ProgramsServices/FellowsProgram/index.htm

Harvard Management Development Program. (n.d.). Higher Education Programs. Retrieved November 10, 2005, from http://www.gse.harvard.edu/ppe/highered/programs/mdp.html

Summer Institute for Women in Higher Education. (n.d.). About HERS. Retrieved November 10, 2005, from http://www.brynmawr.edu/summerinstitute/HERS overview.html

APPENDIX 7.C

Leadership Program Information Chart

Program	Overview	Sponsor	Application Process	Duration	Fees	Class Size	Target Audience	Unique Aspects
Leadership Institutes/Programs								
ACE Fellows Program http://www.acenet.edu/ programs/fellows	Begun in 1965, ACE Fellows spend an extended period of time on another campus, working directly with presidents and other senior leaders to observe how they address strategic planning, resource allocation, development, policy, and other issues and challenges.	American Council on Education	Application form, candidate and institutional profile, confidential evaluations completed by references, form completed by president or CAO	Year-long placement, semester-long placement, or periodic visits	$7,500 fee in 2009–2010, plus a $14,000 professional development budget–$6,000 (varies by duration)	35	The ACE Fellows Program seeks candidates who display a solid record of achievement and some leadership experience as vice president, dean, associate dean, department chair, or another position that required them to assume leadership responsibilities.	Mentoring by senior leadership at another institution.
Harvard Graduate School of Education, Management Development Program http://www.gse.harvard.edu/ppe/highered/ programs/mdp.html	MDP provides innovative and practical ideas about critical management challenges facing midlevel administrators in the early years of their professional careers. The program encourages thinking beyond the confines of one's own discipline and area of administrative responsibility. MDP prepares participants to become more effective managers.	Harvard Graduate School of Education	Institution information, unit information, reference information, current job responsibilities, professional experience, educational background, honors or distinctions, professional challenges statement, anticipated contribution statement, supervisor endorsement, colleague recommendation	2 weeks	$6,885 in 2009, comprehensive fee covering program, materials, accommodations, and meals.	75–80	MDP is designed for deans, directors, and other administrators who are good at leading their units and who want to get even better. MDP is most appropriate for midlevel administrators in the early years of a responsible leadership position.	Critical management issue focus, including human resource management, planning, and effective leadership.

APPENDIX 7.C (Continued)

Program	Overview	Sponsor	Application Process	Duration	Fees	Class Size	Target Audience	Unique Aspects
Leadership Institutes/Programs								
Donna Bourassa Mid-Level Management Institute (ACPA) http:// www.myacpa.org/ pd/mmi/	Now in its 8th year, the institute is an educational program for those desiring to strengthen their skills and understand changing campus dynamics in order to advance in the profession.	American College Personnel Association	No application; registration fee	5 days	ACPA/AFA members: $525; nonmembers: $645 in 2009	50	Midlevel managers	The institute has an open registration process. Admissions are not selective; the institute has a reunion for all classes at annual convention.
President's Academic Leadership Institute (PALI)– University of Missouri System State-Specific Program http:// www.umsystem .edu/pali/	PALI is a systemwide effort jointly sponsored by UM Human Resources and UM Academic Affairs to improve leadership capacity throughout the University of Missouri. PALI offers a variety of programs for academic and administrative leaders.	University of Missouri System	Endorsement from department, essay saying why the program would be of benefit. Application requirements may vary by program.	1 week	No required program costs	Varies	University of Missouri administrators	The programs are specific to one institutional system.
Programs and Institutes of the Student Affairs Administrators in Higher Education (NASPA) http:// www.naspa.org/ programs/ default.cfm	NASPA Programs and Institutes provide a fast-paced highly interactive educational experience focusing on a variety of topics geared exclusively for Senior Student Affairs Officer's needs. Participants leave the institutes with a personal assessment of their leadership and effectiveness styles and specific strategies and tools for implementing initiatives. Institutes are designed for Student Affairs Officers playing a key leadership role and having ultimate responsibility for their organization.	Student Affairs Administrators in Higher Education (NASPA)	Complete registration form.	2-3 days	Costs vary by program or institute.	Varies	Senior Student Affairs Officers	The institute comprises several sessions targeted at Senior Student Affairs Officers. NASPA offers continuing education unit credits for all its professional development programs and institutes.

Academy for Leadership and Development, The Chair Academy http://www.mc.maricopa.edu/other/chair/	The Academy for Leadership and Development offers opportunities to acquire and understand major research and theoretical developments in leadership. Participants have opportunities to develop proficiency in selecting, integrating, and applying appropriate concepts from social and behavioral science and adult education in formulating and implementing approaches to leadership problems and issues. The academy provides a systems approach to transformational leadership. The program is dedicated to long-term change.	The Chair Academy	Registration	10 days	Varies according to location	54	Leaders from colleges and universities internationally as well as domestically	Regional institutes are available.
Executive HR Leadership Program—College and University Professional Association for HR. (The program is not being offered in the current year. Please visit the main CUPA Web site at http://www.cupahr.org/)	Chief human resource officers (CHROs) increasingly are serving as strategic planning partners and advisors to campus constituencies. CUPA-HR's Executive HR Leadership Program supports CHROs in that role. The retreat gives CHROs an opportunity to exchange ideas about important issues that colleges and universities will soon face and the opportunity and tools to address challenges and topics of interest in a small-group, intensive workshop setting.	College and University Professional Association for HR	Those applicants who meet the criteria (HR executives or 15-plus years in HR) are accepted on a first-come, first-enrolled basis until the enrollment limit has been reached.	5 days	No required program costs	NA*	HR executives, or those poised to advance directly into that role, with at least 15 years of HR management experience	The program takes place every 2 years. Information may not be available on the CUPA Web site in years that the program is not being offered.
National Academy for Academic Leadership http://www.thenationalacademy.org/	The National Academy for Academic Leadership educates academic decision makers to be leaders for sustained, integrated institutional change that significantly improves student learning. Its curriculum is based on research and best practices.	The National Academy (and occasional cosponsors)	Request consultation.	Varies	Varies	Varies	Programs are designed for institutional teams working on campus projects and for individuals—presidents, board members, vice presidents, deans, chairs and key faculty members—with role-specific responsibilities and concerns.	The academy programs are geared to the unique institutional contexts and specific needs of participants.

APPENDIX 7.C (Continued)

Program	Overview	Sponsor	Application Process	Duration	Fees	Class Size	Target Audience	Unique Aspects
Leadership Institutes/Programs								
The EDUCAUSE Institute Leadership Program http://net.educause.edu/1091	At the institute, participants examine the realities of information technology (IT) leadership and the characteristics of IT leaders. They work together with institute faculty and fellow participants in highly interactive and intensive sessions to develop and expand the skills needed to be a leader in one's IT organization.	NA*	Complete registration form; first come, first served	1 week	$1,735 in 2009 for Educause members, $1,910 for nonmembers. Accommodations not included.	NA*	The program is designed for individuals who occupy or aspire to senior positions in campus IT organizations.	The target audience is unique.
Leadership Programs for Community College Professionals—Future Leaders Institute (AACC) http://www.aacc.nche.edu/newsevents/Events/fli/Pages/default.aspx	FLI is an innovative seminar designed for midlevel community college administrators who are ready to move into a higher level of leadership.	American Association of Community Colleges	Presidents nominate "rising leaders" on their campus; applicants submit résumé and self-descriptive letter.	5 days	$1,700 in 2009. Accommodations not included.	Varies	Individuals currently in a position that is responsible for multiple employees, including faculty, administrators, and/or staff and probably have titles such as vice president, dean, associate dean, or director.	There are two institutes: one on each coast.
Total = 10								
Leadership Institutes/Programs for Women								
HERS/Bryn Mawr Summer Institute http://www.hersnet.org/HERSHigherEducationResourceServices.htmsishtm.asp	Begun in 1976, the HERS/Bryn Mawr Summer Institute is a residential program that focuses on improving the status of women in the middle and executive levels of higher education administration.	HERS & Bryn Mawr College	Application, two letters of recommendation, current résumé, organizational chart of institution indicating applicant's position, and self-descriptive letter	4 weeks	Residents: $7,900 in 2009; Commuters: $4,900. Fee covers program, materials, meals, and accommodations, if residential.	75-80	Applicants should be women faculty or university administrators who indicate a potential for advancement in higher education administration.	This is a premier national leadership program.

Program	Description	Institution	Application	Duration	Cost	Number	Target	Special Considerations
Center for Women and Leadership Faculty Fellows Program (BVM) http://www.luc.edu/gannon/fellows.shtml	The Gannon Center sponsors a Faculty Fellows Program in Women Studies to encourage research on women and their contributions to society and to promote active learning and scholarship.	Loyola University Chicago	Nomination by applicant's chairperson and dean	1 semester	No required program costs	2	Full-time Loyola faculty	Special consideration given to the study of women and leadership.
Alice Manicur Women's Symposium (NASPA) http:// www.naspa.org/ divctr/women/ manicur.cfm	The Alice Manicur Women's Symposium is designed for women who are contemplating careers as Senior Student Affairs Officers and currently hold midlevel management positions and/or faculty appointments.	Student Affairs Professionals in Higher Education (NASPA)	Application and letter of nomination	1 week	$625 registration fee in 2010 for NASPA members; $725 for nonmembers. Accommodations and meals not included.	50–60	Women aspiring to be Senior Student Affairs Officers	The symposium takes place every 2 years.
National Institute for Leadership Development (NILD) http://www.pc.maricopa.edu/nild/	Through institute programs, women and girls acquire the skills they need to succeed and assume leadership roles in their academic, professional, and personal lives. AAUW's institute now directs the National Conference for College Women Student Leaders, an event that grows in depth and popularity each year. Beyond this college-age program, the institute will develop a breadth of programs addressing women in all stages of life.	American Association for Women in Community Colleges; Maricopa Community Colleges	Registration process	Varies	Varies	Varies	Varies	The programs target a wide range of women and girls.
Higher Ground Women's Leadership Development State-Specific Program For more information please contact the Grace E. Harris Leadership Institute at 804-827-1169 or gehli@vcu.edu	Higher Ground is a dynamic experience for current and emerging women leaders who exhibit the skills, potential, and desire to take significant roles in leading academic institutions, faith organizations, and themselves to a higher level.	Virginia Commonwealth University	Application form and nominator form must be completed.	8 day-long sessions over a 5-month period	NA·	Varies	Women in higher education, faith and community organizations who cross culture, race, ethnicity and faith practice, and who are ready to lead, ready to learn and ready to transform their communities as they transform themselves.	The program is designed for women from higher education and faith-based and community organizations.
Total = 5								

APPENDIX 7.C (Continued)

Leadership Institutes/Programs for Underrepresented Groups

Program	Overview	Sponsor	Application Process	Duration	Fees	Class Size	Target Audience	Unique Aspects
AASCU's Millennium Leadership Initiative http://www.aascu.org/programs/mli/2009/	MLI is a focused leadership development program designed to strengthen the preparation and eligibility of people who are traditionally underrepresented in the role of president or chancellor.	American Association of State Colleges and Universities	AASCU member presidents and chancellors nominate promising senior administrators who apply for acceptance into MLI. The presidential selection subcommittee chooses candidates from education, government, and the private sector.	4-day institute; year-long mentoring program	$1,800 AASCU members in 2009; $2,800 for non-members	33	The next-generation campus chief executive officers in the public and private sectors	The year-long mentoring program component.
LEAP/APAHE Leadership Development Program for Higher Education (LDPHE) http://www.leap.org/develop_ldphe.html	LDPHE increases diversity in senior levels of higher education administration by promoting the leadership and professional development of highly promising Asian Pacific Americans (APAs).	Leadership Education for Asian Pacifics, Inc. (LEAP) & Asian Pacific Americans in Higher Education (APAHE)	Completed LDPHE application form, curriculum vitae or résumé, recommendation from CEO at the applicant's institution, and personal statement regarding desire to participate in the program	Four-day institute	$1,000 includes program, materials, and meals. Accommodations not included.	30	Asian Pacific American administrators, faculty, and staff who have demonstrated a commitment to their personal and professional development and who are motivated to advance their careers in the field of higher education.	LDPHE combines leadership training with personalized attention, a unique understanding of APAs, and invaluable insights of successful APA leaders in higher education.

Program	Description	Sponsor	Application	Duration	Cost	Number	Eligibility	Mentoring
Kellogg MSI Leadership Fellows Program (KMFLP) NAFEO Kellogg Leadership Fellows Program For information contact NAFEO at 202-552-3300 or see http:// www.nafeo.org/ community/ index.php.	The W. K. Kellogg Foundation supports three leadership programs for minority-serving institutions. This program focuses on historically Black colleges and universities (HBCUs) and predominantly Black institutions (PBIs) and prepares exemplary individuals for senior-level leadership.	W. K. Kellogg Foundation and National Association for Equal Opportunity in Higher Education.	Applicants must receive a nomination from the president of their institution, submit two letters of recommendation from a supervisor or colleague, propose a framework for an individualized study program of their own design to achieve specific leadership goals, and curriculum vitae.	1 academic year	No required program costs	10	Current and emerging leaders at HBCUs and PBIs	Each Fellow is matched with a mentor president from another HBCU or PBI (not one's current institution) who will serve as a resource to the Fellow over the Fellowship year, and beyond.
Kellogg MSI Leadership Fellows Program (KMFLP) HACU Leadership Fellows Program http://www.hacu .net/hacu/The_Kel logg_MSI_Leader ship_Fellows_Pro gram_EN.asp? SnID=2	The W. K. Kellogg Foundation supports three leadership programs for minority serving institutions. This program focuses on Hispanic-serving institutions (HSIs) and prepares exemplary individuals for the challenges and rigors of senior-level leadership.	W. K. Kellogg Foundation and Hispanic Association of Colleges and Universities	Applicants must receive a nomination from the president of their institution, submit two letters of recommendation from a supervisor or colleague, propose a framework for an individualized study program of their own design to achieve specific leadership goals, and curriculum vitae.	1 academic year	No required program costs	10	Open to Hispanics who have currently or previously worked at or attended a Hispanic-serving institution, and demonstrate strong ability and potential to rise to a high-level position at an HIS.	Each Fellow is matched with a mentor president from another HSI (not one's current institution) who will serve as a resource to the Fellow over the Fellowship year, and beyond.

APPENDIX 7.C (Continued)

Program	Overview	Sponsor	Application Process	Duration	Fees	Class Size	Target Audience	Unique Aspects
Leadership Institutes/Programs for Underrepresented Groups								
Kellogg MSI Leadership Fellows Program (KMFLP) AIHEC Leadership Fellows Program http://www.aihec .org/resources/ leadership.cfm	The W. K. Kellogg Foundation supports three leadership programs for minority-serving institutions. This program focuses on tribal colleges and universities (TCUs) and prepares exemplary individuals for the challenges and rigors of senior-level leadership.	W. K. Kellogg Foundation and the American Indian Higher Education Consortium	Applicants must receive a nomination from the president of their institution, submit two letters of recommendation from a supervisor or colleague, propose a framework for an individualized study program of their own design to achieve specific leadership goals, and curriculum vitae.	1 academic year	No required program costs	10	The AIHEC Leadership Fellows Program is open to American Indians who currently serve a tribal college or university and who demonstrate strong ability and potential to rise to a high-level position at a TCU.	Each Fellow is matched with a mentor president from another TCU (not one's current institution) who will serve as a resource to the Fellow over the Fellowship year, and beyond.
Total = 5								
Leadership Programs for Women of Color								
National Hispana Leadership Institute http:// www.nhli.org/	This intensive learning experience provides training in public policy; leadership; strategic management; and race, class, and gender issues. The program emphasizes a holistic approach to leadership. Participants reflect on and review their personal history. The NHLI is committed to new paradigms of leadership, not in maintaining the status quo. As such, this program is for women who are ready for profound changes in their personal and professional lives.	National Hispana Leadership Institute and numerous corporate sponsors	Applicants must submit a complete application packet in order to be considered. Regional committee composed of NHLI Alumnae schedule a personal or phone interview and submit its recommendation to the national review committee.	Over a 9-month period, participants meet four times for 1 full week; between sessions, participants must complete assignments.	$3,500 in 2010 for each of the four segments, plus travel costs, or $14,000 total, plus travel costs	22	Participants who are diverse, talented, and accomplished; this program is for women who are ready for profound changes in their personal and professional lives.	As part of the experience, each participant agrees to mentor two Hispanic women for at least 2 years and develop a leadership project that will benefit a minimum of 25 young Latina youth and/or women.
Total = 1								

[a] NA indicates information not available/located.

8

ADVICE FROM THE FIELD
Guiding Women of Color to Academic Leadership

Yolanda T. Moses

This chapter, although brief, took a lifetime to write because it is based on 25 years of lived experience. It is the kind of piece that can only be written from the voice of experience, from the vantage point of having lived to tell the tale. It is a chapter for women on planning their careers in academic leadership, on the individual and institutional barriers and choices that women face, and on suggested strategies for making those choices, navigating barriers, and reaching their goals. It is the story of what I and other women have faced, and what we either have found successful or suggest to you by virtue of having learned the hard way. It is the distillation of career advice through trial and error and ultimately through intentional visioning and planning. While the chapter is applicable to all women in academe, I address it particularly to women of color and situate it in my own experience as an African American woman leader in higher education.

I believe in the importance of, and dedicate part of my work to, the development of an engaged and diverse cadre of institutional leaders for the college and university of the 21st century. The new academy is an institution that will have as one of its characteristics a demographically diverse student body, faculty, and administration. It will also promote a student-centered curriculum that focuses on student-centered teaching and learning and engagement, demonstrating a culture of evidence. My advice to women through this chapter touches upon this changing context and the resulting leadership opportunities for women of color.

Choosing a Path to Academic Leadership: A Traditional or a Nontraditional Path?

The traditional path to academic leadership in American academic institutions has been through the professorate. The newly minted doctoral recipient started a career as an assistant professor. Success in that position was rewarded by tenure and promotion to associate professor and, ultimately, to full professor.

Once tenured, the academic generally could choose to embark either on a lifelong career in teaching and research or on an administrative leadership track. The path to the presidency of a college or university generally led through a department chair position, an academic deanship, and then some time as a provost/vice president for academic affairs.

Until quite recently, a distinguishing feature of this leadership track was that almost the only academics in it were White males. In the last two decades, this has changed somewhat, as affirmative action and other conscious, systematic efforts to identify and encourage potential minority and women faculty members to move up the academic ladder into leadership positions have had a positive, if limited, effect.

The Outlook for Women of Color on the Traditional Academic Path

For women of color, however, progress toward academic leadership in the last decade or more has been a somewhat mixed story. An annual status report, *Minorities in Higher Education, 2001–2002* (Harvey, 2002), published by the American Council on Education (ACE), sheds light on the trends. According to ACE, White men still dominate academic leadership, constituting more than 62% of college and university chief executive officers in 2002 (Harvey). That marks a significant drop since 1990, when they held more than 80% of presidencies. In the same year, women held 21% of all the presidencies and 3.6% of those were women of color (see Table 8.1; Harvey).

When looking at the demographics of those in the traditional path to academic leadership, for women chief academic officers (CAOs)—the position closest in line to the presidency—the proportions of women of color remain unchanged in the last decade (Dean, 2003). The majority of women CAOs are Caucasians (87%), with African American/Black women representing only 8% of women CAOs. Only 2% of CAOs are Latinas, and women from all other ethnicities account for less than 3% of women CAOs (Dean).

TABLE 8.1
Number of College and University Women CEOs of Color

	Number	% of Total CEOs	% of Total Women CEOs	% of Total Minority CEOs
1993	68	2.4	16.5	20.5
2002	103	3.4	15.8	26.7
2003	117	3.6	17	28.5

Source: Harvey, W. B. (2003). *Minorities in higher education: Annual status report.* Washington, DC: American Council on Education.

Currently we see trends that do not bode well for the future. While the minority student population is increasing and the number of women of color receiving doctorates is increasing, there is a growing trend in academe toward hiring faculty in nontenured, often part-time positions. The point made here is that although the number of women of color with doctorates is increasing, they will have added barriers in the traditional academic path because the path itself is changing and the full-time tenure-track appointments are dwindling (see Tables 8.2 and 8.3).

This century will see profound changes in the role of the faculty. By 2015, in addition to changes in student demographics, it is estimated that over one half of America's professors will be eligible for retirement. One of the hallmarks of stability for faculty in American universities is tenure. Tenure was won by faculty to protect their ability to speak their mind without worrying about retribution. Changing demographics among American faculty are deciding, in some very subtle ways, the future of tenure in American universities and colleges. In their article "Assessing the Silent Revolution,"

TABLE 8.2
Number of College and University Women Faculty by Rank

	1981–82	1991–92	1997–98	1999–2000
Full Professor	11,830 (10.3%)	21,168 (14.7%)	32,136 (19.8%)	33,393 (20.9%)
Associate Professor	21,995 (20.8%)	32,320 (27.7%)	43,128 (34.1%)	44,996 (35.5%)
Assistant Professor	37,164 (33.5%)	50,215 (39.7%)	55,832 (45.4%)	58,535 (45.8%)
Instructor and Lecturer	38,372 (42.8%)	42,871 (48%)	41,432 (51.6%)	47,785 (51.3%)
Other Faculty*	11,267 (37.3%)	18,639 (42.7%)	27,937 (45.6%)	29,367 (45.8%)

*denotes full time faculty from institutions without faculty ranks
Source: Harvey, W. B. (2003). *Minorities in higher education: Annual status report.* Washington, DC: American Council on Education.

TABLE 8.3
Number of College and University Women Faculty of Color by Rank

	1981–82	*1991–92*	*1997–98*	*1999–2000*
Full Professor	1,157 (9.8%)	2,200 (10.4%)	4,026 (12.5%)	3,845 (11.5%)
Associate Professor	2,304 (10.5%)	3,743 (11.6%)	5,540 (12.8%)	6,096 (13.5%)
Assistant Professor	4,280 (11.5%)	7,231 (14.4%)	9,439 (16.9%)	10,327 (17.6%)
Instructor and Lecturer	4,655 (12.1%)	6,104 (14.2%)	6,446 (15.6%)	8,070 (16.9%)
Other Faculty*	1,430 (12.7%)	2,918 (15.7%)	4,107 (14.7%)	4,349 (14.8%)

*denotes full time faculty from institutions without faculty ranks
Source: Harvey, W. B. (2003). *Minorities in higher education: Annual status report.* Washington, DC: American Council on Education.

Finkelstein and Schuster (2001) show how changing demographics are reshaping the academic profession. They drew on the major faculty surveys conducted over the past three decades by the U.S. Department of Labor and the U.S. Department of Education. Their first observation is that the new academic generation is substantial in size, increasingly diverse, and female. For example, in 1992, 43.2% of the new generation of faculty was White males, and in 1998 the figure was 36.5%. In 1998 women made up 35.8% among all full-timers and 43.8% among recent hires (Finkelstein & Schuster).

This radical change is really at the heart of "the silent revolution." Finkelstein and Schuster allege that the sharpest difference between the new faculty and the faculty of a generation ago are the kind of academic appointments they hold. In 1992 more than 83.5% of the full-time faculty with 7 or more years of full-time teaching experience held regular or tenure-track appointments compared with only 66% of the new entrants. In 1969 "off-track" appointments were 3%; in the 1990s the majority of hires were off the tenure track (Finkelstein & Schuster, 2001). What does this mean? Additional analysis showed that off-track appointees

- devote about 5 hours a week less to their institutional responsibilities (as much as 10 fewer hours at research universities) than their regular counterparts;
- spend more time teaching, less time in service activities (governance and committee work), and much less time in research; and
- are about twice as likely as regulars to spend no time whatsoever in "informal interaction" with students. The disparity is even greater in professional fields.

In sum, most nontenure-track appointees play highly specialized roles, confined to teaching. The authors suggest that perhaps the days of the full-service faculty who do teaching, research, and service are over. The large question for all of us to ponder is what this means for the quality of academic work, the quality of teaching and advising, and the quality of research. This development requires heightened and continuous scrutiny.

If by 2015 half of the faculty in the United States will be eligible for retirement, and as they are being replaced by more off-track faculty than tenure-track faculty, one wonders what the implications will be for quality faculty-student relationships in the future. One also wonders whether the increasing numbers of women of color in the faculty pipeline will translate into more women of color moving through the ranks and positioning themselves for senior leadership and management roles. This issue of access to tenure-track positions begs us to at least discuss the options of nontraditional pathways to senior academic leadership roles.

But before we do that, I would like to say that the increasing number of part-time and nontenure-track faculty positions makes it more difficult but not impossible to pursue a traditional faculty position as a pathway to senior academic leadership. For example, when I started teaching in 1975 as a doctoral student, I started out as a part-time teacher, then moved to a full-time lecturer for a year, and then moved into a tenure-track position at the same institution. I was what Californians call a "freeway flier," someone who carves out a living by stringing together a series of part-time positions. So, while a person may not start out in the tenure-track faculty position of his or her dreams, a strategy can be to use the experiences from the adjunct or part-time positions to build the requisite research and teaching experience that will prepare the individual to be competitive when a tenure-track position does materialize. Now, let us look at the nontraditional pathways.

The Outlook for Women of Color on Nontraditional Pathways

Nontraditional paths have brought success for some women of color and access to more visible, prestigious career options. Although the data are not all disaggregated to demonstrate similarities and differences between female and male presidents of color, examples of the pathways presidents take emerge from another ACE study, *The American College President: 2002 Edition* (Corrigan, 2002). According to the report, presidents of color

- "were more likely to have earned their degrees in education" (52%) compared with 43 percent of White presidents;

- "had served in their current presidency for 5.5 years," compared with 6.8 years for white presidents and 4.8 years for Hispanic presidents;
- "were more likely to have come from outside education or from another institution" than their counterparts from other racial/ethnic groups. (pp. 21–22)

Collectively, the data reflect the fact that in general, minority presidents tend to come from and also to head 2-year, public baccalaureate or specialized institutions such as historically Black colleges and universities, and are less likely to attain leadership positions in private or public master's or doctorate-granting institutions than their White counterparts (see Table 8.4; Harvey, 2003). I believe that women of color are particularly poised for senior leadership opportunities because they are concentrated in 2-year and 4-year colleges where the anticipated enrollment increases will be the greatest. One of the characteristics of these new students of the 21st century will be their mobility and their need for flexibility. The 2000 census data show that Americans are on the move more than ever before (Schacter, 2001). This means students may not receive their baccalaureate degrees from the same institutions where they began their studies. How will students get the coherence and quality in their curriculum that they need and pay for? How do we guarantee the integrity of the courses and curriculum we offer across institutions and institutional types? These questions are among the major challenges we face.

Ironically, the new for-profit and proprietary institutions have begun to offer mobile and part-time students modularized, high-quality courses,

TABLE 8.4
Percent of Colleges and Universities Led by Minority CEOs,
by Institution Type

	% Led by a Minority CEO	
Institutional Type	*1986*	*2006*
Doctorate Granting	2.4	11.3
Master's	12.8	12.9
Baccalaureate	6.4	13.1
Associate's	8.6	13.9
Special Focus	5.1	15.2
Total	8.1	13.5

Source: American Council on Education. (2007). *The American college president: 2007 edition.* Washington, DC: American Council on Education.

certificates, and programs they cannot receive from more traditional institutions. Technology-based instruction is increasingly used to offer students
programs at times and places suitable to their needs. Even on traditional university campuses, often only the professional schools and colleges in areas
such as health, medicine, and education offer models of flexibility of delivery
of education.

Students are also forcing better articulation among institutions of higher
education. Often students can be discouraged from transferring credits
earned in a community college to a local university. The rationale that staff
of universities often give is that they cannot be sure of the quality of instruction or whether the learning outcomes are comparable. Students, especially
older students, are beginning to vote with their feet, seeking out those institutions, whether traditional or nontraditional, that will fulfill their needs.

The colleges and universities of the 21st century must do a better job of
fulfilling their own mission niche rather than trying to imitate elite private
or large public research universities. There is a need for excellent student-
centered community colleges and regional comprehensive universities, as
well as private liberal arts and elite research universities. Since women of
color in faculty and administrative positions tend to cluster more in the 2-
year colleges and in the 4-year comprehensive universities, they are in a pivotal position to play major leadership roles within these institutions, as they
have taught in them, understand them, and value their missions.

In addition to presidencies, women of color have also increased their
representation in other administrative roles. The number of people in full-
time administrative jobs in higher education increased by more than 15.6%
between 1991 and 1999 (Harvey, 2002).

In summary, women of color have been increasing their numbers in
presidencies, administrative roles, and full-time faculty positions for more
than a decade, but progress has been slow. An estimated 50% of the professorate is predicted to retire over the next 10 to 15 years. The academic leaders
of tomorrow either will be members of the new cohort of faculty, many of
whom are already on nontenure career tracks, or will be graduates from the
burgeoning minority population that is on the way to or has already entered
the higher education system. What will be their pathway to leadership roles?
As mentioned, demographic trends appear to pose an even greater future
challenge to women of color seeking to attain leadership positions in higher
education in the future. What pathway should women of color choose?

While each woman will choose her own path, I offer advice from my
own lived experience, observed experiences of others, and from my careful
study of changing trends in academe. As I said earlier, part-time and adjunct

positions can lead to leadership roles, but they can also lead to dead-end jobs. Although the part-time position is the route I took, I have known women who have taken other paths to the presidency, such as women of color who have come through student affairs and governmental and community relations. I took a traditional path, because frankly when I started out on my journey, I had no intention of becoming a university president. I wanted to be a professor and planned to make revolutionary changes in the university from the classroom. When I did decide to take on leadership roles I was motivated by a set of personal core values that still propel me today. I have always been interested in promoting access and diversity issues in the academy. Each and every leadership role that I have assumed has had those underlying values at the heart of my choices. So, I became chair of a controversial department, dean of a college on a dare, vice president and provost of an institution that did not know how to name and value its diversity, and president of an institution that is known nationally for providing excellent education to smart and deserving poor students. My leadership has all been in service to access and excellence. But at the time that I was taking those traditional leadership steps, they were all in difficult leadership positions that were blazing new trails for diversity and institutional excellence. My mentors, Ann Reynolds, Jewel Plummer Cobb, Johnetta Cole, Niara Sudarkasa, and Paul Weller, all told me that I could not afford to skip any steps toward my senior leadership goal. If you skip a step, they said, that would give search committees the ammunition they need to eliminate you. At that time, women, and especially women of color, had to be twice as good as a White male just to get an interview! So their advice has served me well over the years. In addition, I have followed my own guidelines throughout my career:

- Be prepared—whatever it is you want to do, make sure you are damned good at it!
- Lead from where you are—sometimes you do not have to be in an administrative leadership position. My work on the Academic Senate and key university-wide and systemwide committees as a faculty member stood me in good stead when I wanted to go into an academic leadership position.
- Have a vision of where you want to go and know why you want to do it. So many young men and women have said to me over the years, "I want to be a president" and my reply to them is, "Why?" There are much easier jobs to do than to be a senior administrator or a university president or chancellor. Know why you are doing it. Is it about passion or is it about prestige?

- Once you are on a faculty, be selective about the committees you agree to serve on. Departments and administrators tend to ask women and men of color to serve on every committee having to do with diversity and to be the diversity representative on all other committees. That is a no-no. I have a solution that is win-win: Offer to train the White males to do it, and then get some leadership credit for it!

- Be very selfish about your research agenda. In a research university that is how you are going to get tenure, not through teaching, though it helps to have good teaching evaluations. Unfortunately service is just about off the radar screen in those types of institutions. In teaching institutions, teaching and research count more than they do in research universities. Remember institutions do not hug back! You have to be the keeper of your own career trajectory; no one else can do it for you.

In summary, these positions can often lead to tenure-track faculty positions, but usually not. There are barriers. What follows in the next section is a focus on the specific barriers that women of color encounter on the path to academic leadership.

Barriers on the Paths to Academic Leadership

The demographic trends described in the previous section represent relatively new, potentially formidable barriers in the path of women of color who aspire to academic leadership. But they are not the only obstacles on the route to success. Both my research and anecdotal evidence have contributed to the documentation and understanding of such institutional barriers (Moses, 1989). Key institutional barriers include a problematic hiring and tenure process, the castelike relationship between senior and junior faculty, the difference in culture between the faculty and administrative provinces of academe, unfriendly family policies and practices, and the continued hostile, inhospitable environment for people of color and women in predominantly White colleges and universities (Moses, 1989).

Problems in faculty recruitment and tenure processes. Women and men of color are concentrated on the lower rungs of the academic ladder. Getting up the rungs of that ladder is often very slow and fraught with obstacles. These barriers can have a strong negative impact on their career.

The biggest hurdle is getting into the tenure track. A lot of the best recruitment and retention and tenure practices of colleges and universities around the country are summarized in Caroline Turner's book, *Diversifying the Faculty* (2002).

Once in the door, the retention and tenure process itself is plagued with problems. The traditional tenure process is often not as transparent as it should be. Some institutions have very transparent processes, but many of them do not. Where they are not transparent, they provide an additional hurdle for a woman of color. Even on campuses where they are transparent, these processes and criteria are not necessarily consistent even across programs within the same institution. To date, some of the best case practices are in Turner's book. But in traveling around the country and consulting on issues of diversity and institutional transformation, I have found that the University of Washington, the University of Minnesota, the University of Michigan, the University of Wisconsin, and the University of California (systemwide) are exceptional.

Successful faculty members of color adapt to the ambiguity and develop their own strategies for navigating the tenure track. Members of the inner circle of faculty who have been in a department for some time may have figured out exactly what the criteria are for an assistant professor to become an associate professor, or for an associate professor to become a full professor. When a new faculty member arrives, she really does not understand or know what is expected of her. Without guidelines, it is of course extremely difficult to establish personal priorities that will lead to promotion and tenure. Unfortunately, many of the inner circle who have discovered these secrets are not willing to share them. This is harmful to their colleagues, their departments, their academic disciplines, and ultimately their institutions. It is a practice that benefits no one. When I was first recruited for a tenure-track position, I was lucky to have a female department chair, Joan Greenway. She had been a successful woman in the media and world of television in Australia before she came to the United States. So, not only was she my mentor to guide me through the labyrinth of departmental politics, she understood the politics of the tenure and promotional process from an institutional level. She was my first academic guide and mentor.

Castelike relationships between faculty ranks. The lack of transparency in the tenure process reflects a more fundamental issue: the almost castelike relationship that often prevails between senior tenured faculty and junior untenured faculty. All too often, these two groups do not function as colleagues. In some cases, they hardly interact at all. Unless some formal mentoring system has been established, there is often no systematic way for junior faculty to learn the culture of their department, which is modeled by the senior faculty who are controlling the resources and the policy decisions that can make or break the career of someone who does not figure out how to navigate the system (Moses, 2004). To expand on this statement: Failing to reach out and mentor new faculty members is analogous to inviting someone to visit you and live in your home and then proceeding to ignore the person, although you periodically expect him or her to participate in family life without the person knowing the internal dynamics of the family or how it works. It amazes me how much time and energy a department head may spend to recruit someone who is expected to be a contributing member of the department for 15 to 20 years and then not give the individual any guidance once hired. Ultimately this sink-or-swim tradition sends a signal from the department, intended or not, that the new faculty member is unwelcome. Should the faculty member perceive this and decide the environment is unwelcoming, she might seek employment elsewhere.

There are all kinds of mentoring programs available, and one size does not fit all. The best ones are flexible and allow the mentor and the mentee to experiment with different mentoring styles. In some programs senior mentors are in the department, and in others they are in other programs across the university. In some programs they are not in the university at all. One of my first mentees was a seasoned documentary filmmaker, Carroll Blue, who was hired in the communications department at another university. I mentored her from afar but kept in touch with her for over 10 years until she became a full professor. Today we are colleagues and still talk on a regular basis several times a year. In another instance, a junior untenured professor related her experiences with her assigned mentor. "I was assigned a mentor here at my institution, but he never takes initiative with me. A 'mentor' is supposed to take a definite and personal interest in another's career. Sometimes such relationships can't be 'assigned.' I sought out my own mentors, but I also go in and make myself ask my assigned mentor-guy a few questions now and then, so he can feel like he's doing something." Now that is an example of a junior professor who is taking the initiative on her own behalf. She is so right when she says that mentors should not be assigned if they do not want to do the job!

Lack of clear bridges between faculty and administrative careers. The third institutional barrier relates to the fact that although many women of color choose, or at least envision, their career goal as a top administrative position, there are few clear bridges to get there. Often there are no formal professional development opportunities for them on their campuses. Certainly organizations like ACE's Women's National Network and the now defunct American Association for Higher Education's (AAHE) Women's Caucus provided national opportunities for women to explore administrative and leadership opportunities with formalized mentoring and training programs. In addition there is the Higher Education Research Services (HERS)/Bryn Mawr Summer Leadership Program; the ACE Fellows Program; the Kellogg Fellows Leadership Alliance program (which focuses on developing presidential leadership for minority-serving institutions); and the Millennium Project, a leadership program started by presidents of color in the American Association of State Colleges and Universities. I got mentoring and leadership training from my disciplinary network from senior anthropologists, such as Johnetta Cole and Niara Sudarkasa, and from formal organizations, such as Harvard's Institute for Executive Management, the AAHE Women's Caucus, and the Women of Color Leadership Institute hosted by ACE's Office of Minority Affairs. Yet often many women of color are not part of regional or national networks such as these.

Unfortunately, women of color are still more apt to stumble on the opportunity to test and augment their leadership skills rather than to have an intentional plan. For example, I can recall as a young faculty member the first time I was tapped to take on an administrative assignment, I was admonished by my academic colleagues not to "go over to the other side." However, I had a completely different view of administration than my White colleagues, both male and female. I saw the opportunity to take on an administrative role as the opportunity to change the system to make it better for all of us. I was interested then, as I am now, in creating inclusive learning environments in colleges and universities. My White colleagues, on the other hand, only saw administrative work as a negative imposition on their time and energy at best. So I had little formal mentoring on my campus initially. Mentoring came from senior women of color administrators on other campuses locally and nationally. I happened to meet Jewel Plummer Cobb at a national higher education meeting when I was dean. I had heard that she had been a dean at Douglas College of Rutgers University, so I wanted to talk with her. She had just become president of California State University, Fullerton, in the early 1980s. I followed her around at that meeting and bugged her until she said yes she would meet with me to talk about my future as a dean. We have been friends and colleagues ever since.

The bottom line: I had to create my own mentoring program using women of color and White women and men from all over the United States. I saw these women and men as role models and trailblazers. These women had been successful against the odds. My group of mentors included Gloria Scott, then president of Bennett College; Niara Sudarkasa, then president of Lincoln University, the first liberal arts historically Black university in the United States (what was exceptional to me about Niara is that I remember when she was associate vice president at the University of Michigan in the early 1980s she told a group of women at an ACE women's summit that she wanted to be president at a historically Black college or university—and she did it); Juliet Garcia at the University of Texas at Brownsville and Texas Southmost College; Brit Kirwin, then president of the University of Maryland, College Park; Donna Shavlik and Judy Touchton from the ACE Office of Women in Higher Education; and Johnetta Cole, then president of Spelman College. These people were passionate about their work. They were fierce and courageous in the face of obstacles and opposition. They too were passionate about access and excellence for their students. I wanted to be just like them.

Family unfriendly policies and practices. The fourth institutional barrier for women of all colors is the conflict between their professional and family lives.

Mary Ann Mason, dean of graduate studies, and her research colleague Marc Goulden at the University of California, Berkeley, have been looking at the impact that motherhood has upon the academic careers of women faculty. The project "Do Babies Matter?" is funded by the Sloan Foundation and based on data collected until 1999 by the federal government from 160,000 people who earned their doctorates between 1978 and 1984 and continued working in academe. Mason undertook the study, among other reasons, to answer the question her graduate students had asked her over the years, "Is there a good time to have a baby?" (Wilson, 2003). Mason's research shows that even though women make up nearly half of the PhD population, they are not advancing at the same rate as men to the upper ranks of the professorate; many drop out of the race. In her study on the effects of career on family formation she found that "married with children" is the success formula for men but not for women. For women she found what she calls the "baby gap" (Mason & Goulden, 2004). Only one in three women who take a tenure-track university position before having a child ever becomes a mother. Women who achieve tenure are more than twice as likely as their male counterparts to be single 12 years after earning their PhD, and women who are married when they begin their academic careers are much more likely than men in the same position to divorce or separate from their spouses. They conclude that although men can have both tenure and a family, women cannot. For men, the tenure track and the reproductive track run on parallel lines. For women, they are on a collision course (Mason & Goulden).

Looking back at how I balanced my family and career goals, I was lucky to have a husband who respected my desires to be an academic and to have a family. He wanted the family more than I did, so he did all he could to accommodate me at home. At the university I had the support of the female department chair who worked with me to schedule classes around my first pregnancy. My first daughter (who is now 29 years old, a new attorney, and wondering how she is going to balance work and family life) was born in July, so I had the summer to get ready for the next term. My second daughter (who is now 26) was born in January, and I was able to take off the winter quarter with her and come back in the spring quarter of the same year. We had disability leave, but no family-friendly policies at that time. It is important for women who want a family and an academic career to make sure that their university has such policies spelled out and that the institutional culture does not penalize you if you choose to take advantage of it. For example, at the University of California, Riverside, where I am currently, we have family leave policies on the books, but some women still do not know about them, and some are reluctant to use them for fear of being stigmatized as not being serious scholars and researchers.

I also know women who have chosen the nontraditional pathway to balance career and family. For example, I have a young colleague of childbearing age who consciously chose not to enter the professoriate until after she had children. She intentionally held on to her administrative job, where she had excellent maternity benefits and where she knew it would not hurt her professionally to take time off. ACE's (2005) work on promoting family-friendly policies suggests that this barrier may be coming down. While we see the university slowly changing by at least developing policies to address the conundrum of work and family issues that historically have put all women at a disadvantage in the tenure and promotion process, it remains imperative for women to deliberately map out their career paths—including creating space in that path for personal milestones like having children or taking care of elderly parents.

A continued inhospitable environment. The fifth institutional barrier is the subtle forms of racism and sexism that faculty of color continue to experience on university and college campuses. The behavior is often not overt and therefore very hard to prove that it is really happening. Both Turner (2000) and Boice (1992) say that faculty of color feel the pressure of being the "other," or the *outsider,* as I call them, in more subtle ways. "They feel the pressure to give up their ethnic identity; or are discouraged from studying their own cultures because of doubt about the legitimacy of their research" (Turner, p. 115). Turner and Boice both conclude that entrenched White male elitism is the chief obstacle to treating women and members of minority groups as equals who merit collegial support.

My own scholarly and research history is a case in point. In the 1980s, research on critical race theory and feminist theory was in its infancy and coming of age. As vice president for academic affairs at a California State

University, I intervened in several tenure cases across a range of humanities and social science disciplines where the tenure committees composed primarily of White males could not evaluate the research of their own faculty. Not only could they not review it, they did not even know the names of outside reviewers who could review the work. They had to rely on the names they got from the faculty, and luckily they were open to accepting suggestions from me as well. Today at the University of California, Riverside, I find myself mentoring junior women and men of color who after 25 years still encounter some of the same problems. In one particular case, a young woman of color was brought to the university through the Target of Opportunity Program (this program is still perceived by many faculty as a nontraditional way to hire faculty). When she came up for a review, one senior professor in her research area within the department told her that "critical race theory is not a real scholarly field of research, it is only about political activism." He subsequently did not write her a strong letter of support when she went up for tenure. It was on the strength of her outside letters, and positive discussion by the other members of her department outside her research area, that her dossier was voted as favorable and passed on to the dean. In summary, these barriers continue today, affecting all new faculty who bring new perspectives and points of view that do not fit old or existing departmental and research paradigms. It is very important for new faculty to understand this and develop strong allies outside the department or university if necessary.

These barriers do not necessarily apply only to women of color. In fact, they tend to cast a shadow on the career potential of any junior faculty, including men of color and Euro-American women and men. Such barriers are, as in Lani Guinier and Gerald Torres's (2003) book *The Miner's Canary: Enlisting Race, Resisting Power, Transforming Democracy*, the miner's canary. Miners have traditionally taken canaries with them into mine shafts to serve as warning systems. Canaries, highly sensitive birds, will react and often die if there is something wrong with the air in the mine shaft, such as when a tunnel collapses. So in higher education, the many men of color and women who are blocked from entering and advancing in the academy are canaries: their struggles are symptomatic of something wrong with the climate and institutional processes of the academy itself. The poison in the air is not only deleterious to the women and men of color, but it is deleterious to everyone in the institution. When we block talented individuals from joining and flourishing in our midst, we all suffer the loss of their potential contributions. Although colleges and universities need to recognize and remedy these ills for the health of the institution as a whole, I will now offer advice to women for overcoming these barriers.

Overcoming Barriers: Strategies for Success

Women of color who aspire to academic leadership need to be able to survive and flourish in institutions that are indifferent and even hostile to them. They need to be able to construct a deliberate pathway to the academic leadership or management roles they seek. What follows are institutional survival and personal career strategies. Because nontraditional pathways to academic leadership (while viable) are myriad, I focus my advice on those who will seek the traditional pathway that leads through the academic ranks. This is the advice that I have distilled from a full career of experience, observation, and scholarship, and it has served me well over the years. While I have offered these strategies particularly for women of color in the academy, I share them with all women who are working for institutional change through leadership (Moses, 2004).

Choose the right starting point for you. Begin with selecting an institution that is a good match for you and your personal goals, and follow a series of steps to establish your reputation and your network within that institution and among your colleagues in your own department. Personal career issues to consider include selecting a personal pathway to leadership as early in your career as possible, and then following a series of steps to consciously cultivate certain skills and leadership traits that will bolster your reputation, help you earn the promotions you seek, and assist in preserving your personal strength and health so you can succeed at the tasks you take on.

Choosing the right institution is a crucial first step. In today's competitive academic environment, where the number of attractive jobs seems to be declining, it can be tempting to accept the first job you are offered. But before accepting a position, do your research on that institution and on the department you are being considered for. At the institutional level, read the mission statements and surf the Web sites. Learn as much as you can about the leadership. Who is the president? Who is the provost, and who are the trustees? Find out their track record on issues you care about—such as hiring women and underrepresented minorities, or steps they have taken to create a family-friendly working environment for students, staff, and faculty for both women and men. What are their commitments to the issues that you care about? How have they funded them? Do they have faculty development programs in place?

On the departmental level, study the curriculum and any other policies on departmental initiatives and priorities. When you visit, get a feeling for the student body and meet as many faculty and staff as you can. If you have friends or colleagues who are familiar with the campus, learn what you can from them. Look at the research and professional records of the faculty who will be your colleagues. Are they parochial or cosmopolitan? Does their research overlap or complement yours? Is it basic research or applied research? Are students engaged in service-learning programs within the department? All of the answers to these questions will give you clues to the values of the department and whether or not it is the right fit for you. I had no choice in really doing this in my first position, but when I went to City College of New York (CCNY) as president, one of the first things I did was check whether any faculty in the anthropology department were applied anthropologists or had students interested in the field of political economy. Those academic issues were important to me. A woman needs to know whether her research and scholarship, service choices, and ultimately herself will be accepted. Better to know whether you fit now than to have 7 years of work deemed unworthy of tenure.

Develop a tenure plan. Once you choose an institution and have been hired, sometime during that first semester ask to meet with your department chairperson to develop a specific plan so that you know how you must perform to be promoted or receive tenure. Here I refer to my earlier section on barriers and underscore why it is important for you to take the initiative in bringing clarity to a hidden, vague process. I was lucky in that I had a senior woman who took me under her wing and basically told me not to make the mistakes she had. If I was to give advice here, I would say that it is important to understand the whole process, including levels of votes. For example, if your school has a tenure process that is less rigorous than in the rest of the university, but at some point your tenure dossier must pass through a university panel—you need to plan for that situation. Also, it would be good to know the tenure rates in the department. How many have gone up for tenure in the last 10 years and were awarded/denied?

This strategy of defining a career path early is not widespread on American campuses yet, but it has been promoted by the AAHE's Faculty Roles and Rewards: New Pathways II Project, which examined how institutions are and should be supporting new faculty. One of the principles of good practice the project recommended is that academic departments should communicate expectations for performance to new faculty members (Sorcinelli, 2000).

An example of a career path could be (a) you define a path to tenure that proceeds primarily through research, and (b) your department chair may agree that during your first year or two, you will have a lighter teaching load—and not take any committee assignments—so that you have time to complete your research and write a book or a series of articles or monographs on it. The discussion with the department chair should be as explicit as possible about your goals and should conclude with a commitment from your department chair in writing—in the face of demands to serve on committees or take other detours from your path—that he or she will defend your need to concentrate on your research and writing or whatever priorities you have set.

Build networks and find mentors. Make it a priority to develop and stay in contact with a supportive network of colleagues inside and outside your department. Seek out other women faculty on campus who care about the same issues you care about. They may be able to advise you on questions you cannot or do not want to ask within your own department. Another good networking source may be professional development programs or workshops that are offered to a cohort of new faculty on campus. Participating in these types of activities may give you an opportunity to make and maintain connections with colleagues across disciplinary lines. Organizations such as Black, Asian/Pacific, and Latino faculty and staff associations, or a women of color group on your campus, can provide a safe and secure environment for discussing issues of well-being and survival and enable you to benefit from the experience of others who have been on campus longer than you have. Early in my career I joined the Black Faculty and Staff Association on my campus. Because there were so few African Americans on the campus, the group provided a safe space to discuss issues that affected us as a group. In addition the group welcomed new African American faculty with a reception once a year, raised money for scholarships for students, and hosted holiday gatherings around such national events as Black History Month. It provided me with still another network of support.

Finding and working with a mentor can be another crucial element in moving toward leadership status. In her article "Success in the Ivory Tower" about her study of five Black tenured women at a major research university, Mary V. Alfred (2001) observes:

> By watching, observing and learning the practices of others, these [tenured Black faculty] women developed a frame of reference from which to pattern their own actions and behavior. . . . By interacting with significant members of the culture, the women learned its expectations and its rules and such knowledge made them a member of the culture. (pp. 64–65)

To find a mentor, watch for and seek out people whose behavior you admire, tell them you value their work and want to learn to be like them—whether you admire how they teach, how they engage with students, or how effective they are in advocating programs in their departments. For example, in my own case, as I stated earlier, I was mentored by several people: two on my own campus (one White male, Paul Weller, and one White female, Joan Greenway), and four off campus (Jewel Cobb, Niara Sudarkasa, Johnetta Cole, and Gloria Scott). I saw the mentors on my own campus just about every day. I saw Jewel Cobb about once every 3 months, and the others maybe once a year. In reality, my mentors were women who had overcome great odds to get where they were. Just by watching them and following their careers from afar, I learned a lot. But the advice that each of them gave me was priceless.

Over the years, I find that I have mentored dozens and dozens of women and men myself. It is my way of giving back what was so generously given to me. I believe in helping women and men chart their own destinies. We should all be empowered to make choices that will get us where we want to go. I encourage young professionals wherever I go to get in touch with me and let me see if I can help them or put them in touch with someone who can.

One particular thing I am very proud of, in addition to the individual success of those people whom I have mentored, is the fact that I was a part of a group of presidents of color who saw the need for the establishment of a national program to mentor individuals of color who wanted to be senior administrators and presidents. Called the Millennium Program, it is currently administered by the American Association of State Colleges and Universities.

Know when to say no. As suggested earlier, a junior faculty member who happens to be a woman of color may be deluged with requests to perform tasks in addition to her basic research, teaching, and service responsibilities. You must learn to say no to some of these requests and to be strategic about the times when you say yes. Part of saying no is to resist becoming the all-purpose "woman minority" representative on committees, task forces, and the like. Saying yes strategically means evaluating the demands and opportunities offered to you and investing your time and energy in tasks that will advance your career. One such example is the departmental Curriculum Committee. Usually, serving on this committee is an opportunity to learn how the curriculum is put together and how to work collegially with some of the most influential members of the department. This assignment may give you a good understanding of the rationale for each course in the curriculum and how it contributes to the degree. It also offers an opportunity to gain insight into the politics of your department. For me, serving on my departmental Curriculum Committee and then on the Educational Policies Committee of the Academic Senate gave me the opportunity to learn about campus policies and the way the governance process worked before I became department chair.

Plan your path to leadership. For the reasons discussed earlier in this chapter, leadership opportunities do not just "happen" for women of color in academe. Faculty members who want to move into senior positions on the faculty or in administration must be deliberate about outlining a personal pathway to leadership as early in their career as possible. To be successful requires consciously cultivating certain skills and personality traits that will bolster your reputation, help you earn the promotions you seek, and assist in preserving your personal strength and health so you can succeed at the tasks you take on.

I actually did not begin to plan my administrative career until I was an acting dean. Prior to that, I took on a series of acting positions and projects without seriously planning for my own career. I had not even considered the dean position until a delegation of faculty from my college came to see me and urged me to put my hat in the ring. Only then did I seriously consider it. They persuaded me to allow myself to be nominated for the position, and I was ultimately chosen for the position. After that encounter, I was more deliberate about planning each of my administrative moves. I was the first female dean of the college, I was the first woman dean on the Dean's Council of the University, and under my leadership, nearly half of the 22 department and program chairs appointed in the college were women or underrepresented minorities during the 6 years that I was dean. One of the things I learned from this position was the importance of leadership from the top in setting examples for change.

Whether your goal is to be a department chair, dean, provost, or president, start by deliberately mapping the steps to the goal. This process begins with developing an understanding of the pathways taken by people who are in those positions now. Talk to your dean, provost, or if possible, the president of your institution, or people in other institutions whom you admire, about how they prepared themselves to move into leadership positions. Seek out and gain insights from other women and men of color who are leaders on campus. My graduate years were focused on social activism and scholarship. When I received my PhD, I decided to make the classroom the platform for my social justice stand. I have always been committed to access for underrepresented students (of all kinds) in the academy. It is a core value for me. But when I learned that I could help to make a whole department excellent and focus on student access and success issues, I became a department chair. When I learned I could help to model what an exemplary college looked like that promoted the values of diversity, then I became a college dean (with 22 departments and programs). When I realized I could help to model what an entire academic program looked like that promoted the value of diversity, then I became a vice president for academic affairs and provost. When I then realized that we could model for other universities what an entire institution looked like that had a mission and set of core values based on promoting diversity I became a university president. And finally, when I had the opportunity to provide a forum for national and international conversations on the issue of the value of diversity in a pluralistic society such as ours, I accepted the challenge of being president of an influential national higher education association. The take-home message here is that if you are driven by a passion and a set of core values, then you are less likely to be perceived as a careerist or an opportunist when it comes to making your administrative choices and being very deliberate about those choices.

Develop your leadership style and skills. The ACE Office of Women in Higher Education sponsors a national women's network and offers a range of opportunities to network and learn from other women leaders. Other opportunities for networking and learning leadership skills are available through ACE's Center for Advancement of Racial and Ethnic Equity and the American Association of Community Colleges, which has affiliate groups for women and for minorities, and through HERS, based at Bryn Mawr College in Bryn Mawr, Pennsylvania. AAHE's former Hispanic Caucus has become a separate national organization, the American Association of Hispanics in Higher Education (AAHHE), offering strong leadership and mentoring programs as well.

Make it a point to develop and demonstrate critical leadership skills early in your career. For example, often faculty try to avoid attending meetings because the agenda is not well defined or discussion is allowed to wander far from the meeting's original purpose. Demonstrating that you can run an effective meeting can inspire respect and gratitude from your colleagues. Problem solving is another skill to cultivate. If there is a dispute about who will teach a particular course and at what time, try to be the person who— instead of just arguing—offers a practical solution. Work on your speaking skills. Learn to present your ideas convincingly, in a way that others understand them and will respect you and the ideas even if they don't agree with you. Mastering all these skills can provide a significant boost to your authority among your colleagues. For example, in my own case, early in my faculty career I had participated in a year-long leadership program at the insistence of my mentor Joan Greenway. She said, "You never know when this kind of training will come in handy, and you can use the time to work on your research and publications as well." So, I participated in the program for a year on another campus in the same system, and when I returned to my own home university, I immediately went back to the faculty and focused on my teaching and research. I had no immediate interest in being an administrator. But because I had chaired a departmental committee and had spoken up and been very vocal in senate and university-wide meetings, I had come to the attention of the dean and the provost as someone who certainly had opinions and was not reluctant to speak her mind. You see, that administrative stint gave me ability as a faculty member to "see" and understand the functioning of a university in ways that my peer faculty members could not. Those leadership skills, plus the ones I honed as a community organizer during the civil rights movement, and the ones I learned as a youth leader in my church gave me the skills I needed to be effective in building coalitions and learning how to "work the system." The fact that I have a deep voice as a woman and I have learned how to use that voice to get people's attention and to command respect is another plus!

Take calculated risks. Another way to bolster the perceptions of you as a leader is to take some calculated risks and be seen as an innovator. By calculated risks I mean being conscious about weighing the pros and cons of a decision that has an impact on your leadership options and then deciding what you are going to do based on a decision-making process. Ask yourself questions such as, Will this decision hamper or impede my leadership trajectory? Should I take a leadership role (on the academic side) before I am a full professor? Will this hurt my chances or help me in the long run? In other words, weigh the investments of time, effort, and other risks against the benefits to be garnered from taking on such an assignment in terms of knowledge, visibility, networking opportunities, monetary compensation, and institutional appreciation. Remember, for the most part, institutions do not hug back, meaning you must think about your decision in terms of whether it is the right opportunity for you at that time.

At one point fairly early in my career, I was asked to chair a department that appeared on the verge of closure. Uncertain about whether to take on this task, I asked the dean who encouraged me. With the help of senior faculty—men and women—I took on the challenge. In short order, I was able to turn the department around and demonstrate my leadership capabilities—including the particular skill of turning a failing program into a stronger department. As I mentioned earlier in this chapter, I took over as chair of the women's studies program and a recently merged ethnic studies department consisting of four different programs: American Indian studies, African American studies, Asian American studies, and Hispanic American studies. I actually felt flattered when the dean of the College of the Arts (Liberal Arts) asked me to take on this troubled constellation of programs and forge a department out of them. My colleagues in the anthropology program told me that I was committing professional suicide by taking on such a troubled program. But I saw it as a challenge and an opportunity to bring a new cutting-edge concept in programming to the college and university.

My university was primarily a polytechnic university where most of the students majored in engineering, agriculture, architecture, or business. So selling these programs as a major was out of the question. Instead I had a vision for creating five different minors and several certificate programs that would be useful to students going into professional fields. This was at a time when California was just starting to deal with multicultural issues in the workplace in the early 1980s.

So when I met with the disgruntled faculty of the five programs and told them about my vision for a new ethnic and women's studies department, they bought it after a lot of back-and-forth and negotiating the core values of this new department. Once the faculty bought into my vision, we set out to create this unique set of programs. We developed some of the first interdisciplinary courses on campus, five minors, and we became one of the few departments across the United States that integrated issues of race, class, and gender and sexuality into our curriculum. Because of my experience with the Academic Senate, we were able to put a large number of our courses on the general education list in a variety of categories.

Be self-confident. A leader must perceive herself as confident and be perceived by others as trusting in herself and in her instincts. Participating in leadership training and networking can also help with the task of building self-confidence. It can be difficult, but another way to enhance your self-confidence is to stay on task—to focus on the things that are important to you and succeed at them. As you work with people in your department or institution, and as you expose yourself to other leaders, you are likely to realize at some point that you have been developing leadership skills and you were hardly conscious of doing so.

One concrete way to build self-confidence is to attend and become active in your disciplinary professional meetings so that you know at all times what is cutting-edge work, nationally and internationally, in your field. García (1997) also notes that involvement with professional organizations is important at the social/personal level as well as the scholarly/academic level. At the social/personal level the professional organization provides women of color, who are often isolated on their individual campuses, a network to meet other faculty of color and a circle of friends to call upon for advice. At the

scholarly/academic level these organizations can often provide research partners, a place to test new ideas, and the opportunity to talk to people who
truly understand your research (García).

In my own case, I have been lucky enough to have been involved in the
American Anthropological Association (AAA) since I was a graduate student.
In the mid-1970s the Mellon Foundation gave the Association of Black
Anthropologists a grant to bring a group of graduate students to the national
meetings. That year, in 1972—I will never forget it—the meeting was held
in Toronto, Canada. It was my first professional meeting, and I have been a
member ever since. It was also the first meeting where I saw Johnetta Cole
and Niara Sudarkasa as young assistant professors of anthropology who were
actively involved in social justice issues not only in their research areas but
also within the AAA. Over these past 30-plus years, I have gotten to know
all the Black anthropologists and the other anthropologists of color. I even
had the opportunity to ask Johnetta Cole (former president of Spelman College and current president of Bennett College) and Niara Sudarkasa (former
president of Lincoln University) to be my mentors. We have been friends
and colleagues now for over 30 years. Over the years, I have given papers and
served on key committees and task forces within the association. Again, I
brought my leadership skills from my community life and the university to
bear. In 1992 I was elected president of the Anthropology and Education
Section of the AAA because of the visibility and timeliness of the topics of
the sessions that I organized within the larger association. I was elected by
the membership to serve on the executive board from 1993 to 1995 and was
then elected president of AAA from 1995 to 1997. I was the first African
American president of the AAA in its 100-year history. Of course it is not
necessary to become president of your professional or disciplinary association, but your involvement at any level will raise your stock in your home
department. And if you are not appreciated in your current department, it
will help you move on to your next position. Remember, if you aspire to
senior academic leadership, you are going to have to demonstrate that you
are a leader far beyond the walls of your department. This can also mean
working on your own campus on key committees as well.

Be passionate about your work and true to your beliefs. Hopefully, you have
made the right choice of an institutional base and can be enthusiastic about
implementing the institution's mission. Demonstrating how much you care
about your students and the issues you are committed to can energize your
students and your colleagues. Realize that if you find it hard to be passionate
about your work, you may have chosen the wrong academic niche or institution—and that you may have to move on to another college or university.

There are strategic ways to do that as well so that you minimize any damage to your career. A good mentor can help you with that kind of transition. For me, I knew that it would be hard to turn down the offer of the presidency of CCNY when it was offered to me because I had always been true to its mission "to educate the whole people." CCNY was started by the city of New York in 1847 to educate immigrants and children of immigrants and poor, bright, and smart students. By 1993, the year I became president, it had become a world-class doctoral-granting institution still serving the poor and underserved students of New York City and the world. The day I went for my first on-campus interview I learned about all the problems of an urban campus, but in spite of all of those problems, I knew that it was the presidency for me. Ultimately, they chose me—and I chose them too. It was a wonderful and difficult presidency for me. Every day for 6 years I went to work to tackle those problems. I felt good about being there and making a contribution to the legacy of such a place.

Finally, take care of your physical and emotional self. There will always be papers to correct, grades to record, discussions and lectures to prepare, and scholarly articles and books to write. But when the weekend comes, take some time off. When it is time for vacation, get away from your work. It is essential to build time into your routine to be reflective. A burned-out faculty member does no favors to either her students or herself. Early in my faculty career, when my two daughters were small children, my husband and I used to take a vacation away from them so that we could have time for ourselves. Over time I actually took that model one step further, by taking periodic vacations away from both my children and my husband. It took me a while, but I learned not to feel guilty about it. It worked wonders for my rejuvenation. And it gave me the energy I needed to return for the next round of opportunities and challenges of academic administration. I have other colleagues who plan special getaways for themselves to retreats or spas and they have standing reservations to go every year! We owe that kind of care to ourselves. We all have our own ways of maintaining and restoring emotional balance. Spending time with women friends, with family, or with professional friends outside your institution can help.

Conclusion

Those of us who have devoted many years, even decades, to defining and following our pathway to leadership in academe know that the path for women of color in the future will not be easy either. But we who have gone before can help point out the barriers and some strategies for going over, around, and under them as we work on long-range strategies to completely knock those barriers down!

Women of color who want to become academic leaders will need to overcome conservative economic and societal trends, such as the backlash against affirmative action, as well as demographic change, declining higher education budgets, and competition for the most prestigious jobs at the most prestigious institutions (if indeed that is where they want to go). At the same time, they must contend with remaining institutional barriers such as racism and sexism to gain full participation. Cathy Trower (Trower & Chait, 2002) believes that "change will come either from outside, perhaps initiated by trustees who span the corporate and academic worlds, or from inside, through grass-roots efforts of new faculty who bring with them different and diverse views, values and beliefs about work" (p. 7). You must see yourselves as these new leadership pioneers with the vision and skills to forge new leadership models that will work in the new academy.

Do not forget, as a result of conscious efforts such as affirmative action, enlightened self-interest on the part of universities and colleges, the sharing of learning experiences among women of color, and even learning from the mistakes of our women pioneers, that the doors to women's leadership have begun to open a little wider. In this chapter, I have endeavored to share my own story with you. Women of color can push the doors open even more if they understand that they must be responsible for defining their own goals and creating the path to reach them while making connections and collaborating with the ever-growing pool of women in this country who share their values and their goals. These are the values and goals that target the creation of a new kind of leadership that strives for transformational change for all of higher education.

References

Alfred, M. V. (2001). Success in the ivory tower: Lessons from black female tenured faculty at a major research university. In R. Mabokela & A. L. Green (Eds.), *Sisters of the academy: Emergent black women scholars in higher education* (pp. 57–80). Sterling, VA: Stylus.

American Council on Education. (2005). *Creating flexibility in tenure-track faculty careers focus of new report from American Council on Education.* Retrieved March 11, 2009, from http://www.acenet.edu/AM/Template.cfm?Section=Search& template=/CM/HTMLDisplay.cfm&ContentID=18235

Boice, R. (1992). *The new faculty member: Supporting and fostering professional development.* San Francisco: Jossey-Bass.

Corrigan, M. (2002). *The American college president: 2002 edition.* Washington, DC: American Council on Education.

Dean, D. R. (2003, November). *America's women chief academic officers and their presidential aspirations.* Paper presented at the meeting of the Association for the Study of Higher Education, Portland, OR.

Finkelstein, M. J., & Schuster, J. (2001, October). Assessing the silent revolution: How changing demographics are reshaping the academic profession. *AAHE Bulletin, 54*(2), 3–7.

García, M. (Ed.). (1997). *Affirmative action's testament of hope: Strategies for a new era.* Albany, NY: SUNY Press.

Guinier, L., & Torres, G. (2003). *The miner's canary: Enlisting race, resisting power, transforming democracy.* Cambridge, MA: Harvard University Press.

Harvey, W. B. (2002). *Minorities in higher education 2001–2002: Nineteenth annual status report.* Washington, DC: American Council on Education.

Harvey, W. B. (2003). *Minorities in higher education 2002–2003: Twentieth annual status report.* Washington, DC: American Council on Education.

Mason, M. A., & Goulden, M. (2004, November–December). *Do babies matter (Part II)? Closing the baby gap.* Retrieved March 11, 2009, from http://www.aaup.-org/AAUP/pubsres/academe/2004/ND/Feat/04ndmaso.htm

Moses, Y. T. (1989). *Black women in academe: Issues and strategies.* Washington, DC: American Association of Colleges and Universities.

Schacter, J. P. (2001). *Geographical mobility: March 1999 to March 2000. U.S. Census Bureau, Current Population Reports, Series P20–538.* Washington, DC: U.S. Government Printing Office.

Sorcinelli, M. D. (2000). *Principles of good practice: Supporting early career faculty.* Washington, DC: American Association for Higher Education.

Trower, C. H., & Chait, R. P. (2002, March–April). Faculty diversity: Too little for too long. *Harvard Magazine,* 33–37, 98.

Turner, C. S. V. (2000). Defining success: Promotion and tenure-planning for each career stage, and beyond. In M. Westport (Ed.), *Succeeding in an academic career: A guide for faculty of color* (pp. 111–140). Westport, CT: Greenwood.

Turner, C. S. V. (2002). *Diversifying the faculty: A guidebook for search committees.* Washington, DC: Association of American Colleges and Universities.

Wilson, R. (2003, December). How babies alter careers for academics: Having children often bumps women off the tenure track, a new study shows. *The Chronicle of Higher Education, 50*(15), A1.

9

WOMEN AND THE QUEST FOR PRESIDENTIAL LEGITIMACY

Rita Bornstein

L
egitimacy is the sine qua non of a successful college presidency (Bornstein, 2003). Beginning with the search and assimilation processes, continuing through the years of institution building and, finally, the next presidential transition, effective presidents must have the respect and support of their constituents. Stakeholders accord legitimacy to a president they view as a good fit with the institutional culture and as an effective leader (Hollander & Julian, 1978). Legitimacy cannot be taken for granted but ebbs and flows with a president's decisions and actions. It often requires repair. When legitimacy with one of a president's key constituencies—faculty or trustees—is lost and beyond repair, the presidency is in trouble. However, once leaders gain legitimacy, constituents give them more leeway to act on their behalf (Gamson, 1968; Hollander & Julian).

A Higher Hurdle

Female presidents face the same legitimacy hurdles as their male counterparts, but for women, the legitimacy bar is higher. Women must overcome structural and gender-based cultural biases and discrimination; many carefully monitor their own attitudes and behaviors to avoid reinforcing sex stereotypes. Expectations for the role of college president are based on traditional male models, and the position is located within taken-for-granted gendered structures.

I am grateful to Ellen Kimmel and Rachel Setear for their insightful comments and suggestions on the manuscript, and to Jim Eck for his assistance in analyzing the survey data. Rita Bornstein is President Emerita and Cornell Professor of Philanthropy and Leadership Development at Rollins College.

Gendered expectations of leadership are not unique to higher education but exist in most institutions where men have traditionally held the chief executive officer (CEO) position. For example, Alice Eagly points out that the symphony conductor role "has a thoroughly masculine image. . . . [making it difficult] for people to reconcile their ideas of what a conductor should be like with their ideas of what a woman should be like. This disjunction makes the role especially challenging for women, but fortunately there are some women willing to take on this challenge" ("Gender and Leadership," 1998, p. 107). Despite the common disjunction between stereotyped expectations and actual leader performance, it is unlikely that scholars and practitioners can reconceive academic leadership until women represent more than a token number of presidents and establish themselves as effective within existing systems. In her groundbreaking 1977 book, *Men and Women of the Corporation*, Rosabeth Moss Kanter notes that tokens are "both highly visible as people who are different and yet not permitted the individuality of their own unique, non-stereotypical characteristics" (p. 211).

Judith Glazer-Raymo (1999) takes a pessimistic view of the potential of women to overcome the barriers to their progress and calls the metaphorical glass ceiling impermeable. She attacks the cultural myths that embody assumptions of the "inevitability of women's progress, the autonomy of their choices, and the fairness of the reward system," while they underestimate "the tenacity of obstacles deterring women's upward mobility." Glazer-Raymo also points out that those who are invited to participate in the system are expected to "adapt to existing institutional norms" (pp. 196–197).

Although formidable barriers remain, women have made progress in gaining and retaining the top leadership role in academic institutions. According to a 2002 survey by the American Council on Education (ACE), the proportion of women in college presidencies more than doubled between 1986 and 2001, from 9.5% to 21% of all presidents (Corrigan, 2002). Despite this impressive advance in opportunity, many women experience significant challenges to their legitimacy—challenges less likely to affect their male counterparts. For example, the presidential search committee may find that

- there are fewer women candidates in the applicant pool, making the selection of a woman appear to be an affirmative-action decision;
- women candidates may seem less qualified than men candidates because they have traveled nontraditional career paths or taken longer to reach the senior level of administration;
- initially, women candidates may not appear "presidential" because of their own lack of confidence and the stereotyped expectations of campus constituents;

- after their hire, women presidents may mishandle management problems at the start of a presidency because they lack the mentoring that might have prepared them for this role; and
- women presidents may be seen as inept in developing relationships of importance to the institution, because many women are averse to the external requirements of the presidency.

This is not to suggest that women are always afflicted with such challenges (and men never are). In fact, there are ways in which the experience and background of women presidents may have given them better tools to adapt easily to a new institutional culture and to exert leadership accepted by constituents. Some women move into a presidency with the bona fides, confidence, expertise, and adaptability to achieve and maintain the legitimacy necessary to build their institutions and leave a significant legacy. In a survey of 377 presidents I conducted in 2002 (Bornstein, 2003), which had a 48% response rate, women and men did not report differences in their quest for legitimacy except in two areas: (a) women were more likely to experience their gender as an impediment to legitimacy, unless at a women's college where it facilitated their legitimacy; and (b) women were more likely to take an adaptive and situational approach to leadership.

Based on this survey, interviews with 13 presidents, extensive scholarly research, and my own 14 years of experience as a college president, I have proposed a series of factors that influence a leader's success in the three stages of a presidency: gaining legitimacy as a new president, making legitimate change, and assuring a legitimate transition at the conclusion of a presidency (Bornstein, 2003). The factors in legitimacy that I have identified interact differently in each presidency, and each factor can serve as an impediment to or facilitator of legitimacy. With the number of women presidents increasing, it is important to understand how the factors in presidential legitimacy affect women and how these factors become conflated with gendered expectations for leadership. Women presidents who understand the embedded biases and impediments to legitimacy that they face can work with their constituents to overcome or manage these obstacles.

Enough women have now completed successful long-term presidencies to provide evidence that gender does not by itself undermine the influence and accomplishment of college and university leaders. Does this record of achievement mean that women no longer find gender an impediment to acceptance and influence in their presidencies? It does not. Have these successful women presidents experienced leadership differently from male presidents? We do not know. Is there a possibility that we are at a tipping point where search committees begin to believe that the academy has had its share of women presidents and return to reproducing the traditional look and style of presidential leadership? That is a possibility. In fact, between 1998 and 2001, "the percentage of women presidents declined at almost all types of private institutions and at public baccalaureate institutions" (Corrigan, 2002, p. 16).

Much of what we think we know about women presidents is based on anecdote and informal observation, and needs to be tested systematically. The research on higher education leadership has been conducted primarily by and about men, and although research by women is gaining ground, what exists on women leaders is contradictory and inconclusive. There are few comparative studies. Our conceptions of leadership may change significantly as women presidents increasingly become subjects of research and women become "interpreters of organizational life and leadership in the academy" (Bensimon, 1993, p. 472).

Achieving Presidential Legitimacy

Gaining presidential legitimacy is dependent on the intersection of five factors: individual, institutional, environmental, technical, and moral. Some of these factors appear to be of special importance to a woman's quest for legitimacy, but without a great deal more data, our understanding of the relationship between legitimacy and gender is limited to inference. My own experience (Bornstein, 2003) in a successful 14-year presidency provides one case study of the impediments and facilitators to legitimacy faced by a new and nontraditional president at a liberal arts college. I had a number of special legitimacy hurdles because I was the first woman president, the first Jewish president, and the first from a development vice presidency. Men with nontraditional backgrounds also have legitimacy problems, and with more information on how successful presidents, both men and women, handle these challenges, we could provide better guidance to new leaders from all backgrounds.

Individual Legitimacy

This factor refers to the prestige and relevance of the background, experience, and personal characteristics that a president brings to the position and to the institution. A number of roads may lead to the college presidency, but the traditional academic route, the royal road (Birnbaum & Umbach, 2001), confers the greatest individual legitimacy. Many women have taken a circu-itous route to administration, which puts them at a disadvantage as presiden-tial candidates. Family obligations may have required them to step off the career track for a while, creating professional potholes that are difficult to repair. According to the ACE survey, women presidents have spent an aver-age of 5 years out of the full-time job market compared with 2 years for their male counterparts (Corrigan, 2002).

Women often have difficulty navigating the "cultural barriers" and "structural impediments" to their pursuit of academic careers. A series of interviews with senior women faculty at the University of Minnesota, Twin Cities, conducted by Shirley Clark and Mary Corcoran (1993), uncovered disadvantages in their early preparation or their careers. These disadvantages included "lack of sponsorship . . . , exclusion from the collegial culture, and significant 'role-overloading' with marital and child-care demands." As a result, the researchers conclude, "Although women are no longer excluded, their place may be limited to some middle-range of career success" (pp. 410–411).

On paper, women may not appear qualified for a presidency and often fail to make the final cut, but women also may bring to the position strengths that are not evident on their résumés. Mary Catherine Bateson (1990) writes of the creative potential and adaptability that arise from the interrupted and discontinuous lives led by many women. Men, says Bateson, tend to operate on a single track, while women's lives make them more comfortable impro-vising creative and flexible solutions to the problems arising in our fluid and discontinuous society. These qualities of flexibility, adaptability, and creativ-ity are very appropriate for the current academic environment.

An increasing number of presidents have not traveled the royal road and are chosen for the other experiences and skills they bring. The number of presidents with experience outside higher education grew from 10% in 1986 to 15% in 2001 (Corrigan, 2002). Such presidents, both women and men, have a legitimacy handicap that must be overcome, but many of them do very well. In fact, experience in external relations may explain the rapid increase, up from 8% in 1986 to 27% in 2001 (Corrigan), in the number of women presidents at 2-year colleges where such skills are highly prized. Reporting on a discussion among women presidents, Brown, Van Ummer-sen, and Sturnick (2001) suggest that some women are drawn to struggling institutions where conventional qualifications are less of an issue and where their strengths are needed. They say also that when women fail in one presidency, they are less likely than men to seek another since "a failure may leave a first-time woman president feeling incompetent or embarrassed" (pp. 10–12). Women presidents serve 2.2 fewer years than men and are less likely, 18.8% compared with 26.6% of men, to hold a second presidency, in part because of lifestyle issues and the strain on their personal lives (Brown et al.).

To increase the pool of women with traditional qualifications for the presidency, the academic pipeline must be unclogged. In its December 3, 2004, edition, *The Chronicle of Higher Education* reported that although women earn 51% of all PhDs, they constitute only 38% of college and university faculties and just 28% of the faculties at research institutions. In America's elite universities, men make up over 70% of professors and 60% of assistant professors (Wilson, 2004). In 2004, of 32 offers of tenure in the arts and sciences at Harvard University, just four went to women. Exacerbating the chilly climate for women, in early 2005, Harvard's president said publicly that women may be innately less able than men to succeed in science and mathematics, and he downplayed the role of bias in explaining the dearth of women in science and engineering at elite institutions. A faculty standing committee on women at Harvard responded that his remarks "serve to reinforce the institutional culture at Harvard that erects numerous barriers to improving the representation of women on the faculty, and to impede our efforts to recruit top women scholars" (Hemel, 2005, p. 1).

Academic institutions, corporations, and governments have all made progress in preparing and selecting women for leadership, but the challenges, identified by Kanter in 1977, persist. People in positions of power tend to reproduce themselves when making decisions about mentoring, hiring, and promoting. Partly in response to the institutionalized male bias, especially at top institutions, many women PhDs are finding alternative employment opportunities such as teaching at community colleges, working in business and industry, or freelancing. Until women move through the academic pipeline in sufficient numbers, they will be underrepresented in presidential candidate pools, and those chosen from nontraditional career paths will continue to have legitimacy challenges.

Another pipeline problem that constricts the number of qualified women presidential candidates is the attitude of women in academic vice presidencies. Although this role is the most legitimate launching pad for a presidency, especially at prestigious institutions, Diane Dean (2003) has found that 63% of women chief academic officers do not wish to be presidents. This is not because they do not believe they could be hired as presidents—73% of them believe they could if they sought the position. They express three major reasons for their disinclination to seek a presidency: (a) they believe that the presidency will distance them from "the academic heart" of an institution, (b) they do not wish to engage in the fund-raising and socializing required of a president, and (c) they want more balance in their life than the all-consuming presidential schedule allows.

Dean is currently gathering comparative data for men, but her research results on women are consistent with a larger social trend. A survey of corporate women not yet in senior positions reveals that 25% of them do not aspire to those jobs. They are opting out because they want time with family, they lack confidence in their ability, or they reject the stereotypical male model of leadership (Kellerman & Rhode, 2004). These issues cross many professional fields. In an interview focusing on methods of increasing the number of women leaders of symphony orchestras, Alice Eagly suggests that "the anticipation of gender prejudice causes many women to hesitate to apply for higher-level positions until their qualifications are exceedingly good—in fact, better than those of the men who apply" "(Gender and Leadership," 1998, p. 110). The evidence suggests that the quest for individual legitimacy is more challenging for women presidents than for men.

Institutional Legitimacy

This factor relates to the internal structural and cultural contexts in which a president and her constituents experience the search and transition processes, governance, and other norms and traditions.

There are many pitfalls, especially for women, and most especially for the "first" woman president. The first woman in a presidency is viewed from a male-normed perspective, and constituents may perceive differences in personal and leadership style negatively. As Hollander (1992) observes, "women begin with an initial hurdle to attaining legitimacy" resulting from "the effect of expectations about a prototype" (p. 72). The first woman president is an oddity, a novelty, even a cultural misfit. Constituents may feel that she does not look or act like a president. They scrutinize her critically—her clothes, language, family arrangements, and management style. Judith Rodin has said that being the first female president of the University of Pennsylvania, indeed the first in the Ivy League, was an opportunity and a burden (Basinger, 2003).

In one women's college, the first woman president was compared unfavorably with her dignified male predecessors because, one alumna said, "she is short with short gray hair that is not in the least bit attractive, and wears godawful clothes" (Leatherman, 1992, p. A17). After being ousted, this president wrote, "Women are defined more by how they look . . . than by what they can do. . . . There was no way for [constituents] to have another sense of how a different new president . . . might look and act" (Hall, 1993, p. 19).

Gender appears to be an impediment for some women, especially those who are the first to be appointed president in a coeducational institution. In my 2002 survey on presidential legitimacy, 9 of the 34 women respondents (26%) indicated that gender had been a handicap in their quest for legitimacy. Another 8 of the respondents presided over single-sex institutions where, according to some respondents, being a woman was an advantage.

In addition to cultural fit, institutional legitimacy includes the ability to work within the structures and habits of board and faculty governance. Women are often at a disadvantage in managing this aspect of legitimacy because of the unequal power relations in our social institutions, which can diminish the authority of a president. Male trustees are often unaccustomed to interacting with women in positions of leadership, and they are less likely to develop the social, travel, and sports relationships with women presidents that characterize their relationships with male colleagues. Thus, the relations of many woman presidents with their boards remain formal.

In faculty governance, men also are accustomed to dominating, in part because of their seniority and numbers and in part because women faculty often lack the experience and confidence to exert leadership. Here, too, instead of talking informally over coffee, women presidents may have to depend on formal mechanisms to involve themselves in faculty matters. New women presidents must find alternate ways of establishing their authority and clarifying their expectations in order to establish mutually reinforcing and respectful relationships. Fortunately, as more women move into positions of leadership in the corporate, government, and nonprofit worlds, and these interactions become more familiar and comfortable, the unease between women and men in positions of power will diminish.

Key to institutional legitimacy is the extent to which constituents, especially faculty, perceive the president to be a good fit with a college's culture and norms. Male and female presidents have failed to gain or have lost their legitimacy and then their jobs, some within the first year or two, based on a real or perceived lack of cultural fit. Women have the added burden of overcoming expectations derived from a history of male presidents. In every case, the legitimacy of a president's vision and goals for change depends on the leader's ability to connect them organically to the organizational culture.

Those presidents who do not fit into the culture have been characterized as alien tissue that is rejected, like an unsuccessful graft (McLaughlin, 1996). Because women presidents are more likely to be viewed as outsiders, as alien tissue, they must work harder to achieve a good fit and the legitimacy that depends on it. Ann Die (1999), former president of Hendrix College, writes, "Many presidents get off on the wrong foot—and will continue on the wrong foot—because their articulated vision cannot be embraced by most of their stakeholders" (p. 35). Failure to appreciate and fit into a culture impedes the legitimacy and the leadership potential of presidents. In my study, in response to a survey question about why presidents lose their jobs, one woman president wrote: "The cases that especially strike me are those in which a president wants to do things that an institution truly needs, but does not grasp the distinctive culture of the place and is thus unable to sing its song in key."

Presidents are judged effective leaders, says Estela Bensimon (1991), if they are seen as taking the role of the faculty, which involves "a sharing of key faculty values, beliefs, and patterns of thinking" (p. 641). Those who are interactive and consultative in their leadership style may have a better chance of being accepted than those who are distant and bureaucratic. Presidents also may find that a high level of consultation is the most effective way of working with trustees. Of course, some presidential actions and decisions will be interpreted as inimical to faculty interests and, as a result, as failing to connect with the traditions and culture of the institution.

Institutional legitimacy is a challenge for every president, and although women face gender-based impediments, they also bring unique strengths. All presidents, however, must struggle to promote change within the cultural context and decision-making structures of their particular institutions.

Environmental Legitimacy

Every president is faced with the vicissitudes of the external environment— the economy, enrollment patterns, legislation, public opinion, terrorism, war. Major projects and campaigns have been torpedoed by economic collapse, and institutional planning and growth have been stalled by severe declines in enrollment and revenue. The leadership challenge is to maintain the institution's equilibrium through rough times and to generate momentum when times are good. It also requires that leaders ensure that their institutions are responsive to trends affecting higher education, although not overly reactive to passing student interests. Many women have not been mentored or prepared sufficiently for the wide array of critical challenges that can sweep through an institution and require a president's attention. Some believe that women need better mentoring on such issues as risk assessment and reading campus politics and campus culture (Brown et al., 2001). Although men are faced with similar problems, they appear to have a broader and deeper network of mentors and colleagues to seek advice from.

Prior to my own presidency, I had learned many important leadership lessons from the CEO of each institution I was associated with. While we never formalized a mentorship relationship or called it by that name, those CEOs gave me opportunities for growth and achievement, and they instructed me through their behavior. When I assumed my presidency, I brought with me the extraordinary experience of having watched and worked closely with a successful, long-term president. He was always available to discuss problems and offer advice.

Constituents look to the president to set the tone and chart a course for the institution even, or perhaps especially, when there are many environmental challenges. A president who vacillates or exhibits uncertainty, confusion, or indecisiveness in the face of such challenges is viewed as weak, a special problem for women, whose inclination is to consult widely before making important decisions. On the other hand, unless an institution is in crisis, a president dare not make significant changes without first establishing a convincing case, ensuring transparency, and involving faculty and trustees in the decision-making process. Presidents who have the necessary skills to manage in unpredictable environments are more likely to achieve legitimacy, which rests on leader competence as well as fit.

Technical Legitimacy

This factor refers to the president's ability to manage the institution, which includes internal and external responsibilities such as budgeting, faculty relations, fund-raising, and lobbying. The president's actions and decisions are perceived as competent or incompetent, effective or ineffective. The first woman to hold a presidency is violating norms about the gender appropriateness of the position. Performing tasks associated with her male predecessors, the new female president is diminished by the stereotyped expectations and low status assigned to her by constituents. Wishing to appear decisive and competent, women presidents may respond precipitously to internal or external challenges.

Constituents will withhold legitimacy until the president demonstrates her expertise and competence through task-relevant successes (Yoder, Schleicher, & McDonald, 1998). In one encouraging study, women business leaders "gained credibility and legitimacy by achieving results" (Rosener, 1990, p. 125). In another, women who displayed technical competence and provided "expertise in managing difficult, complex organizational programs and changes" were more likely to gain "follower acceptance or legitimacy" (Rusaw, 1996, p. 24).

Most studies find no difference in the leadership effectiveness of women and men (Birnbaum, 1992; Freeman, 2001; Hollander, 1992; Kabacoff, 2000), although some identify modest differences in leadership behavior.

Kabacoff, in a study of male and female corporate CEOs and senior vice presidents, found that men were seen as "more restrained in emotional expression" (p. 4) and women as more emotionally expressive, energetic, and intense, with a greater interpersonal orientation. Kabacoff identifies these perceived differences as stemming from sex-role stereotypes that nevertheless did not affect respondents' views of leadership effectiveness.

Another leadership issue is emotional intelligence, defined by Daniel Goleman (1995) as the ability to control impulsiveness, persist in the face of frustrations, regulate one's moods, and empathize with others. In his analysis of the characteristics necessary for effective leadership in the U.S. presidency, Fred Greenstein (2000) writes that without emotional intelligence "all else may turn to ashes" (p. 200). Higher education is replete with stories about presidents using intemperate language or exhibiting inappropriate emotional behavior, generally resulting in a loss of legitimacy and position. It would be useful to know if there are differences between male and female leaders in emotional intelligence, as there appear to be in what Kabacoff calls emotional expressiveness. An understanding of the interrelationship of emotional intelligence, gender, and leadership effectiveness would be an important contribution to our thinking about the college presidency.

Studies that have found women leaders to be more generative, interactive, consultative, relational, empowering, and connected than male leaders (Bensimon, 1993; Jablonski, 2000; Rosener, 1990; Rusaw, 1996) may simply be describing the nurturing role prescribed for women in a patriarchal society. These qualities may smooth the way for change but also may have the unintended consequence of making a president seem indecisive or weak. On the other hand, women presidents may strive for a male-normed leadership style, the only model they know—tough minded, decisive, and authoritative. Women as well as men have been fired from presidencies because of their authoritarian manner and failure to listen to faculty. In some cases, women presidents believe themselves to be participatory and empowering as leaders, while their faculties characterize them in opposite terms: directive and controlling, instead of participatory; and hierarchical and bureaucratic, instead of empowering (Jablonski, 2000).

When women are underrepresented in positions of leadership they often face resistance, lowered status, and questions about their competence (Yoder et al., 1998). In a study of women managers, Rusaw (1996) found that those who established credibility exhibited three key behavioral patterns: a track record of success, technical competence, and a service ethic. According to Rusaw, women overcome bias and gain acceptance as leaders by working hard to achieve recognition for their competence. In her study of women managers in federal agencies, Rusaw found that earning credibility among constituents requires developing task and relationship skills and using them appropriately for the context created by organizational norms.

In Becker (2002) a woman dean writes of the challenge she faced in being appointed to follow a male predecessor. She notes that faculty anxiety about her appointment was in response to the lack of a male authority figure: "The potential for anarchy is always present in patriarchal structures, because there is a perception that no defining order exists—that no rules, no cohesion can be maintained—without the father at the top" (p. A15). She goes on to suggest that women are rarely trained to be as tough as they need to be in high-visibility positions. In her own case, she writes, "It was important to project the image of a woman who was not afraid . . . and to try to become such a woman in fact" (p. B15). Susan Resnick Pierce recalls that as a new president, "I came in and behaved, whether I knew what I was doing or not, as if I did. I can remember taking deep breaths before I walked into a room, had a moment of absolute calm and said, 'be presidential' (whatever that meant), and sort of get myself into a mindset for a role" (S. R. Pierce, personal communication, 2002).

Many women suffer from the imposter syndrome, the sense that they are not qualified or competent for the job and will be unmasked as a fake (Topping & Kimmel, 1985). When these feelings of inadequacy represent an unrealistic self-appraisal, they can also lead to lowered effectiveness (Brems, Baldwin, Davis, & Namyniuk, 1994). There is some evidence, however, that for women and men the imposter syndrome diminishes with increasing achievement (Topping & Kimmel).

The college presidency is an all-consuming position with responsibilities for management of the enterprise, implementation of change, and development of resources. As Dean (2003) has demonstrated, not every woman has the appetite for such a broad-ranging position and many eschew the pace and demands of the presidency, especially the external requirements for socializing and fund-raising. This is true of many men as well, but it may be that male competitiveness and the drive for professional advancement outweigh those considerations. We do know that despite the special challenges to their legitimacy, successful women presidents leave a solid record of acceptance and achievement. Technical competence is a vital factor in presidential success.

Moral Legitimacy

This factor includes ethical behavior as well as devotion and service to the mission and values of the institution. There are all too frequent instances of presidential misbehavior, and the culprits are generally, although not exclusively, men. For example, in 2004 a woman, well known in her former presidency and maintaining her innocence, was indicted for "using her position to orchestrate a $5 million fraud scheme" to secure student financial aid loans that students later had to pay off (Ghezzi, 2004, p. D1). Whatever the disposition of such situations, examples of misconduct by women presidents are rare. Why is this? We need to understand more about the relationship between gender and ethics, and this is an area where leadership studies from other professions could be applicable. It may be that women tend to behave more ethically, that standards for the behavior of women are higher, or that women presidents always feel under scrutiny. Whatever the reason, most women presidents appear to understand the importance of internalizing the institutional ethos and the necessity of being above reproach.

A subtler aspect of moral leadership is the significant challenge to personal authenticity presented by a presidency. As women seek pathways to good decision making and to their acceptance as influential leaders, they may find the necessary compromises of the presidency distasteful. Some examples of inauthenticity are suppression of personal and political opinions to protect the integrity of the institution and its constituents; chameleon-like behavior reflected in subtle changes in language and demeanor with different constituent groups; and asymmetrical relationships that are like reciprocal friendships in appearance but freighted with the president's agenda—lobbying, fund-raising, and so forth. Successful, long-term presidents find ways to maintain their authenticity and integrity but "the need to act as the embodiment of the institution diminishes the president's individualism" (Bornstein, 2004, p. B16). The challenges to authenticity may help to explain the dislike of socializing and fund-raising expressed by so many female chief academic officers (Dean, 2003). However, presidents who have gained legitimacy exemplify the highest standards of moral behavior, and while suppression of the authentic self in service to a mission may sometimes be distasteful, it is not immoral.

The factors in achieving legitimacy (individual, institutional, environmental, technical, and moral) have a particular weight for women because they are often conflated with issues of gender. Despite these challenges, increasing numbers of women, from traditional and nontraditional backgrounds, apply for presidencies, are selected, and are successful.

Legitimacy and Institutional Change

Presidents seek to leave a legacy based on significantly enhanced institutional quality, reputation, and financial resources. Such improvements depend on the positioning and needs of an institution when a new president takes over, as well as the skill with which the newcomer approaches change. Presidents have little control over institutional decision making, which can be chaotic and anarchic (Cohen & March, 1974), but they can develop strategies to move a change agenda. The four interrelated factors that can promote or retard the legitimacy of institutional improvement efforts are presidential leadership, governance, social capital, and fund-raising. To be effective, a president must exhibit a leadership style consistent with the culture and needs of the institution, involve trustees and faculty through accepted governance systems, develop a strong network of trusting relationships with constituents (internal and external), and generate the philanthropy necessary to support innovation and change.

Presidential Leadership and Change

One of the many myths surrounding the presidency is that the right person, with the right vision, can lead an institution to new heights of excellence, recognition, and financial sufficiency. Ironically, faculties yearning for just such visionary presidents quickly grow disenchanted with leaders who arrive at a university or college ready to implement their vision and goals without concern for institutional history or culture. In the academy, to become institutionalized, change initiatives have to develop through a process perceived as legitimate. Presidents have an important leadership role to play in establishing frameworks for strategic planning, developing consensus around goals and needs, and providing incentives for implementing change. Although colleges and universities have been characterized as prototypical "organized anarchies . . . a problem to describe, understand, and lead" (Cohen & March, 1974, pp. 2–3), presidents must behave as though they are rational systems amenable to systematic planning. And, although the university president has been compared to the driver of a skidding car, whose marginal judgments, skill, and luck "may possibly make some difference to the survival prospects for his riders" (Cohen & March, p. 203), presidents must assume that their leadership can make a difference.

Presidents successful in repositioning their institutions through innovation and change are comfortable providing leadership in this context of chaos, complexity, and ambiguity. As Bateson (1990) suggests, an unpredictable, chaotic environment may favor women over men. We need more information about whether women react more nimbly to environmental perturbations and more creatively in anticipating new trends because of their experience with competing demands, multiple responsibilities, and circuitous career trajectories. Since women leaders are thought to be especially adept at relationship building, they may be better able to employ their networks to test and validate a compelling narrative (Birnbaum, 2002) with the power to unite and motivate the institution's constituencies. Bensimon (1991) reports that presidents who communicate, consult, and acknowledge faculty governance are taking the role of the faculty and therefore are able to gain approval and support for the changes they propose. Presidents who take the role of the faculty are also perceived to be effective leaders.

Although studies indicate that women and men are equally effective as leaders, it is not yet clear whether they would lead differently in a nongendered role and system and whether differences in leadership behavior would be viewed as the result of individual personality and experience. Faculties say they prefer collaborative leadership, but their underlying assumptions about good leadership are based on a more authoritarian *Father Knows Best* style. Women presidents are expected to have a different leadership style from men but are criticized as soft if they show themselves to be consultative consensus builders rather than authoritarian change agents.

Glazer-Raymo (1999) calls for adoption of "new institutional prototypes that replace hierarchical management, in-house rivalries, and ladder climbing with non-bureaucratic, responsive models . . . where women may enjoy different roles unconstrained by adversarial and competitive relationships" (p. 207). The generative leadership model developed by Sagaria and Johnsrud (as cited in Jablonski, 2000) encourages participation, creativity, empowerment, trust, and collaboration. Astin and Leland (1991) propose a nonhierarchical model of feminist leadership, with the leader "as a catalyst or facilitator" (pp. 8, 11) who promotes collective planning and action toward the accomplishment of the community's goals. In the words of one successful woman president, "That's leadership—looking, seeing, identifying, acting. Nothing happens unless you have a lot of people who want to make a place better. You have to tap into that. People want to be given permission, encouragement, and support" (S. R. Pierce, personal communication, 2002). A study of successful women managers suggests that in certain organizational settings so-called feminine qualities may actually be more effective in leadership. The leadership style of the women in this study is called interactive and involves "encouraging participation, sharing power and information, enhancing other people's self-worth, and getting others excited about their work" (Rosener, 1990, p. 120).

Sally Helgesen (1990) offers a compelling metaphor for women's ways of leading. Based on her observational study of four successful women executives, she reports that they lead from within an organizational web of inclusion. These women created a model much like a spider's web with themselves in the center of things, different from the traditional hierarchical, top-down model of leadership. The interrelated weblike structure enhanced the flow of information and communication and resulted in stronger relationships and better teamwork. It in no way diminished the leader's authority. Helgesen suggests that this way of leading is more suited to the information age than the hierarchical structure, which was more appropriate in the industrial era.

The hierarchical and interactive perspectives on effective leadership are often referred to as *transformational* and *transactional.* One of the most contested issues in the leadership literature is whether transformational or transactional leadership is more effective in promoting change. Although there is some disagreement about the definition of these terms, for the most part transformational refers to charismatic, visionary, authoritative leadership, and transactional to collegial, interactive, and collaborative leadership. Typically, men are identified with a strong, visionary top-down transformational style, although some scholars find women more transformational in that they inspire and nurture group commitment to institutional goals. Jill Ker Conway (2001), former president of Smith College, has a different view: "To me, the argument for including women was one of equity and utility, not some biologically based transformative capacity. I thought the executive role very little modified by the sex of the person who played it" (p. 125). Transactional leadership has been characterized pejoratively by some as reactive leadership that "responds to the consensus reflections of constituents" (Fisher & Koch, 1996, p. xi). A gendered perspective assumes a male model of visionary, authoritative leadership as transformational, and a female model of inclusive, collaborative leadership as transactional.

As useful as they may be for purposes of analysis, these two styles are not dichotomous but are part of a continuum of behaviors available to female and male leaders as called for by different institutional circumstances (Bass, 1985; Birnbaum, 1992; Hollander, 1987; Northouse, 2001). Each institution is unique and each changes over time. The appropriate leadership style for one situation may be inappropriate in another. Eagly ("Gender and Leadership," 1998) reports that according to theorists there is no one generally effective leadership style. "Some situations," she says, "call for a more autocratic, directive style, and others call for a much greater component of communication, consensus building, and participation. . . . The ideal leader therefore would shift from one style to another, after an astute sizing up of the style that would be optimal in each situation" (p. 108). Steven Sample (2002), president of the University of Southern California, agrees. He writes, "Leadership is highly situational and contingent; that is, what works for me as a leader may not work for you, and what works for me as a leader today may not work for me tomorrow" (p. 25).

My 2002 survey on legitimacy questioned presidents about leadership style. Forty-nine percent of the 182 respondents considered themselves to be transformational, 28% transactional, and 23% both. Forty-one percent of the women presidents indicated that they are transformational *and* transactional compared with just 25% of the male presidents. This is an important gender difference in presidents' perceptions of good leadership as contextual. The difference might be construed as reflecting the adaptability many women develop through their complicated career paths and personal lives. The comments that respondents made about this issue are instructive. These presidents do not regard the two styles as contradictory, dichotomous, or mutually exclusive, but view good leadership as transformational or transactional, depending on the context or situation. Many see themselves as having applied both styles of leadership: the transformational to establish their vision and the transactional to enact change.

In my own examination of legitimacy in the academic presidency, I apply the term *transformative* to leadership that I have defined as "the exercise of either or both presidential authority and constituent collaboration, as appropriate to the situation" (Bornstein, 2003, p. 99). From this perspective, a repertoire of leadership behaviors is available to women and men, and successful leadership is less a matter of style or gender than it is a good match between a president and an institution. Kelly and Duerst-Lahti (2000) call this a world in which "traits and behaviors exhibited by leaders, and actors at all levels and positions, can be seen as suitable for the socially situated context in which they occur regardless of the biological sex or sexual orientation of the person who happens to be the leader or actor at that moment and place" (p. 262). Transformative presidents can lead successful and legitimate change by working thoughtfully within the contexts of their institutions, and women may hold an advantage in this area because of their flexible and adaptable approach to leadership.

Governance and Change

For change initiatives to be accepted as legitimate and to become institutionalized, they should be validated through the formal board and faculty governance systems. Although processing change through governance is time-consuming and the outcomes are unpredictable, inclusiveness in decision making legitimates the president's change agenda. However, as Nannerl Koehane (1998), former president of Duke University, points out, "Caught between . . . trustee authority and faculty prerogatives, presidents can some-times feel more like the rope in a game of tug-of-war than a chief executive officer" (p. 14).

It is important for new presidents, especially women, to be consultative and to operate within the structures of an institution's governance culture. Once legitimacy is achieved, a president has more latitude, although Tierney (2001) believes that genuine shared governance is necessary for sustained, successful reform. Koehane (1998) compares the modern campus to a demo-cratic political system, with extensive checks and balances governing rela-tionships among the board, faculty, and administration. The president sets the agenda and involves appropriate stakeholders in the processes necessary to create change. Where such a cultural climate exists, the governance system can facilitate rather than sabotage change.

Many presidents and scholars consider faculties to be obstacles to change: "The innate academic conservatism of tenured, senior faculty at American institutions of higher education reflects many things, including their own significant managerial role and their insulation from the forces of the marketplace" (Fisher & Koch, 1996, p. 155). For example, when presi-dents propose changes to the curriculum, based on changing student inter-ests and preferences, faculty may feel that their expertise and control are being compromised and refuse to cooperate. Fortunately, as noted in the section on institutional legitimacy, those presidents seen as taking the role of the faculty through their behaviors and actions are "able to gain approval and support for proposed changes" (Bensimon, 1991, pp. 651–652).

Social Capital and Change

Successful change and institutional improvement define a president's legacy, but to implement new initiatives a president must rely on significant internal and external social capital. Social capital is the accretion within a community of honest and cooperative behavior, shared norms, and a "prevalence of trust" (Fukuyama, 1995, p. 26). Rusaw (1966) considers trust an essential leadership skill, necessary for successful and effective task completion.

According to Coleman (1988), groups with extensive trust are able to accomplish much more than comparable groups without it. This view is reinforced in an ACE study of change in higher education institutions. The authors found that in the absence of trust, "stakeholders will focus on pre-serving rights and privileges rather than taking risks to create a future with the common good in mind" (Eckel, Green, Hill, & Mallon, 1999, p. 9). Distrust, they say, makes organizations dysfunctional (Eckel et al.). With a network of trusting relationships, a president can develop a consensus for change.

A president's most trusting relationships must be with the board, faculty, and administration. These are the connections necessary to ensure presidential legitimacy and to build support for change. Birnbaum (1992) asserts that a president who has secured the support of all three constituencies is considered successful and "has a claim to being a good leader." Based on evidence that women are especially good at cultivating relationships, they should be well suited for attaining legitimacy, building social capital, and generating consensus for change. Women, says Rusaw (1996), earn respect through "developing interpersonal relations skills as leaders" (p. 24). However, if women resent the time and the inauthentic behaviors involved in building social capital, they may neglect the relationships so vital to presidential success.

Without internal and external social capital a president cannot reposition or strengthen an institution. In fact, without it a president cannot survive in office. Dissatisfaction with a president's actions accumulates in the institutional memory and eventually reaches a tipping point where it jeopardizes the presidency. Overwhelmingly, respondents to my 2002 survey on legitimacy said that the loss of faculty or board support is a major reason presidents lose their job. Such a loss of support depletes the trust necessary for social capital, and failure to sustain social capital delegitimizes a presidency.

No changes can be sold and implemented without the enthusiastic support and involvement of the president's senior team. Three values are key to the relationship between presidents and their administrators—expertise, mutual respect, and loyalty (Bornstein, 2000). Loyalty to the president is critical because senior administrators can undermine the president's legitimacy, sometimes unwittingly, through their conversations with trustees, faculty, alumni, and others. Women presidents may inherit or hire senior administrators who are burdened with stereotyped expectations for leadership. It takes courage, confidence, and patience to build a well-functioning team despite such misgivings. Women, especially, have to guard against several dangers: failing to delegate appropriately out of concern for the quality of outcomes; the tendency of senior administrators to delegate up some of their thorniest problems; and enabling what Judith McLaughlin has called sibling rivalry, where senior people complain about each other to the president (J. McLaughlin, personal communication, 2002). The top team is also key to positioning the president. What the senior administrators say publicly and privately helps to shape the perceptions that constituents develop about such things as their president's style, competence, and concern for faculty and students. The wrong signals can quickly delegitimate, even terminate, a presidency.

Fund-Raising and Change

Change requires resources, available from a variety of sources: government, tuition, endowment, investments, commercial ventures, patents, subsidiaries, grants, contracts, and philanthropy. Most of this funding is directed to activities outside the president's direct control, while philanthropy provides the most flexibility in support of the president's change initiatives. The president has final approval of fund-raising priorities, makes most of the big solicitations, and can allocate new resources to strengthen or create programs, staff, and facilities (Bornstein, 2003). Conway (2001) notes that in her early years as president of Smith College, "Since the faculty was almost fully tenured, I could change Smith's culture only by raising new resources" (p. 66).

The uncertainties of the economy, state funding, and student markets have made philanthropy increasingly vital to an institution's strategic positioning and operations. Fund-raising is the aspect of the presidency that in an increasingly competitive environment is most likely to affect a president's longevity and legacy. But despite the growing importance of fund-raising to the legitimacy of a president and to the quality and reputation of an institution, most new presidents are unprepared for the task. According to an ACE survey, over half of presidents of most types of institutions indicated "a desire to have had more experience in this area" (Ross & Green, 2000, pp. 27–30).

Successful fund-raising depends on the external social capital established by a president. This capital is built on relationships of trust and confidence, although the president must always seek opportunities to solicit the next gift. The lack of authenticity in so many of these relationships is objectionable to many presidents—female and male. Dean's (2003) research shows that the majority of women in an academic vice presidency do not want to do the socializing and fund-raising required in a presidency. Certainly the endless round of social events and the time invested in cultivating relationships with fund-raising prospects absorb so much of a president's time that family relationships and prior friendships often suffer from a lack of attention. My own approach to this necessary aspect of the presidency was to indulge my keen interest in other people and the development of their ideas and values. I enjoyed the stimulation of interpersonal interaction and used the constant round of activities to build and synthesize a narrative about the college, its history, accomplishments, and aspirations. If women are to be successful at securing and maintaining university and college presidencies, they need to acquire the kind of experience in and comfort with external relations that most faculty and academic administrators do not have.

Presidents must spend a great deal of time in building relationships with trustees, alumni, corporate executives, and other prospects that enable them to be successful at fund-raising. People generally do not make major gifts to an institution unless they believe in the president. For them, the president is the embodiment of the institution. Although presidents often seek to make their mark through academic improvement (e.g., program development, student selectivity, faculty recruitment, rankings), the key criterion of success tends to be their fund-raising record.

To strengthen the quality and reputation of a college or university, to reposition it in the higher education marketplace, and to sustain these advances, presidents need to ensure that changes are perceived as legitimate. They have to manage this process in a chaotic environment, with diffuse decision-making processes, in a system inherently resistant to change. To that end, female as well as male presidents must engage with the factors involved in creating sustainable institutional change. This means finding the most appropriate leadership style, patiently working through faculty and board governance, building and rebuilding social capital, and raising a lot of money and deploying it strategically. All presidents have legitimacy challenges that can impede innovation and change. Women may have the advantage of adaptability and relational skills, but they face additional hurdles stemming from their own attitudes and biases as well as from traditional male-created and male-normed institutional structures and attitudes.

Legitimacy in the Succession Process

The final stage of a presidency is the succession process. The presidential succession process is significant because it signals a college or university community's ability to maintain its equilibrium while undergoing significant change. An institution's legitimacy is at stake if the legitimacy of the presidential succession process is compromised. So too is the legitimacy of the exiting and incoming presidents. I have compared this delicate process to the rites of passage from the anthropologists van Gennep (Kimball, 1968) and Turner (1969/1990), emphasizing the stages of separation, transition, and incorporation, which often overlap.

The announcement of the current president's planned departure signals separation, the first rite; the period of search, selection, and testing of the successor is transition, the second rite; and finally, the new president's symbolic investiture as leader during the inauguration ceremony, followed, one hopes, by acceptance into the culture, which is the third rite of passage, incorporation (Bornstein, 2003).

Separation

Presidents are often reluctant to give up the visibility and perquisites of the position, even after a decade or more and a solid record of accomplishment. Their life and relationships are woven around their institution, and they are addicted to the challenges and opportunities of the presidency. Some cannot imagine another phase in their life. Depending on their age, incumbents might be drawn to another presidency, a different professional opportunity, a faculty position, or retirement. Since women presidents on average serve fewer years than men and are less likely to hold a second presidency, they may be more comfortable than men in leaving the position. Women may be less motivated than men by the prestige and personal advantages of the presidency, and feel less diminished by retiring or taking a faculty position. They also may be more likely than men to step down for the good of their institution rather than for their own benefit. Syndicated columnist Ellen Goodman (n.d.) writes that the graceful exit "begins with the vision to recognize when a job, a life stage, a relationship is over—and to let go."

On announcing her retirement from Duke University's presidency after 11 years and a recognized record of accomplishment, Nannerl Koehane said that she was looking forward to the "next stage of my life [and] returning to the library, the study, and the classroom" (Fogg, 2003, p. A28). After 10 years, Judith Rodin resigned from a very successful presidency at the University of Pennsylvania, saying, "I'm not tired, and I don't think the job is overwhelming. I'm still full of energy. It's just that the timing is right" (Basinger, 2003, p. A23). After 10 successful years as president of the University of Puget Sound, Susan Resnick Pierce retired to spend more time with her family and to "write in a genre other than memoranda and other than on long plane rides" (S. R. Pierce, personal communication, 2002). Jill Ker Conway (2001) writes, "Moving toward my tenth year at Smith, I felt an intense longing to live in another self. My drive had switched suddenly toward the creative, while my current life was managerial" (p. 117).

When I announced my resignation after 14 years in the presidency, I had plenty of energy, but I had completed all I had been asked to do to strengthen the college and believed that it was time for new leadership. My departure announcement shook the college community and I was surprised by the anxiety and disruption it caused. A leadership change is a momentous event for an institution. As Deal and Kennedy (1982) point out, any change in leadership threatens a culture and leaves employees confused, insecure, and angry. In this phase of succession, it is up to the incumbent president to reassure employees and help ease the transition. This I did. By leaving while still respected by my constituents, I had the exhilarating experience of being feted and flattered as I prepared to exit.

Transition

Once a new president is selected, board members redirect their attention to other responsibilities, assuming that they have chosen a person who will know how to manage the transition and be an effective leader. Boards tend to be oblivious to a new president's need for support in the transition into the institution, as well as during change, in crisis, and at exit. Presidents, on the other hand, do not ask for support and direction, not wishing to appear inadequate to the task. Women may feel especially vulnerable when requesting advice, worried about exhibiting stereotypical inadequacies.

In most institutions, unless the search and transition processes are perceived as flawed or illegitimate, the office of president confers immediate legitimacy. This is transitory, however, for, once selected, a new president undergoes a period of testing and scrutiny during which constituents watch for missteps and for signs that this person does not belong (Bornstein, 2003). Donna Shalala, president of the University of Miami, has referred to this as the "Gotcha!" phase (Lindsay, 2002). The inevitable period of testing a new president's appropriateness for the institution is hazardous but is a key element of the rites of passage (Bornstein, 2003).

My early years in the presidency were fraught with suspicion and hostility. There was a palpable sense that I did not fit into the college or the wider community. An influential administrator was heard to comment, "This college is not ready for a Jewish woman president." Despite the sniping, I immersed myself in the culture, established an effective management team, developed influence with faculty and trustees, and embarked on creating relationships with those who could provide the resources we so badly needed. This period could have been eased for me and for the institution had there been an assimilation plan for my transition into the college.

Every presidential transition would benefit from an assimilation plan that provides ongoing assistance to the new president in becoming acculturated to the new environment and in learning the job. Such planning, if routinized in higher education, would help ensure the legitimacy of women and men in a new presidency.

Transition planning should also take into account the needs and goals of the departing president. If the president who is leaving has had a successful tenure and wishes a nonintrusive institutional affiliation, some mutually agreeable arrangement can be made. Departure rituals to celebrate the outgoing president's contributions are very important to the community. Deal and Kennedy (1982) point out that such ceremonies place an institution's culture "on display" and "keep values, beliefs, and heroes" in the "minds and hearts" of constituents (p. 63). This is true, as well, of the new president's inauguration. Throughout the transition, the departing president must remain upbeat and enthusiastic about the new president and not opine negatively on her or his utterances or actions.

New presidents are often hired for skills and experiences lacking in their immediate predecessor. One commonly accepted belief is that presidents are at a disadvantage if they follow successful and beloved presidents. Constituents tend to make comparisons of leadership style, management effectiveness, fund-raising ability, and other characteristics. For this reason, it may benefit a new president to be different in as many ways as possible—background, race, sex, and so on. From this perspective, a candidate of the opposite sex might have an advantage. When tokenism is replaced by a critical mass of women in the presidency a candidate's sex may be irrelevant. In my own experience as a new president, the "big shoes" that I had to fill belonged to a man who was very different from me. This was helpful in that it made comparisons almost impossible. My successor was a man with a very different background and personality from mine, which I think enabled him to escape the big shoes comparisons.

Incorporation

Whetten and Cameron (1991), based on a series of interviews, report being "impressed with the tendency of faculty and administrators to demarcate their institution's history into presidential eras. . . . Their recollections of what transpired on campus during each term was strongly colored by their overall evaluation of the effectiveness of each president" (p. 463). Successful presidents acknowledge and build on the achievements of their predecessors but chart their own goals and create their own unique legacy. Women participating in an ACE roundtable discussion suggested that just as each college and university has its own myth, successful presidents have their own myths (Brown et al., 2001). I became known as a builder—of the college's quality and reputation, as well as of endowments, budgets, and buildings. At my farewell gala, a dean performed a rap number that he wrote, titled "Rita, the Weapon of Mass Construction."

A new president must achieve legitimacy before being fully incorporated into the institutional culture. The inauguration is the formal and symbolic incorporation of the new president into the institution. The event celebrates the institution and its heroes and announces a new era. However, the new president does not have legitimacy until accepted by constituents. This is the final step in the rites of passage that characterize the presidential succession process. Careful transition planning would help to ensure the successful incorporation of a new president; it is especially important for a woman because she confronts higher hurdles at every stage in the rites of passage.

Legitimacy, Gender, and the Presidency

The presidency is a perilous perch, and presidents need to be vigilant about gaining and maintaining legitimacy. Located in a social and institutional context characterized by stereotyped roles, norms, and expectations, the presidency presents special challenges for women. Despite these challenges, higher education institutions and their constituent groups—for example, trustees, faculties, students, alumni—benefit from having women and men at the leadership level.

To ensure that the increased number of women in college and university presidencies is not a passing phenomenon, the academy needs to reinvent itself. The role and dimensions of the presidency should be reconceived. Women aspiring to have an academic career and a family should be assisted by a more flexible tenure clock, child care facilities, and flexible work schedules. Women with administrative talent should be encouraged to consider the presidency a worthy career goal and be provided with experience, training, support networks, and mentors. Women presidential aspirants should seek relevant experience and develop attitudes and behaviors necessary for success. Women presidents need to stifle feelings of inadequacy and demonstrate their competence by developing strategies, balancing budgets, meeting enrollment goals, raising money, managing problems, avoiding crises, and leading their institutions.

To ensure legitimacy, a woman president must learn and identify with the institutional culture, effectively manage her institution in response to environmental pressures and trends, and serve as a moral exemplar in every dimension of her work and life. To implement change successfully, she must be adaptable in her leadership style, effective in her use of governance, able to build a large store of social capital, and adept at fund-raising. When her goals have been accomplished, the president needs to move on, work with constituents to plan a smooth transition, and assist in the acculturation and incorporation of her successor. While these strictures apply also to male presidents, gendered expectations and definitions for the leadership role make legitimacy more problematic for women.

Today's presidents are often criticized for not measuring up to the heroic, outspoken, and visible leaders at the helm of America's universities and colleges in an earlier era. This larger-than-life male model of leadership reflects the style of the corporate titans of that period and was appropriate for fueling the growth and quality of the higher education enterprise. Those educational titans were academic entrepreneurs and public intellectuals, but their leadership style is inappropriate in the current environment.

Presidents now have multiple and diverse constituencies and the challenge of creating a sense of community and a shared vision for the future. Today's presidents also are confronted with constant demands for involvement in civic, economic development, and professional projects, which, coupled with the incessant round of fund-raising and lobbying, distance them from the day-to-day activities of their institution. As the number of women in presidencies increases and the range of presidential activity expands for women and men, we are likely to see changes in constituent expectations for the role. Relationship building, engagement, and collaboration may become the gold standard for leadership, along with adaptability and an authentic and balanced life. Presidents may lead more effectively from the center of the metaphorical web (Helgesen, 1990) than from the top of the traditional ladder. Margaret Jablonski (2000) suggests that what was called "a woman's leadership style in the twentieth century has now become the new leadership for the twenty-first century" (p. 255). Transformative leadership may become the norm for women and for men.

Presidential legitimacy is vital for the legitimacy and reputation of an institution. All presidents are called upon to be academic leaders, financial managers, fund-raisers, public intellectuals, civic leaders, and ethical standard bearers. Women bring to this challenge their own life experiences, talents, values, and interests, which may be similar to or different from those of their male colleagues. They serve as role models for students, the majority of whom are female, and they bring new ways of thinking and acting to higher education leadership. It is not a question of whether women or men are better suited for the presidency, but rather what experiences and attributes the position requires in the 21st century.

The following is a recapitulation of the questions I have raised, focusing first on the position itself and leadership style. Is it possible to develop a nongendered description of the college presidency? Should the presidency be reconceived for the 21st century? How effective is a transformative leadership style (adaptable, contextual) compared with transformational and transactional styles? Are women presidents more adaptable than men, and does this work to their advantage in the position? Do women presidents tend to be relational, collaborative, and empowering, while men presidents tend to be authoritarian? Are there differences in emotional intelligence? Are women and men presidents similar or different in the ethical standards they observe? Are there differences in fund-raising ability? Do women have an easier or more difficult time than men do when stepping down from a presidency?

There are also questions about the pipeline to the presidency. Are male academic vice presidents and provosts more likely than women to aspire to a presidency? Are men more likely than women to apply for a presidency because of a competitive spirit and drive for professional advancement? Are women with nontraditional careers less likely than similarly situated men to apply for presidencies? Have male and female candidates had similar or different amounts and types of mentoring?

Despite many unanswered questions about legitimacy, gender, and leadership, there are talented, dedicated, and successful female as well as male presidents at the helm of the nation's universities and colleges. It may be time to reevaluate and redefine the presidency to make it more attractive to potential candidates, but our immediate goal should be to increase the proportion of women in the pipeline and in the position. If we accept the view that there is a continuum of leadership behaviors available to men and women, then presidents can perform in ways suitable for the requirements of the institutions that hire them. The academic presidency is a challenge and an honor. Greater diversity in the role will expand our conceptions of the presidency and its place in higher education.

References

Astin, H. S., & Leland, C. (1991). *Women of influence, women of vision: A cross-generational study of leaders and social change.* San Francisco: Jossey-Bass.

Basinger, J. (2003, July). Rodin to resign from Penn presidency [Electronic version]. *The Chronicle of Higher Education, 49*(43), A23.

Bass, B. M. (1985). *Leadership and performance beyond expectations.* New York: The Free Press.

Bateson, M. C. (1990). *Composing a life.* New York: Penguin.

Becker, C. (2002, January). Trial by fire: A tale of gender and leadership. *The Chronicle of Higher Education, 48*(20), B15. Retrieved December 30, 2005, from http://chronicle.com/weekly/v48/i20/20b01501.htm

Bensimon, E. M. (1991). The social processes through which faculty shape the image of a new president. *Journal of Higher Education, 62*(6), 637–660.

Bensimon, E. M. (1993). A feminist reinterpretation of presidents' definitions of leadership. In J. S. Glazer, E. M. Bensimon, & B. K. Townsend (Eds.), *Women in higher education: A feminist perspective* (pp. 465–474). Needham Heights, MA: Ginn Press.

Birnbaum, R. (1992). *How academic leadership works: Understanding success and failure in the college presidency.* San Francisco: Jossey-Bass.

Birnbaum, R. (2002). The president as story-teller: Restoring the narrative of higher education. *The Presidency, 5*(3), 32–39.

Birnbaum, R., & Umbach, P. D. (2001). Scholar, steward, spanner, stranger: The four career paths of college presidents. *The Review of Higher Education, 24*(3), 203–217.

Bornstein, R. (2000). A president's guide to fund-raising success: Relationships are key. *The Presidency, 3*(2), 25–29.

Bornstein, R. (2003). *Legitimacy in the academic presidency: From entrance to exit.* Westport, CT: American Council on Education/Praeger.

Bornstein, R. (2004, July). The authentic, and effective, college president. *The Chronicle of Higher Education, 50*(47), B16.

Brems, C., Baldwin, M. R., Davis, L., & Namyniuk, L. (1994). The imposter syndrome as related to teaching evaluations and advising relationships of university faculty members. *Journal of Higher Education, 65*(2), 183–193.

Brown, G., Van Ummersen, C., & Sturnick, J. (2001). *From where we sit: Women's perspectives on the presidency.* Washington, DC: American Council on Education.

Clark, S. M., & Corcoran, M. (1993). Perspectives on the professional socialization of women faculty: A case of accumulative disadvantage. In J. S. Glazer, E. M. Bensimon, & B. K. Townsend (Eds.), *Women in higher education: A feminist perspective* (pp. 399–414). Needham Heights, MA: Ginn Press.

Cohen, M. D., & March, J. G. (1974). *Leadership and ambiguity: The American college presidency.* New York: McGraw-Hill.

Coleman, J. S. (1988). Social capital in the creation of human capital. *American Journal of Sociology, 94*(Supplement: Organizations and institutions: Sociological and economic approaches to the analysis of social structure), S95–S120.

Conway, J. K. (2001). *A woman's education.* New York: Knopf.

Corrigan, M. E. (2002). *The American college president: 2002 edition.* Washington, DC: American Council on Education.

Deal, T. E., & Kennedy, A. A. (1982). *Corporate cultures: The rites and rituals of corporate life.* Reading, MA: Addison-Wesley.

Dean, D. R. (2003, November). *America's women chief academic officers and their presidential aspirations.* Paper presented at the annual conference of the Association for the Study of Higher Education, Portland, OR.

Die, A. H. (1999). Going the distance: Reflections on presidential longevity. *The Presidency, 2*(3), 32–37.

Eckel, P., Green, M., Hill, B., & Mallon, W. (1999). *Taking charge of change: A primer for colleges and universities.* Washington, DC: American Council on Education.

Fisher, J. L., & Koch, J. V. (1996). *Presidential leadership: Making a difference.* Phoenix, AZ: American Council on Education and Oryx Press.

Fogg, P. (2003, March). Duke's president to leave office [Electronic version]. *The Chronicle of Higher Education, 49*(27), A28.

Freeman, S. J. M. (2001). Women at the top: "You've come a long way, baby." In S. J. M. Freeman, S. C. Bourque, & C. M. Shelton (Eds.), *Women on power: Leadership redefined* (pp. 27–60). Boston: Northeastern University Press.

Fukuyama, F. (1995). *Trust: The social virtues and the creation of prosperity.* New York: Simon & Schuster.

Gamson, W. A. (1968). *Power and discontent.* Homewood, IL: Dorsey Press.

Gender and leadership: A review of pertinent research. (1998, April). *Harmony: Forum of the Symphony Orchestra Institute, 6,* 100–110.

Ghezzi, P. (2004, December). College's ex chief pleads innocent: Morris Brown scheme denied [Electronic version]. *Atlanta Journal-Constitution,* D1.

Glazer-Raymo, J. (1999). *Shattering the myths: Women in academe.* Baltimore: Johns Hopkins University Press.

Goleman, D. (1995). *Emotional intelligence.* New York: Bantam.

Goodman, E. (n.d.). *Broadly speaking: Words from women writers.* Retrieved December 30, 2005, from http://www.storycircle.org/quotes/alpha/g.html

Greenstein, F. I. (2000). *The presidential difference: Leadership style from FDR to Clinton.* Princeton, NJ: Princeton University Press.

Hall, E. W. (1993). *Virtual reality in academic life.* Paper presented at the conference of South Carolina Women in Higher Education Administration, Furman University, Greenville, SC.

Helgesen, S. (1990). *The female advantage: Women's ways of leadership.* New York: Doubleday.

Hemel, D. J. (2005, January 19). Summers draws fire for remarks on women. *The Harvard Crimson.* Retrieved December 30, 2005, from http://www.thecrimson.harvard.edu/article.aspx?ref=505362

Hollander, E. P. (1987). *College and university leadership from a social psychological perspective: A transactional view.* Presented at the Invitational Interdisciplinary Colloquium on Leadership in Higher Education, Teacher's College, Columbia University, New York.

Hollander, E. P. (1992). The essential interdependence of leadership and followership. *Current Directions in Psychological Science, 1*(2), 71–75.

Hollander, E. P., & Julian, J. W. (1978). Studies in leader legitimacy, influence, and innovation. In L. Berkowitz (Ed.), *Group processes* (pp. 115–151). New York: Academic Press.

Jablonski, M. (2000). The leadership challenge for women college presidents. In J. Glazer-Raymo, B. K. Townsend, & B. Ropers-Huliman (Eds.), *Women in higher education: A feminist perspective* (2nd ed., pp. 243–251). Boston: Pearson Custom Publishing.

Kabacoff, R. I. (2000). Gender and leadership in the corporate boardroom. *Management Research Group.* Retrieved December 30, 2005, from http://www.mrg.com/documents/APA2000.PDF

Kanter, R. M. (1977). *Men and women of the corporation.* New York: Basic Books.

Kellerman, B., & Rhode, D. L. (2004, Fall). Viable options: Rethinking women and leadership. *Compass. Center for Public Leadership,* 2(1), 15–17, 37.

Kelly, R. M., & Duerst-Lahti, G. (2000). Toward gender awareness and gender balance in leadership and governance. In G. Duerst-Lahti & R. M. Kelly (Eds.), *Gender power, leadership, and governance* (pp. 259–271). Ann Arbor: University of Michigan Press.

Kimball, S. T. (1968). Gennep, A. V. In D. L. Sills (Ed.), *International encyclopedia of the social sciences* (Vol. 6, pp. 113–114.). New York: Macmillan.

Koehane, N. O. (1998). More power to the president? *The Presidency,* 1(2), 12–17.

Leatherman, C. (1992, December 12). Female president's style upsets Converse College alumnae. [Electronic version]. *Chronicle of Higher Education, 39*(17), A17.

Lindsay, J. (2002, January 16). *Controversies abound in the ivory tower as new Harvard president tangles with faculty.* Retrieved December 30, 2005, from http://community.seattletimes.nwsource.com/archive/?date=20020116&slug=harvardi6

McLaughlin, J. B. (1996). Entering the presidency. In J. B. McLaughlin (Ed.), *Leadership transitions: The new college president* (pp. 5–13). San Francisco: Jossey-Bass.

Northouse, P. G. (2001). *Leadership: Theory and practice.* Thousand Oaks, CA: Sage.

Rosener, J. B. (1990, November–December). Ways women lead. *Harvard Business Review, 68*(6), 119–125.

Ross, M., & Green, M. F. (2000). *The American college president.* Washington, DC: American Council on Education.

Rusaw, A. C. (1996). Achieving credibility: An analysis of women's experience. *Review of Public Personnel Administration, 16*(1), 19–30.

Sample, S. B. (2002). Unlocking the power of contrarian leadership. *The Presidency,* 5(2), 25–27.

Tierney, W. G. (2001). Why committees don't work: Creating a structure for change [Electronic version]. *Academe, 87*(3), 25–29.

Topping, M. E. H., & Kimmel, E. B. (1985). The imposter phenomenon: Feeling phony. *Academic Psychology Bulletin,* 7, 213–226.

Turner, V. (1990). Liminality and communitas. In J. C. Alexander & S. Seidman (Eds.), *Culture and society: Contemporary debates* (pp. 147–154). Cambridge, UK: Cambridge University Press. (Reprinted from *The ritual process: Structure and anti-structure,* pp. 94–130, by V. W. Turner, 1969, Chicago: Aldine)

Wilson, R. (2004, December). Where the elite teach, it's still a man's world. *The Chronicle of Higher Education, 51*(15), A8–A14.

Whetten, D. A., & Cameron, K. S. (1991). Administrative effectiveness in higher education. In M. W. Peterson (Ed.), *Organization and governance in higher education* (pp. 459–469). Needham Heights, MA: Ginn Press.

Yoder, J. D., Schleicher, T. L., & McDonald, T. W. (1998). Empowering token women leaders: The importance of organizationally legitimated credibility. *Psychology of Women Quarterly,* 22, 209–222.

IO

ASSIMILATION, AUTHENTICITY, AND ADVANCEMENT

Crafting Integrated Identities as Academic Leaders

Diane R. Dean, Susan J. Bracken, and Jeanie K. Allen

The chapters in this volume have addressed many strategies that women employ in the quest for successful careers in academe, as well as the difficult choices they face when negotiating their personal and professional lives. This culminating chapter focuses on the deep tension between the compulsion to assimilate and the desire for authenticity. It uses a framework from the field of cognitive psychology to elucidate the foundation of this tension, enumerates the potential hazards of assimilation, and poses strategies for navigating assimilation, authenticity, and advancement.

The Psychosocial Origins of the Assimilation Imperative

Organizations uphold a clear and normative definition of what a leader is like and what a leader does, and all individuals who move into leadership roles enact their acculturated view of a leader to some degree (Kanter, 1993). This process of conforming to social norms—assimilation—accompanies and aids career advancement. Bornstein (see chapter 9) conceptualizes the assimilation imperative as the necessary process of gaining legitimacy among one's constituents. By meeting the organization's cultural expectations in terms of preparation, knowledge, capacities, and behavior, academic leaders gain respect and support among their constituencies. For example, leaders gain individual legitimacy based on the relevance and prestige of their personal characteristics, professional background, credentials, and experience. They gain institutional legitimacy based on their conformity to organizational culture (Hollander & Julian, 1978; McLaughlin, 1996) and the degree to which their own recruitment and hiring adhered to traditional practices. Throughout their employment within the organization, their moral legitimacy emerges from their ethical behavior, adherence to the institutional mission and values, and adherence to a democratic versus dictatorial leadership style. Without meeting the organization's cultural expectations for the traits and behaviors of a leader, one cannot legitimately enter or thrive in leadership roles. Assimilation, therefore, becomes a professional imperative.

Cognitive psychologists interpret the assimilation imperative as the need to convey a group identity story that will be readily accepted by the members of the organization. The need for self-identification and group identification are essential features of human beings (Gardner, 1995). All people define themselves according to their membership in various groups, such as race, gender, religion, socioeconomic strata, families, and ethnic cultures. These groups provide strong sources of identity through either shared attributes or shared rituals, values, and attitudes. The modern workplace too has become a primary source of an individual's identity (Gabelnick, Herr, & Klein, 1998), providing a shared experience that helps members "think about and feel who they are, where they come from, and where they are headed" (Gardner, p. 3). One of a leader's primary responsibilities is to embody and convey the organizational identity story through his or her words, actions, symbols, and examples, which should reflect the organization's past, affirm its present, and shape its options for the future (Gardner). Leadership, cognitive psychologists posit, results from a complex and interactive relationship between leaders and followers that originates in this human need to construct and affirm self and group identities (Gardner). Assimilation, therefore, becomes the act of embodying and conveying an identity story for the organization.

Modern colleges and universities fulfill a wide array of functions and purposes. Each has its own nuanced culture. Each operational area within the institution (e.g., student affairs, finance and administration, development and external affairs, and individual colleges or academic departments) also can have its distinct professional culture or group identity. Yet American higher education as a whole has a single overarching identity story that all colleges and universities share: the advancement, preservation, and perpetuation of knowledge (Newman, 1854). Because leaders convey the organization's identity story, it remains important to colleges and universities that their president and senior academic leaders exude an academic identity and have faculty or scholarly experience. Even though more relevant presidential skills may be found in other areas of the organization, such as development and external affairs, the majority of presidents continue to come from academic careers (American Council on Education [ACE], 2007; Corrigan, 2002), which Bornstein calls *the royal road* (see chapter 9, p. 211).

Unfortunately, little in faculty life directly prepares one for the type of responsibilities required in the presidency and senior leadership. Success in the academic world relies upon what Lipman-Blumen (2000) calls *direct achieving styles*: mastering one's own tasks, excelling, competing, outperforming, taking charge. The behavioral attributes of individualism, competition, and transactional relationships permeate the way in which individual faculty conduct their work; pervade the dynamics through which academic units vie within their organization for the resources necessary to their survival; and shape the way in which colleges and universities compete with each other for prestige, rankings, resources, and enrollments. Not incidentally, these are the same behaviors and attributes associated with masculine leadership styles. Founded by and for men, the academic world propagates career architectures and rewards behaviors that are masculine in their nature and origin, suited to the men who once exclusively pursued them. Consequently, these behaviors and attributes continue to form the basis of legitimized leadership behavior in academe.

The Costs of Assimilation

Women's increasing presence and participation in academia has not neutralized masculine leadership norms nor has the increasing need for leadership that incorporates feminine achieving styles, such as empowering, networking, persuading, collaborating, contributing, and mentoring (Lipman-Blumen, 2000). Colleges and universities remain deeply gendered structures (Glazer-Raymo, 1999), where women feel compelled to heed the assimilation imperative in order to attain career advancement, success, and legitimacy. Assimilation offers real gains but not without a price. In the following sections, we consider six costs of assimilation. Most women in academe will likely face one or more of these during their career.

Work-Life Imbalance

Women who seek to balance and integrate American family life and a career in academe face unique difficulties (Colbeck, 2006; Creamer, 2006; Mason, Goulden, & Wolfinger, 2006; Wolf-Wendel & Ward, 2006). As they struggle to conform to a male-normed professional life, they also must respond in their personal lives to strong American cultural expectations and definitions of women. For example, child care, elder care, and domestic chores still fall largely to women, as do many of the assorted clerical and social management responsibilities that accompany family life. The resulting time demands become a constant source of stress and imbalance for which male-normed academic career architectures offer little relief. Tarule and her colleagues (see chapter 2) have suggested that work-life imbalance originates in the public-private separation between the historical spheres of women's (domestic, private) and men's (vocational, public) lives. Academic leadership, as a public domain role, remains resistant to the integration of the personal—or whole person—dimensions of a leader's life. Academic women, as they point out, frequently face choices that keep the diametrical differences between the public and private domains present in their daily consciousness, such as balancing the scheduling of family duties (doctor appointments, school transportation) with professional duties (committee meetings, advising appointments).

To this we add: The different valuations of the historical spheres of women's and men's lives deter the integration of the two. Higher education. professional cultures fail to perceive any sense of elasticity in an individual's roles, so that the demands of the private domain are seen as encroachments on the professional domain. Because women's private roles (domestic and family) have a substantially lower valuation in our society (Waring, 1989), when women refer to or reveal their private identities in the workplace, it subtracts from—not adds to—their professional identities. At the same time, the nurturing and serving behaviors associated with women's private roles conflict with the individualism, competition, and direct achieving styles they are expected to assimilate and project in academe. *The Balancing Act,* volume 1 in this series (Bracken, Allen, & Dean, 2006), reveals how women either diminish or deny their family roles and personal issues while at work, opt to work intense hours to meet the needs of both domains, or forego family life altogether to concentrate on meeting the demands of their professional identity and responsibilities.

The tensions are no less difficult in reverse. Vast portions of American society still view women's professional ambitions as somehow not fully feminine and criticize women who seek a family life and a successful career (Fels, 2004). The need to work for wages is viewed distinctly from, and more sympathetically than, the need to realize one's potentialities and interests through a career. The same perception of inelasticity for women's roles operates in reverse, so that having a professional identity subtracts from—not adds to—women's private identities. With such inverse proportionality, academic women who have a spouse, partner, or family quickly learn to build a wall separating their personal and professional lives to minimize cultural penalties for holding multiple roles, yet thereby also diminishing the potential for achieving any real integration or balance between the two.

Inconsistent Expectations

Men and women who seek leadership roles in academe must acquire and incorporate the capacities and characteristics expected by their professional culture, yet their starting points are not even. Because academic leadership is male normed, simply being male gives men a boost. College and university communities may perceive men as fulfilling expected leadership characteristics whether or not they actually demonstrate such capacities. Being female, on the other hand, visually contradicts leadership expectations. Because women do not completely *look* the part according to academic cultural expectations (they are not men), they must demonstrate an even higher level of ability than their male peers in order to gain the same level of legitimacy and acceptance (see chapters 1, 4, 5, and 9). Women have to prove they belong (Eckert, 1998), more so than men do.

Paradoxically, even though women must meet male norms of leadership, they receive inconsistent reactions and reviews when they behave according to those expectations (see chapter 1). Women leaders must carefully navigate the razor's edge between being seen as either too tough (gender inconsistent) or not tough enough (too gender consistent; Brown, Van Ummersen, & Sturnick, 2001). Women who are the first anything—professor, program coordinator, department chair, dean, provost, or president—feel that razor's sharpness most keenly (see chapter 9), as do women of color who often break gender and color barriers with their career advancement, and women in faith-based institutions where religious beliefs require female submissiveness (see chapter 4). Ironically, while women have difficulty gaining leadership legitimacy regardless of whether they assimilate masculine behaviors, men can assimilate feminine behaviors into their skill repertoire and still meet the acculturated definition of leadership (see chapters 1, 2, and 9). This illuminates the point that expectations are inconsistent between men and women and suggests that traits (gender) may matter more in academe's acculturated definition of leadership than actual behaviors do (masculine or feminine leadership attributes).

Inequitable Rewards

Numerous studies and panel reports abound on the inequities of academe experienced by students, faculty, and staff, and based upon differences such as gender, race, and socioeconomic strata. For women in the academic career pipeline, findings have shown that in colleges and universities across the nation, women continue to receive inequitable acknowledgment, support, resources, pay, and promotions for their performance (Fogg, 2006; Henig, 2006; Wilson, 2006). Women hold only a minority of senior academic and leadership positions (ACE, 2007; *The Chronicle of Higher Education*, 2008a, 2008b; Corrigan, 2002; Dean, 2003) and remain relegated to midlevel careers. Despite decades of evidence, the disparities continue. For women in academic leadership who had to meet higher hurdles in demonstrating competencies and achievements (see chapter 9), the injustice of such inequities calls women to question and doubt whether advancement is worth their efforts (Dean, 2003).

Imposter Syndrome

The imposter syndrome occurs when successful, high-achieving individuals erroneously believe themselves inadequate for their own jobs and attribute their success to external causes instead. Individuals manifesting this syndrome experience an inability to internalize or take credit for their accomplishments, an inaccurate self-perception that they are somehow professional frauds and a fear that others will expose them (Clance & Imes, 1978; Clance & O'Toole, 1987; Imes & Clance, 1984; Langford & Clance, 1993; Topping & Kimmel, 1985). Although research demonstrates that women and men suffer from this syndrome (Bussotti, 1990; Dingman, 1987; Harvey, 1981; Langford, 1990), it is thought to be particularly common among women. Scholars suggest that sex-role stereotypes precondition young girls in early childhood and adolescence to believe that they are less competent than they actually are (Broverman, Vogel, Broverman, Clarkson, & Rosenkrantz, 1972; Rosenkrantz, Vogel, Bee, Broverman, & Broverman, 1968). Yet professional contexts in adult life can also create or certainly exacerbate this delusion. Academic culture—with its inconsistent gender expectations and inequitable rewards—presents ripe conditions for women to disassociate their accomplishments from their own actions and abilities and perceive themselves as fraudulent.

Diminished Self-Efficacy

Diminished self-efficacy naturally accompanies the imposter syndrome. Sloma-Williams, McDade, Richman, and Morahan (chapter 3) base their work on Bandura's (1997) definition of self-efficacy as a belief in one's sense of agency, a catalyst for leadership, the origin of goal-setting behavior, and the capacity to organize actions and follow through. Healthy self-efficacy builds upon experiences of professional domain mastery, which necessitates that individuals objectively assess and attribute the effects of their actions to themselves (Bandura). Conversely, diminished self-efficacy feeds off a lack of such mastery experiences or a failure to attribute one's successes to one's own actions and abilities. Whenever women—or men—cannot logically anticipate the results or effects of their actions, diminished self-efficacy may result. In academia, the dissonance stemming from inconsistent behavioral expectations and inequitable rewards for women can wreak havoc on their sense of agency and self-efficacy, particularly when combined with the compulsion to separate the public and private spheres of one's life, fracturing and penalizing the whole self.

Inauthenticity

Assimilation is an advancement strategy that can result in a less-authentic leadership style that doesn't integrate—and may occasionally violate—women's competencies or preferences. Masculine leadership attributes simply feel inauthentic for many women, who then struggle to validate their own leadership styles[1] (chapter 8; Amey & Twombly, 1992). At times, behavioral expectations violate feminine behavioral norms, such as when leaders must engage in relationships that are insincerely political or covertly asymmetrical and laden with the leader's agenda (chapters 2 and 9). Assimilation can result in intellectual authenticity as well, such as when women (and men) adopt the cultural majority's view and lose their own view, a phenomenon that Tarule, Applegate, Early, and Blackwell (chapter 2, p. 44) call *sympathetic resonance*.

A sense of inauthenticity also arises directly from the forced separation of public and private selves. Academic women must suppress their personal roles while in the public sphere and suppress their professional roles while in the private sphere or face cultural penalties for holding multiple roles. This false dichotomy denies a whole and genuine sense of self.

Gender Dissonance: The Fruit of Assimilation

Cognitive dissonance (Festinger, 1957) refers to the resulting tension when an individual's behavior, thoughts, feelings, or opinions conflict with his or her established behavior, knowledge, values, and attitudes. For women in academe, the assimilation necessitated by advancement to academic leadership evokes a similar tension. Each person has multiple facets of identity, such as gender, sexuality, race, religion, political allegiance, social class, and a full range of intellectual abilities and various interests, preferences, and skill competencies. The self sits at the focal point, coordinating the image resulting from the light refracted through the facets. Unfortunately, assimilation strategies weaken or block out entire facets, creating an incomplete, inauthentic self. College and university cultures compel assimilative behaviors by reinforcing male-normed career architectures that frustrate attempts to achieve work-life balance, upholding inconsistent behavioral expectations between men and women and bestowing inequitable rewards. For women, feelings of fraudulency, inefficacy, or inauthenticity may result. We propose the term *gender dissonance* (see Figure 10.1) to capture the contradictions and resulting conflict that women face in such contexts of disparity.

The Quest for Authenticity

The compulsion to assimilate into an organizational or group culture has strong psychosocial roots intended to maintain group cohesiveness through

FIGURE 10.1
Contributors to Gender Dissonance

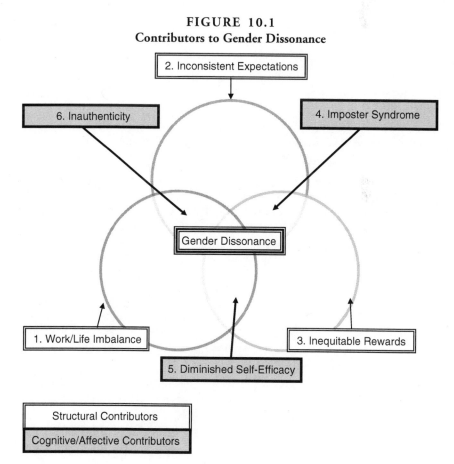

a shared identity. As a professional strategy, assimilation integrates individuals into organizational culture and facilitates career advancement for those who can embody and convey the group identity story. Yet assimilation in academe comes at a cost for women and can lead to gender dissonance: an incomplete, inauthentic sense of self. How can women attain legitimacy, enter, survive, and thrive in leadership roles in colleges and universities while preserving the multiple facets of their identity and core values? Cognitive psychologists suggest that dissonance can be resolved by either changing the conflicting beliefs or behaviors, acquiring new information that reduces the conflict, or accepting or reducing the importance of the dissonance (Festinger, 1957). Roughly following these lines, we pose several structural, cognitive, and affective changes toward reconciling assimilation, authenticity, and advancement.

Structural Changes

Structural contributors to gender dissonance include work-life imbalance, inconsistent expectations, and inequitable rewards. Each involves a contradiction within the campus culture that manifests itself in the organizational structure, in this case working conditions, performance expectations, and distribution of resources and rewards. We can indeed reduce dissonance in beliefs and behaviors by changing the campus policies and practices that bind us. In chapter 4, Wood calls for data, deliberate honest discussions, and decisions to expose inequities on campuses and effect change. Pointing to the Nine Presidents coalition (Harvard, Massachusetts Institute of Technology, California Institute of Technology, Princeton, Stanford, University of California–Berkeley, University of Michigan, University of Pennsylvania, and Yale), as a model, she shows how committed campus leadership can create more gender-equitable (and family-friendly) policies that benefit all members of the campus community. Yet we need not view these solutions as lying outside of ourselves and wait for others to take action. We can claim the role of solution seekers and advocates of equitable work environments.

Cognitive Changes

Dissonance also can be eliminated by acquiring new information or beliefs that increase consonance (Festinger, 1957), or more specifically, acquiring new information or beliefs that support a woman's sense of self. The imposter syndrome and diminished self-efficacy are governed by self-perceptions that are fueled by misinformation coming from the organizational structure. Women's ambitions, self-efficacy, and sense of accomplishment have been diminished by a pervasive and accumulated lack of recognition for their accomplishments, abilities, and talents (Fels, 2004). Implementing structural changes that would create equitable expectations, recognition, and rewards, as suggested here, would be a powerful force for improving self-efficacy and women's sense of adequacy. However, we need not wait for action at the structural level to provide the necessary recognition that shapes self-concepts. Acquiring new information or beliefs from other sources can achieve the same result (see chapter 3). Women can be agents of their own change by building informal and formal support networks and by seeking professional development opportunities, each of which would encourage and support women's development and success, provide positive feedback, acknowledge abilities, and reconnect one's actions and accomplishments. Such new information and positive experiences would help women develop self-beliefs and attitudes necessary to survive and thrive in academic leadership.

Affective Changes

Finally, dissonance can be reduced by changing the importance attached to dissonant beliefs or behaviors (Festinger, 1957), or more specifically, changing how we think about differences in masculine and feminine leadership attributes. Women can create greater consonance for themselves by deconstructing the assimilation/authenticity tension, recognizing that leadership is a socially constructed role, and not allowing the role to replace who they are as individuals. Eddy (in chapter 1) proposes a multidimensional model of leadership that moves beyond traditionally male attributes and toward greater gender fluidity. Taken from a feminist standpoint, Eddy's model acknowledges the differences between masculine and feminine leadership styles, without ranking the value of such differences, and acknowledges that the attributes of each leadership style offer varying advantages in different contexts. We can invoke this multidimensional model into being by controlling how we study, write, think, and speak about leadership.

Academe in the modern age requires leadership that encompasses masculine and feminine attributes. For example, contemporary college and university management calls for greater participation, better relationships, and more power sharing between academic units. Issues in education planning and policy, such as improving access and affordability, require greater collective—not competitive—behaviors. While formal leadership roles do necessitate a certain measure of authority, employment remains a negotiation of sustained transactions between individuals and the organization, and academe continues to revere individualism. If we can conceptualize leadership behaviors as simply various achieving styles required for the task at hand

(Lipman-Blumen, 2000) rather than in terms of masculine/feminine dichotomies, we can reduce the importance of acting in gender-inconsistent ways. Women and men can remain authentic to their identities and preferred achieving styles and also can accept responsibility, legitimacy, and intentionality to act in ways required for the context and task.

Conclusion: A New Identity Story

When social movements and legislation challenged gender and racial barriers and introduced women and people of color to academe en masse, assimilating into cultural norms was necessary for acceptance and success. As these newcomers moved through the academy and entered leadership, they did so as what Kanter (1993) calls *tokens*: highly visible people who were different from the majority and not permitted the individuality of their own unique, nonstereotypical characteristics. Many of these pioneers assimilated into and replicated the identity story necessary to gain legitimacy and the support of their constituents, facilitating advancement but resulting in gender dissonance and diminished personal authenticity. Although many ethnic minorities remain underrepresented in higher education, collectively women of all colors have achieved a numerical presence in academe equal to men's. Still, their presence has not been enough to dislodge the compulsion to assimilate. Colleges and universities understand the benefits of diversity in education and scholarly thinking, yet many have not made the leap to understand the benefits of a collective leadership capacity composed of diverse leadership styles and strengths. Rather than continuing to rely on assimilating to a received tradition (bending new information, people, and behaviors to fit our acculturated views of leadership) we need accommodation (forming new leadership norms and identity stories that build upon the past and add the synthesized, collective strengths of the present).

In rising to leadership, Gardner (1995) observes, a leader can choose to convey a familiar and formulaic identity story that will be readily assimilated by the group or choose to invent a new story with distinctiveness and power but risk affronting and alienating those who adhere to the current story. The best approach lies somewhere in the middle. Innovative "leaders benefit from the ability to build on stories that are already known . . . and to synthesize them in new ways" (p. 291). Effective leadership begins not with wanting to change an organization but rather with honoring and understanding the organization, becoming a part of it before attempting to change it (Gabelnick et al., 1998).

We envision a new identity story on the horizon for academe that would sidestep behavioral norms based in traits and behaviors originating in gender and ethnicity and would instead embrace what Joseph (1995) calls a new paradigm of community based on shared values and a compelling vision. We need not wait for the "right" leader to come along and bring that identity to our campuses. Leadership is cocreated. Organizational members' needs and desires interplay with the contours of leaders' identity stories, influencing and interpreting them (Gardner, 1995). Women and men can alter the American academic identity story by maintaining awareness of multiple dimensions of identity and their intersections, celebrating and valuing these differences, and questioning what we define as normal. Campuses can influence socially constructed leadership norms by seeking leaders who embody and convey the importance of multidimensionality and difference, and they can effect real change in their organizational cultures by altering management practices and policies (Burke & Litwin, 1989) to ensure equitable working conditions, performance expectations, and distribution of resources and rewards. Rather than having campus leadership in which everyone strikes the same note in sympathetic resonance, we would have one in which everyone plays his or her own individual notes in beautiful symphony.

Note

1. Some women authentically exhibit and prefer masculine leadership attributes, whether through nature or nurture.

References

American Council on Education. (2007). *The American college president: 2007 edition.* Washington, DC: American Council on Education.

Amey, M. J., & Twombly, S. B. (1992). Revisioning leadership in community colleges. *The Review of Higher Education, 15*(2), 125–150.

Bandura, A. (1997). *Self-efficacy: The exercise of control.* New York: Freeman.

Bracken, S. J., Allen, J. K., & Dean, D. R. (2006). *The balancing act: Gendered perspectives in faculty roles and work lives.* Sterling, VA: Stylus.

Broverman, I. K., Vogel, S. R., Broverman, D. M., Clarkson, F. E., & Rosenkrantz, P. S. (1972). Sex role stereotypes: A current appraisal. *Journal of Social Issues, 28,* 59–78.

Brown, G., Van Ummersen, C., & Sturnick, J. (2001). *From where we sit: Women's perspectives on the presidency.* Washington, DC: American Council on Education.

Burke, W. W., & Litwin, G. L. (1989). A causal model of organizational performance. In *1989 Annual: Developing human resources* (pp. 277–288). San Diego: Pfieffer.

Bussotti, C. (1990). The impostor phenomenon: Family roles and environment (Doctoral dissertation, Georgia State University, 1990). *Dissertation Abstracts International, 51,* 4041B.

Choi, J., Price, R. H., & Vinokur, A. D. (2003). Self-efficacy changes in groups: Effects of diversity, leadership and group climate. *Journal of Organizational Behavior, 24,* 353–372.

The Chronicle of Higher Education. (2008a, September). Number of full-time faculty members by sex, rank, and racial and ethnic group, fall 2005 [Electronic version]. *Almanac 2008–09, 55(1),* 24.

The Chronicle of Higher Education. (2008b, September). A profile of college presidents, 2006 [Electronic version]. *Almanac 2008–09, 55(1),* 27.

Clance, P. R., & Imes, S. (1978). *The imposter phenomenon among high-achieving women: Dynamics and therapeutic intervention.* Retrieved January 1, 2008, from http://www2.gsu.edu/~wwwaow/resources/ip_high_achieving_women.pdf

Clance, P. R., & O'Toole, M. A. (1987). The impostor phenomenon: An internal barrier to empowerment and achievement. Women and Therapy. *Feminist Quarterly, 6(3),* 51–64.

Colbeck, C. L. (2006). How female and male faculty with families manage work and personal roles. In S. J. Bracken, J. K. Allen, & D. R. Dean (Eds.), *The balancing act: Gendered perspectives in faculty roles and work lives* (pp. 31–50). Sterling, VA: Stylus.

Corrigan, M. (2002). *The American college president: 2002 edition.* Washington, DC: American Council on Education.

Creamer, E. (2006). Policies that part: Early career experiences of co-working academic couples. In S. J. Bracken, J. K. Allen, & D. R. Dean (Eds.), *The balancing act: Gendered perspectives in faculty roles and work lives* (pp. 73–90). Sterling, VA: Stylus.

Dean, D. R. (2003, November). *America's women chief academic officers and their presidential aspirations.* Paper presented at the annual meeting of the Association for the Study of Higher Education, Portland, OR.

Dingman, D. J. (1987). The impostor phenomenon and social mobility: You can't go home again (Doctoral dissertation, Georgia State University, 1987). *Dissertation Abstracts International, 51,* 4041B.

Eckert, P. (1998). Gender and sociolinguistic variation. In J. Coates (Ed.), *Language and gender: A reader* (pp. 64–75). Oxford, UK: Blackwell.

Fels, A. (2004). Necessary dreams: Ambition in women's changing lives. New York: Pantheon.

Festinger, L. (1957). *A theory of cognitive dissonance.* Stanford, CA: Stanford University Press.

Fogg, P. (2006, September). Panel blames bias for gender gap. *The Chronicle of Higher Education, 53(6),* A13.

Gabelnick, F., Herr, P., & Klein, E. (Eds.). (1998). *The psychodynamics of leadership.* Madison, CT: Psychosocial Press.

Gardner, H. E. (1995). *Leading minds: An anatomy of leadership.* New York: Basic Books.

Glazer-Raymo, J. (1999). *Shattering the myths: Women in academe.* Baltimore: Johns Hopkins University Press.

Harvey, J. C. (1981). The impostor phenomenon and achievements: A failure to internalize success (Doctoral dissertation, Temple University, 1981). *Dissertation Abstracts International, 42,* 4969B.

Henig, S. (2006, September). Female scientists trail men in earning patents. *The Chronicle of Higher Education, 53*(2), A57.

Hollander, E. P., & Julian, J. W. (1978). Studies in leader legitimacy, influence and innovation. In L. Berkowitz (Ed.), *Group processes* (pp. 115–151). New York: Academic Press.

Imes, S. A., & Clance, P. R. (1984). Treatment of the impostor phenomenon in high achieving women. In C. M. Brody (Ed.), *Women therapists working with women: New theory and process of feminist therapy* (pp. 69–85). New York: Springer.

Joseph, J. (1995). *Remaking America: How the benevolent traditions of many cultures are transforming our nation's life.* San Francisco: Jossey-Bass.

Kanter, R. M. (1993). *Men and women of the corporation* (2nd ed.). New York: Basic Books.

Langford, J. (1990). The need to look smart: The impostor phenomenon and motivations for learning (Doctoral dissertation, Georgia State University, 1990). *Dissertation Abstracts International, 51,* 3604B.

Langford, J., & Clance, P. R. (1993). The impostor phenomenon: Recent research findings regarding dynamics, personality and family patterns and their implications for treatment. *Psychotherapy: Theory, Research, Practice, and Training, 30*(3), 495–501.

Lipman-Blumen, J. (2000). *Connective leadership: Managing in a changing world.* Oxford, UK: Oxford University Press.

Mason, M. A., Goulden, M., & Wolfinger, N. H. (2006). Babies matter. In S. J. Bracken, J. K. Allen, & D. R. Dean (Eds.), *The balancing act: Gendered perspectives in faculty roles and work lives* (pp. 9–30). Sterling, VA: Stylus.

McCormick, M. J., Tanguma, J., & Lopez-Forment, A. S. (2002). Extending self-efficacy theory to leadership: A review and empirical test. *Journal of Leadership Education, 1*(2), 2–15.

McLaughlin, J. B. (1996). Entering the presidency. In J. B. McLaughlin (Ed.), *Leadership transitions: The new college president* (pp. 5–13). San Francisco: Jossey-Bass.

Murray, L. R. (2003). Sick and tired of being sick and tired: Implications for racial and ethnic disparities in occupational health. *American Journal of Public Health, 93,* 222–226.

Newman, J. H. (1854). *The idea of a university.* Retrieved January 1, 2008, from http://www.fordham.edu/halsall/mod/newman/newman-university.html

Pajares, F. (2002). *Self-efficacy beliefs in academic contexts: An outline*. Retrieved January 22, 2005, from http://www.emory.edu/EDUCATION/mfp/efftalk.html

Rosenkrantz, P. S., Vogel, S. R., Bee, H., Broverman, I. K., & Broverman, D. M. (1968). Sex-role stereotypes and self-concepts in college students. *Journal of Consulting and Clinical Psychology, 32*, 287–295.

Singer, M. (1991). The relationship between employee sex, length of service and leadership aspirations: A study of valance, self-efficacy and attribution perspectives. *Applied Psychology: An International Review, 40*, 417–436.

Topping, M. E. H., & Kimmel, E. B. (1985, Summer). The imposter phenomenon: Feeling phony. *Academic Psychology Bulletin, 7*, 213–226.

Waring, M. (1989). *Counting for nothing: What men value and what women are worth*. Wellington, New Zealand: Bridget Williams Books.

Wolf-Wendel, L., & Ward, K. (2006). Faculty work and family life. In S. J. Bracken, J. K. Allen, & D. R. Dean (Eds.), *The balancing act: Gendered perspectives in faculty roles and work lives* (pp. 51–72). Sterling, VA: Stylus.

Wilson, R. (2006, November). AAUP report blames colleges for gender inequity among professors. *The Chronicle of Higher Education, 53*(11), A11.

ABOUT THE EDITORS AND CONTRIBUTORS

Jeanie K. Allen is assistant professor of behavioral science and interdisciplinary studies at Drury University in Springfield, MO, and coeditor of the Women in Academe series.

Jane Henry Applegate is professor of English education at the University of South Florida.

Peggy J. Blackwell is dean and professor of education at Zayed University, United Arab Emirates.

Rita Bornstein is president emerita and Cornell Professor of Philanthropy and Leadership Development at Rollins College.

Susan J. Bracken is assistant professor of adult education at North Carolina State University in the Department of Adult and Higher Education, and coeditor of the Women in Academe series.

Diane R. Dean is assistant professor of higher education administration and policy at Illinois State University, and coeditor of the Women in Academe series.

Penelope M. Earley is professor of education and director of the Center for Educational Policy at George Mason University.

Pamela L. Eddy is professor of educational administration and community leadership at Central Michigan University.

Leila Gonzalez Sullivan is the W. Dallas Herring Professor of Community College Education at North Carolina State University and executive director of the National Initiative for Leadership and Institutional Effectiveness.

Janelle Kappes is a senior coordinator for Senior Transition and Parent Programs at Arizona State University, where she also completed her doctoral degree in higher education.

Sharon A. McDade is director of the ACE Fellows Program at the American Council on Education (ACE) and associate professor of higher education administration at George Washington University.

Page S. Morahan is codirector of the Hedwig van Ameringen Executive Leadership in Academic Medicine (ELAM) Program for Women and codirector of the Foundation for Advancement of International Medical Education and Research (FAIMER) Institutes at Drexel University College of Medicine, where she is also professor of microbiology and immunology.

Yolanda T. Moses is professor of anthropology; special assistant to the chancellor for excellence and diversity; vice provost for conflict resolution at the University of California, Riverside; and past president of the American Association for Higher Education.

Rosalyn C. Richman is codirector of the Hedwig van Ameringen Executive Leadership in Academic Medicine (ELAM) Program for Women at Drexel University.

Lorraine Sloma-Williams is assistant director of alumni programs at George Washington University.

Jill Mattuck Tarule is associate provost and professor of education at the University of Vermont.

Caroline Sotello Viernes Turner is professor of educational leadership and policy studies at Arizona State University.

Claire Van Ummersen is vice president of the Center for Effective Leadership at the American Council on Education (ACE).

Diane F. Wood is assistant professor of family and consumer sciences and education at George Fox University.

INDEX

Abbhul, S., 50, 51
academic administration, women in, 1–2
academic careers, agency as applied to, 4–5
academic leadership
  barriers on paths to, 189–95
  guiding women of color to, 181–206
  integrated identities and, 238–49
  mentoring women in, 128–44
  overcoming barriers in, 196–205
  professional strategy and personal choice
    on path to, 1–7
  underrepresentation of women in, xi
academic medicine and dentistry, women in,
  50–71
academic sciences, treatment of women in,
  14
acculturated view of leader, 34
acquired competencies, 9
action, suggestions for building, 6–7
administrative careers, lack of clear bridges
  between faculty and, 191–93
advocacy
  community colleges and, 110–11
  suggestions for building, 6
affective changes, dissonance and, 247–48
agency
  as applied to academic careers, 4–5
  defined, 4
  personal, 4–5
Aiken, J., 34
Alfred, Mary V., 198
Allen, J. K., 1, 238, 241, 253
Allen, W., 149
Allinson, C. W., 132
American Anthropological Association
  (AAA), 204
American Association for Higher Education
  (AAHE), 191
  Faculty Roles and Rewards: New Path-
    ways II Project, 197
  Women's Caucus, 191, 192
American Association of Colleges and
  Unversities (AACU), 168n2

American Association of Community Col-
  leges (AACC), 98, 105, 107, 109, 110, 111,
  117, 120, 123, 201
American Association of Hispanics in Higher
  Education (AAHHE), 201
American Association of State Colleges and
  Universities (AASCU), 151–52, 192
American Association of University Profes-
  sors, xiii
The American College President: 2002 Edition
  (ACE), 185–86
American Council on Education (ACE), 2,
  128, 129, 150n, 151, 182, 186n, 194, 209,
  240, 243
  Center for Advancement of Racial and
    Ethnic Equity, 201
  Office of Minority Affairs, 192
  Office of Women in Higher Education,
    201
  Women's National Network, 191
American Council on Education (ACE) Fel-
  lows Program, 149–80, 155–57, 192
  importance of, 166
  women of color and their perspectives on,
    157–64
Amey, M. J., 8, 10, 12, 99, 117, 119, 130, 244
Anderson, D. R., 132, 141
Anderson, E. L., 150n, 167
Anthony, W. P., 139
Applegate, Jane Henry, 3, 31, 244, 253
apprenticeships, 114–15
Armstrong, S. J., 132
assimilation, 238
  costs of, 240–45
  gender dissonance and, 244–45
  psychosocial origins of, 238–40
Association of American Medical Colleges
  (AAMC), 50, 51
Astin, H., 34, 47, 222
authenticity, quest for, 245–48
authentic style of collaboration, 22
authoritative leadership, men in, 12
awareness, suggestions for building, 5–6